# KIM NOVAK
## *on Camera*

# KIM NOVAK
## *on Camera*

Larry Kleno

SAN DIEGO • NEW YORK
## A. S. BARNES & COMPANY, INC.
IN LONDON:
### THE TANTIVY PRESS

First Edition
Manufactured in the United States of America

For information write to:

A.S. Barnes & Company, Inc.
P.O. Box 3051
La Jolla, California 92038

The Tantivy Press
Magdalen House
136-148 Tooley Street
London, SE1 2TT, England

**Library of Congress Cataloging in Publication Data**

Kleno, Larry.
　　Kim Novak on camera.

　　1. Novak, Kim.　2. Moving-picture actors and
actresses—United States—Index.　I. Title.
PN2287.N58K55　　　791.43′028′0924 [B]　　　79-17591
ISBN 0-498-02457-7


1 2 3 4 5 6 7 8 9　84 83 82 81 80

# CONTENTS

# Acknowledgments

The author is deeply grateful to the following:

Jim Backus, Martin Balsam, Julian Blaustein, David Bowie, Michael Brandon, Coral Browne, Paddy Chayefsky, Michael Conrad, John Conte, Ellen Corby, Joe De Santis, Charles Drake, Larry Gates, Hermione Gingold, Virginia Grey, Edith Head, Marcel Hellman, David Hemmings, Alfred Hitchcock, James Wong Howe, Freida Inescort, Richard Johnson, Elsa Lanchester, Jack Lemmon, Joshua Logan, Delbert Mann, Dean Martin, Walter Matthau, Peter Medak, Dolores Michaels, Alvy Moore, Patti Page, Otto Preminger, Dory Previn, Aldo Ray, Alejandro Rey, Cliff Robertson, Sutton Roley, Rosalind Russell, Jules Schermer, Benno Schneider, Milton Selzer, George Sidney, James Stewart, Susan Strasberg, Shepperd Strudwick, Mary Tamm, Billy Wilder, and Estelle Winwood.

ABC Television; Academy of Motion Picture Arts and Sciences and The Margaret Herrick Library; Alfred J. Hitchcock Productions; William Banks; Bond Street Books; Budget Films; Loraine Burdick; Myron Braum; The Bryna Company; CBS Television; Philip Castanza; William Chapman; Chapman's Picture Palace; Cherokee Books; Cinemabilia; Robert Coburn; Robert Coburn, Jr.; Columbia Pictures Corporation; Oliver Dernberger; Directors Guild of America, Incorporated; Joan Doty; Eddie Brandt's Saturday Matinee; John Engstead; Filmways Corporation; Doug Hart; Michael Hawks; Jess L. Hoaglin; Hollywood Poster Exchange; KCOP Television; KHJ Television; KTLA Television; KTTV Television; Talbert Kanigher; Kimco Pictures Corporation; Paula Klaw and Movie Star News; Larry Edmunds Book Shop; Leguan Films; Lopert Pictures Corporation; Loews, Incorporated; Metro-Goldwyn-Mayer, Incorporated; Tina Michael; Mirisch Corporation; NBC Television; Paramount Pictures Corporation; Playboy Productions; RKO Radio Pictures Corporation; Screen Gems, Incorporated; Seven Arts, Incorporated; William Eben Stephens; The Estate of Ray Stuart; Sudan Productions; United Artists Corporation; Warner Brothers, Incorporated; Franciene Watkins; Winchester Film Productions Limited; David L. Wolper Productions; and World Film Services Limited.

The Keane painting originally credited to Walter Keane in previous publicity was in actuality painted by Margaret Keane. It is reprinted in this book with the kind permission of the artist Margaret Keane McGuire.

Very special thanks to:

Felisa Ortega with love.

And to:

L. Allan Smith for generous assistance.

Heartfelt appreciation to:

William J. Dyerly for friendship, encouragement, and his constant belief that this book would become a reality.

And to:

Ella Smith, a cherished friend, who gave me the confidence that can only come from a gifted writer.

# Foreword

I agree thoroughly with your perception—"Kim
Novak was highly underrated as an actress."
This all added to her good taste in choosing to
spend her time in the real animal world up north
and ignoring the animals that populate the mental
state called Hollywood.

George Sidney

# KIM NOVAK
## *on Camera*

Part I

# *Achievement*

**Keane painting of Kim Novak.** *Reprinted courtesy of Margaret Keane.*

# 1

The noted artist Margaret Keane once painted a portrait of Kim Novak. The Keane paintings of wide-eyed children are still extremely popular, and the artist's conception of Kim showed a little girl standing wistfully in front of a barbed-wire fence. In the background were open sea and a sky full of gulls.

At the time, Kim said:

That little girl is just like me. The fence, I think, represents the walls everyone has in life. The child's back is to it, almost as if she is giving up. If she had looked a little further, she would have found a place where the fence is down and she could reach the freedom of the sea and the gulls. The special places of life are walled off to her because she doesn't want to tear down the fence.

Some years later, she would say of her career:

I think it is essential for all who work in Hollywood to get away from it for awhile. If you become slightly more aware of what is going on outside, you can offer so much more. The one thing you must fight in Hollywood is the constant pressure placed upon you from within the industry to conform to its current way of thinking.

At first, Kim allowed herself to be fenced in by the studio because she thought it was for her own good. She was considered a property, and there were times when she felt as though she were one. Like an over-strict parent, the studio supervised all of her activities, telling her what to do and what not to, allowing her no freedom beyond its invisible barbed wire.

As she put it:

This can kill all desire to improve, to experiment. In Hollywood, they constantly imply that if you don't play along with them according to their rules you will make yourself unhappy. What is happiness, anyway? A matter of a particular mood, a particular environment, a particular person being with you at a particular time. Moods change like the climate, and so do places and people. You can be happy in a city one year, and miserable in it the next. In the long run, you can only hope that your happiness ratio will exceed your capacity for making yourself unhappy. That's all I ask from life, no more.

Eventually, she rebelled. She said, "I'm a human being, not a puppet." And, as her stature grew, so did her ability to find loopholes in the barbed wire. Finally, there was no barbed wire at all.

\*        \*

Kim Novak was one of the last stars built up by a major studio at the end of the star system. Angered by Rita Hayworth's actions when she was the reigning queen at Columbia and reluctant to work, Harry Cohn said, "I'll make a star out of the next girl who walks into my office, whoever in hell she is." Kim was the next girl through the door. Her timing was perfect.

Cohn, next to Louis B. Mayer, was probably the most powerful studio boss in town, but it is doubtful that he could have made a star out of just anyone. A person has to have something to start with which the public will accept and want. Although she was lacking in acting experience, Kim had the combination of looks and personality that only a star brings to celluloid. She generated a kind of sex appeal that was provocative because it also seemed innocent.

Cohn, however, insisted that he was totally responsible for Kim's success. Years later, during one of their contract hassles, he would say, "I could have taken a two-bit whore and made her a star just as I did Kim. In fact, if you wanna bring me your wife or your aunt, we'll do the same for them."

It's true Cohn could take credit for a lot—the grooming, the publicity, and good roles in important pictures. But, if Kim didn't have that special something that defines a star, she would never have gotten further than some of the others who were under contract at the time. Jody Lawrance, Betsy Palmer, May Wynn, Dianne Foster, and Lucy Marlowe were all promising hopefuls at Columbia. Stardom didn't happen for them.

Kim Novak set a record for going far and fast. Audiences responded to her magnetism with 3,500 fan letters a week. She grew from an insecure and floundering novice to the complete and respected professional she is today. Statements from actors, directors, producers, cameramen, and other film craftsmen who were interviewed for this book will bear that out. As these words are being written, a little less than twenty-five years since her movie debut, Kim Novak's charisma on the screen is still strong.

\*　　　\*

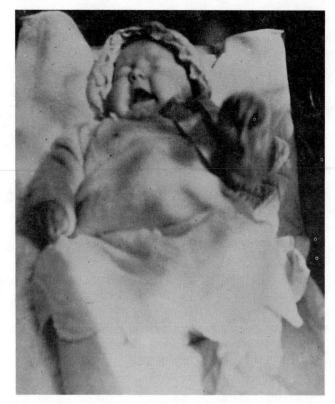

Earliest photo, four months old

Her beginning said it all: Monday's child is fair of face. Marilyn Pauline Novak was born in Room 313 of Chicago's Saint Anthony's Hospital on 13 February 1933, at 3:13 a.m. It is small wonder that she has always felt the numbers three and thirteen are lucky for her.

Her parents, Blanche and Joseph Novak, already had one child, three-year-old Arlene, and were hoping for a boy. Her father, a second-generation Czech, had been a teacher in Oregon. When he relocated in Chicago, he found he would have to attend college

16

Sixteen months old, with older sister Arlene

much and was constantly trying to please him and win his approval. However, she did not always succeed. One of the things that displeased him most was the fact that she was left-handed. He continually badgered her to use her right hand, but his badgering was in vain. She was left-handed and remained so.

Her older sister was the favored child. Marilyn always felt she was in Arlene's shadow, and it caused her to be timid and insecure. She was so shy, in fact, that people seldom noticed her.

The Novaks were concerned that Marilyn's marks in school were not as good as her sister's. About her school days, she said:

I hated school! I hated being told what to do. I had a strong feeling not to go along with anything unless I believed in it. I'd rather take the bad grades, which is what I did. They never liked me—neither the teachers nor the pupils. I was always in the last row or the next-to-the-last row, according to the marks. I was seated with the jerks!

Those school days left permanent scars. Because she was plain, the other kids thought of her as homely and stupid. She would later remember:

I was always afraid of people and felt a lot of rejection. Even before I went to school I never seemed to fit in with anything, even in my own family. My childhood was comparatively happy in spite of the fact that I was a loner. My parents weren't rich, but they were a devoted couple and always gave my sister and me the best they could. I just felt there was something wrong. I think psychiatrists are right when they say that most of the disturbances of adult life are caused by a disturbed childhood. My sister, Arlene, was older by three years. We got along fine and I adored her, but, because of the age difference I was never accepted by her friends. I wasn't jealous of my sister. It was just that she did everything better than I.

One of Marilyn's earliest dreams was to become a veterinarian. Animals were her friends. She could give them love and never fear that they would hurt her in the way people did. She would never lose this love for animals.

for another year in order to teach there. Before reaching this goal, he fell in love with Blanche Marie Kral, also of Czechoslovakian descent, and gave up the idea of teaching. They were married, and he took an office job.

Joe had always been a lover of nature. Basically an earth person, he loved animals and looked forward to the day when he could take his family back to Oregon and grow old with nature around him. That day never came. He remained in Chicago and kept his job as traffic claims clerk for the Chicago-Milwaukee-St. Paul and Pacific Railroad, mainly because Blanche didn't want to leave her family and Chicago.

It is not surprising that Kim, too, would be an earth person. Eventually, she would adopt her father's dream of a way of life that would fulfill her needs for a peaceful existence. Her quest would lead her to the Big Sur country where she could commune with nature and animals.

Marilyn Novak grew up in a Polish middle-class neighborhood in Chicago. She loved her father very

Four years old, with Arlene

First Communion, with Arlene

While their daughters were still in grammar school, the Novaks sent both of them to take piano, singing, and dancing lessons. Marilyn didn't like these because she was too scared to show off in public. The rebellious "Mickey," as she was nicknamed, wasn't about to do anything that was forced on her, and, since her parents had no intention of pushing her into something she didn't want, the lessons were dropped. She did, however, love painting, and her parents encouraged her in this. Today, an accomplished artist, she still finds painting a soothing antidote to the stresses of life.

Marilyn retreated to her own world. It was a world of beauty in which she didn't have to get along with the other kids or be hurt by them. Later, she would say about this period, "There is such a thing as being very lonely but liking to be alone. I preferred this way of life." She had her dolls and her animals. They became her true friends. She developed a great fondness for clowns because "They're always laughing and smiling,

even in the face of tragedy." She had one favorite that she dubbed her kissing clown, and he was a special friend. She took him along with her when she first started modeling, years later, to kiss him for good luck before a shooting session.

The one thing that ultimately had the greatest influence on Marilyn came through a department store meeting place for teenagers. It was called The Fair Teens and became a mecca for young people in the Chicago area. She attended a club meeting and became a regular for the next four years. It opened up a whole new world for her.

The manager of the club was a beautiful young fashion director named Norma Kasell. She would play an important role in the life of the future star. Later,

Eleven years old

High school graduation

when Kim was established in films, Mrs. Kasell became her personal manager and Mrs. Kasell's husband, Hollee, became her business manager.

Among the activities within the club were modeling and radio shows. It was Hollee Kasell who noticed the blonde Marilyn and said to his wife: "That kid is sexier in jeans than the others in evening gowns. Why don't you use her?"

About this period, Kim said:

I guess my career really began when I joined a Chicago teen group called The Fair Teens Club. Norma Kasell, who originated and directed the club, saw possibilities in me, and she helped me to become a model. That was the starting point.

Mrs. Kasell gave the young Marilyn her first feeling of belonging and being wanted for herself. Marilyn was still shy and insecure, and the feelings of inferiority were not easily overcome. But she began to assist in fashion shows and, upon Mrs. Kasell's suggestion, entered a modeling contest for a $400 scholarship to the Patricia Stevens Professional Modeling School.

She won. In addition to the scholarship, she also won her first title: "Miss Rhapsody in Blue." The victory gave her a new lease on life. For the first time, she felt as if she had excelled at something. It was an exhilarating feeling, unlike anything she had known.

The modeling course was followed by a summer job showing sports dresses in another department store at ten dollars an hour. Marilyn's modeling career had begun, and she was kept busy with assignments. Her main asset was the fact that she looked years older than her true age of fourteen.

Although she won another beauty contest (as "Queen of Lake Michigan") and the world was beginning to take notice, her inferiority complex was not completely shaken off. Her mother was in favor of the modeling career only because she wanted her daughter to develop poise and self-confidence. For Marilyn, the modeling jobs were merely to earn spending money.

During the period between William Penn Grammar School and Farragut High School, her goal in life changed. While she had originally wanted to become a veterinarian, now that people were interested in her, she became interested in them. She thought seriously of becoming a nun. Part of this came from the influence of her Grandmother Kral, a devout Catholic, whom Marilyn adored.

While school had never been much fun for Marilyn, things changed when she enrolled at Wright Junior College. She joined the Alpha Beta Mu Sorority and was very popular. The one-time gangling teenager had grown into an adult beauty. She stood five feet six inches and measured 37-23-37. Her voice was low and sexy.

Someone in the sorority suggested she model for advertisements and, although she didn't like the artificiality of it, the money was good and she gave it a try. Boys had also discovered Marilyn Novak and her popularity soared. She spent a year and a half at Wright until she quit in order to take a full-time modeling job.

From her first modeling days until the time she left Wright Junior College, she held a number of jobs, none of which she found particularly appealing. She worked in a Christmas card factory, clerked in a dime store, ran an elevator, and even groomed horses. Of them all, she enjoyed being around horses the most. She also worked briefly as a dental assistant. She would later tell the story in this way.

> I was working as a dentist's assistant, or nurse, back in Chicago. One day, the laundry delivered the wrong white uniform, but there was nothing to do but wear it—even though it was a couple of sizes too small. Well, who came in that afternoon but the dentist's wife. It was a warm summer day, but the look she gave me cooled things off! The next morning, the dentist handed me a check for two week's pay, and said he could get along without a nurse.

Marilyn was hired by an appliance manufacturer to demonstrate washing machines and refrigerators in large stores, on a summer sales tour of the country for Thor Appliances. She was given the title "Miss Deep Freeze" and raised temperatures as she gave out rhythmical sales pitches in that low, sexy voice.

After five weeks, the tour ended in San Francisco. Marilyn had a return train-ticket back to Chicago but never used it. Instead, she and another girl, Peggy Dahl, rerouted their tickets so they could visit Los Angeles and see some of the local sights. Thus, the unemployed twenty-year-old model, Marilyn Novak, arrived in Hollywood in 1953.

During their vacation, Peggy's mother came out from Chicago to keep an eye on her, and the three of them checked into the Beverly Hills Hotel, taking turns sleeping on the floor so they wouldn't have to pay

Maid of Honor at sister's wedding

for another room. There were no plans for a screen career, and, as Kim remembers it:

> Do you know what we wanted to do in Hollywood? The only thing? We wanted to swim in the Beverly Hills Hotel pool. We stayed there a whole week with Peggy's mother. I didn't know the first thing about acting, or movie studios or anything like that. I was a model. If you want to get a job as a model, you just go to an agency and leave some pictures of yourself, and if they need your type they call you. That's all I did. I knew exactly what my acting limitations were. I could open a refrigerator door gracefully, and that was it, period. I could see where a lot of time might go by before any movie studio would want a girl to open an icebox.

Nineteen years old, with Siamese cat Mei Som Sin

"Miss Deep Freeze" demonstrating refrigerators

But a lot of time didn't go by. Marilyn had fallen in love with California and the climate at first sight. When Peggy's mother finally decided it was time for them to return to Chicago, Marilyn was determined to stay a while longer.

She had saved $500 from her Miss Deep Freeze tour, so she moved to a less expensive apartment and registered with the Caroline Leonetti Agency for modeling jobs. The agency came through with a few, then sent her on an interview that would prove to be a turning point in her life.

It happened that RKO needed some models to back up Jane Russell in a musical number for *The French Line*. In an inspired moment, the casting department thought maybe real models might look more like models than actresses trained for the part. Marilyn Novak was among the interviewees and was hired. She was one of a score of lovelies and beauty-title holders making their movie debuts.

Marilyn would be among eighteen girls in the musical number, "Any Gal From Texas," in which Mary McCarty shared the spotlight with Russell, center-screen. She would walk regally down a long staircase and sing one line, "Cannot give a canapé away," as the camera caught a fast glimpse of her face and figure.

*The French Line*, directed by Lloyd Bacon, was filmed in technicolor and 3-D. Dance numbers were staged by Billy Daniel, (not to be confused with singer Billy Daniels) who would be an important figure in the career of the young model. The movie was thin on plot, with Jane Russell as the richest gal in Texas who goes

to Paris incognito to avoid fortune hunters. A big Paris-style fashion show with a musical number wrapped things up.

Although made in 1953, the film wasn't released immediately because of the difficulties Howard Hughes, who owned RKO at the time, had with the Production Code Office. The problem resulted because of one of Russell's scanty costumes (weighing seven ounces) which showed a little too much of the amply endowed star to satisfy the Code people. Seven years later, Helen Westcott would wear this same costume in *Studs Lonigan* with no static. When *The French Line* was finally released in mid-1954, it was advertised as "the costume and that dance" to lure moviegoers to the box office.

Soon after completion of *The French Line*, Marilyn would make a brief return to RKO—this time for *Son Of Sinbad*, which top-billed Dale Robertson, Sally Forrest, Lili St. Cyr, and Vincent Price. It was to be a Howard Hughes spectacle of beauty, fun, and adventure. They needed girls, girls, and more girls, and featured what was termed as Hollywood's prize collection of screen beauties.

Producer Robert Sparks interviewed 653 girls to select 127 finalists who would work in the film. Marilyn would be among the lucky ones chosen from the Miss Universe contenders and other beauty-title holders. In addition to the languorous charmers in the harem and the Oriental dancers, Sparks needed a group of female "Raiders" for the film. The famous forty thieves of the Arabian Nights tales were changed from brigands to beauties. They were now explained by the fact that they were the daughters of the notorious Baghdad bandits. That was reason enough.

Marilyn was cast as one of the Raiders and was among the fiery beauties who had to employ the devastating green fire to drive the forces of the mighty Tamarlane from the beseiged Baghdad. *Son Of Sinbad* was shot in technicolor and Superscope. Although it was completed in early 1954, it would not see release until 1955, by which time Marilyn Novak would have gone on to better things.

An actress who worked on both *The French Line* and *Son of Sinbad*, Dolores Michaels, remembers:

When I first met Kim, and she was still Marilyn Novak then, we were both models. We were doing The Home Show. She was working for a freezer company and I was working for some boat company. During this time, we saw each other, but only in passing, as models do.

We both worked in The French Line, but our scenes were

*The French Line*

23

at different times. I had a fast day or two on it and she had about the same amount of time. I worked during the beginning portion and she came on it later.

Oddly enough, our next meeting was also on the RKO lot. We came right out of *The French Line* and went into an epic titled *Son Of Sinbad*. I got the job through a modeling agency that sent me over to RKO Casting and I think Marilyn was referred to the studio by the agency she was signed with. I remember a lot of girls traipsing over there for interviews. They were looking for beauties, and, considering the quality of the film, they certainly needed them.

Marilyn came on *Son Of Sinbad* after I was already there. She was unusually beautiful. When she walked on that set, which was loaded with beautiful girls, everyone was awed by her beauty. It was during the making of this movie, when there were long periods of time where everyone sat around waiting for setups, that I got to know her.

We were the newest ones. The other girls, who had been assigned to the film, had been there longer and had become fairly well acquainted with each other. They were like a small sorority—all off in separate little groups. Because I knew a little more than she did about film sets, I felt fairly protective. She seemed so shy. I don't know if she was really shy or simply not exuberant. I've never really decided. I'm not positive because what I got from her originally was something I mistook for vacuity or lack of focus. But she obviously was focused. She was serious. She wasn't all that chatty and really didn't mix with the groups on her own.

Claire Kelly was on that film and Joanne Jordan played the head of the harem. Claire had become a friend of mine, and, when Marilyn came in, I sort of brought her into the group. Since we were cast as "Raiders," we all had the same costumes and wore orange pants (which we referred to as our 'orange crepeys'), white crepe blouses with cummerbunds, boots and orange headgear. The funny thing was that Marilyn and I were constantly being mistaken for one another particularly from the rear. We both had hair styles that were exactly the same (a pseudo-poodle cut which was the vogue in those days) although she was more platinum.

Marilyn and I were the only two who didn't have cars. At the time, I was living in Beverly Hills and she was some place in the West Hollywood area. So we shared cabs. I paid the fare myself (although she always wanted to pay her share) because I had to go in her direction anyway. I always felt she'd be eaten alive in this town and I kept thinking she's got to save her money because she's going to have to get back to Chicago. Are you ready for this?

Most of our conversations were just winsome talk about how things went on the set that day. I had a feeling that she was from a lower-middle class family and I didn't think she was terribly bright. But, obviously, she was. I think she was essentially ill-at-ease and absolutely vulnerable. What I took for lack of intelligence was the fact, I think, that she was really a reclusive girl. In retrospect, because I did most of the talking, there wasn't much of a chance for her to say a lot. It was very hard to get feedback from her because of her basic shyness.

I really would be interested in knowing what that personality was all about. I think it's intimately more compli-cated than anyone in this town can tell you. What is interesting is that she really is a bit of an enigma. She's a woman, obviously, of talent. In addition to her acting career, there's talent in her painting. And she's one of the few that walked away. I don't know what her situation was when she left but she cut out in good time. I think she had geared herself to do pretty much what she wanted. She has led a rather quiet life but certainly not a dull one.

She has shown great development. She was sensitive to the fact that as an actress she wasn't total. The kind of heaviness she had as a person, she was constitutionally not equipped to handle. When Harry Cohn took over, that had to be murder—absolute murder. She went through a lot of very heavy and nasty people during her rise to stardom. I never saw her in the same light as Marilyn Monroe simply because she didn't have the frivolity or the obvious insanity. She had, perhaps, some of the eccentricities and neuroses but not the open-hearted insanity that Monroe had. Kim was there to do the best job she could and stick with the business at hand.

Years later, we met at a party. Kim was indeed successful, and, by that time, I had stopped acting. We chatted for quite a while. She was much more outgoing at this point and we laughed about the days at RKO.

I think she's had an incredibly interesting life. I would not have predicted upon our first meeting, despite the great beauty, that she would ever have become the star she is. I just wouldn't have counted on it because she was so vulnerable. And what I originally interpreted as vacuity was finally, to Harry Cohn, sexuality.

But nice she was, I thought. Always, terribly, terribly nice.

---

If Kim had mapped out a plan to get into films, it probably wouldn't have worked. She would later say, "I never wanted to be a movie star. It was an accident." Her only previous acting experience was one word of dialogue when she said, "Hello" before exiting in a class production of *Our Town* at Wright Junior College.

Billy Daniel, choreographer on *The French Line,* is the man who helped open the first door to her promising future. He had noticed her during the shooting, had liked her, and wanted to see her get ahead. He introduced her to agent Wilt Melnick who was with the Louis Shurr Agency. Melnick saw her possibilities but felt she was a little overweight. She signed a contract with the agency with the proviso that she would take off ten pounds before it was enforced.

Ten days later, minus the poundage, Marilyn Novak was introduced to Max Arnow, who was the casting director for Columbia Pictures. Arnow had a feeling that she could be Columbia's answer to Fox's Marilyn Monroe in the sex-symbol race between the studios. A screen test was arranged.

Because she wasn't being tested for any particular part, Marilyn wasn't terribly enthusiastic when she

*The French Line,* **with Jane Russell and Mary McCarty**

was informed that she was to be screen-tested. She had no idea what was involved, and, on the day of the scheduled test, was two hours late. When she arrived at the studio, the enormity of her offense hit her. More than forty people—including the director, cameraman, makeup crew, script girl, and assorted representatives of the other arts and crafts that create a motion picture scene—had been waiting for her in various stages of patience or impatience.

She was embarrassed and confused. Marilyn was handed a scene from *The Moon Is Blue* and could hardly hold it, let alone read it. It was the late actor Robert Francis (who had a promising screen career that ended in a tragic plane crash) who came to her rescue. He ran through the lines with her and tried to assure her that she couldn't miss. But she almost did. As she recalled it:

> It was over my head. I was supposed to read a scene that Barbara Bel Geddes [who would later play a supporting role in *Vertigo*] had made famous on Broadway, and I knew I wasn't her. I didn't know who I was, or what to do, and I was just terrible. If Bob hadn't carried me through, I never would have finished. I just wanted to hide somewhere. Poor Bob, he was so considerate.

Marilyn was still too self-conscious and did not register well because she was attempting to act for the first time. Richard Quine (who would later guide her through four films) directed. As luck would have it, she was to get a second chance with another test on the same day.

This time, she would be alone on screen in a two-minute monologue from *The Devil Passes*. Whereas in the first scene she appeared dressed in something with a Peter Pan collar and looking demure (as required), the second test would show her in quite a different light. This time, decked out in a gown that reportedly had been worn by Rita Hayworth, she felt different about this character and said:

> It required an earthy girl who stood before a fireplace and told what she wanted from life. The words were just the way I felt. I told what I wanted out of life: to love and be loved. It was very tender. What she said rang a bell within me. I agreed with her outlook, so I was practically myself.

Marilyn could not be totally convincing unless she believed in what she was doing. Fortunately, this time she did. Quine's patience and sensitivity were assets which further eased her tensions.

When Harry Cohn finally viewed the test, he gruffly said, "She can't act. She mumbles and I can't hear her."

Screen test at Columbia

Fortunately, Marilyn Novak had two men in her corner. They were Max Arnow and Production Chief Jerry Wald. Arnow volunteered, "She'll never be able to act, but that doesn't matter. She's got star quality." Wald countered with, "Don't listen, just look." Harry Cohn looked. The result was that Marilyn was signed to a stock contract starting at $100 a week.

Her parents were not overjoyed or even overly enthusiastic about the whole thing. She had gone against their advice by remaining in California. Mrs. Novak would way, "I never could see that sort of business." The Novaks would have been pleased if she had returned to Chicago, married, settled down, and raised a family as her sister was doing. But fate had something else in store for Marilyn. And she had a mind of her own.

# 2

Although things were happening for Marilyn Novak, and plans were being made by Cohn and the higher-ups at Columbia, she was not terribly impressed with the whole thing. She took it lightly, commenting, "When they said I was signed, I thought, 'Well, for six months, and that will be that.'"

But Columbia was roaring into gear with its new find. Her teeth were capped, her hair was restyled, she was put on a rigid diet and exercised in a gym class, and, in addition, acting lessons (which she paid for from her paltry salary) took up the rest of her time.

When she was turned over to the still photographers, her visual impact was immediate. There was obviously a love affair between her and the camera. Fan-magazine editors were ecstatic over the pictures of her that reached their desks, and there were demands for interviews before she ever faced a motion picture camera.

The publicity department also struck pay dirt. Scanning the questionaire she had filled out after signing her contract, they discovered she liked bicycling and concocted a story that she'd been discovered by Louis Shurr while cycling in Beverly Hills. For years after, eager young starlets would ride their bikes to Shurr's office hoping the same thing might happen for them.

It was Max Arnow's secretary who suggested she give up her apartment and move into the Studio Club a few blocks away from Columbia. This was a YWCA dormitory where young women seeking careers could get a room and meals for $19.50 a week. It had been a haven for a number of promising screen personalities who went on to better things—among them, Marilyn Monroe, Rita Moreno, and Evelyn Keyes.

At first, Marilyn didn't like the idea and protested at living with so many strangers. She agreed to the arrangement only because she realized she could walk to the studio and use the money saved for dramatic training. However, after moving in, she felt at home and stayed the full three years allowed, even after she'd been starred in a number of films.

\* \*

Marilyn Novak had been told she was to undergo training for at least a year before she'd make a picture. Three months after that statement, she was called to test for *Pushover* and given the role which would bring her fame. Her first reaction was one of terror. The old complex came to the fore again. "I just know I can't do it," she said, and worried herself sick and sleepless the night before the production began. It was all she could do to make herself walk on the set.

Producer Jules Schermer remembers:

At the time I produced *Pushover* (originally titled *The Killer Wore A Badge*) for Columbia, we knew that it wasn't going to be a big picture because we only had a budget of $500,000 to do it. In those days, we did small pictures for the lower half of a double bill. That's all *Pushover* was ever intended to be. We were fortunate enough to get Fred MacMurray for the male lead and that took $60,000 right off the top for his salary. We had some good actors such as Phil Carey, E. G. Marshall, and Paul Richards for smaller roles, but we needed a female lead. Obviously, we couldn't pay top dollar.

We looked over the contract list and interviewed about ten girls for the role. I remember a damned good actress, who was under contract to the studio, named Dianne Foster, but she wasn't right for the part. Out of all the girls, only one, Marilyn Novak, pleased me. I guess I would have to say that she fell into the sex symbol category, as far as a description goes, because she oozed with sex appeal which we felt the role needed.

We made a number of tests—both to see her on camera and to find an appropriate director for her. We finally got a guy, Richard Quine, who seemed right. He had patience and took an interest in getting the very best out of her. While I was aware she didn't have the experience some of the other girls had, I stuck with my original feeling about her and the role was hers.

There were still problems with the script. Roy Huggins, who wrote the original, did not give me exactly what I wanted and I didn't like the ending. So I took some things from a previous film that I had done on the lot (*Framed* with Glenn Ford and Janis Carter) and borrowed from that. If you ever watch the film, you will see that much of it is the same—even to the ending—with the same dialogue which also worked for *Pushover*. When Huggins eventually saw a rough cut of the latter he said, "You've ruined my picture"—because of what I had borrowed from *Framed*. Fortunately, nobody else thought so.

Kim was not an actress when we started shooting. The face was beautiful. The body was great. She photographed sensationally. But she couldn't show any emotion. So we kept her dialogue to a minimum. When you can't act, you react—which is what we counted on.

We did the filming on the Columbia lot in Burbank. At one point, I remember seeing Kim standing in the rain, getting soaking wet, at the main studio in Hollywood. I knew she had to be in Burbank and I asked her, "Why aren't you at the location?" She explained that she was trying to get a cab and was waiting to flag one down. I was amazed that nobody had thought to provide a ride for her. I arranged for the assistant director to pick her up and see that she was brought back home each night, so her transportation problems were taken care of for the duration of filming. Because we didn't shoot day for night, there was quite a bit of night shooting and she'd have had a helluva time getting back and forth.

One of the first scenes to be shot was a love scene with Kim and MacMurray. Naturally, she was very nervous about the whole thing. But she held her own. There was only one problem that I remember during the whole production. It was a scene in which Kim had to walk up to a car, get in, and back out. She just couldn't shift gears. When I asked her if she knew how to drive, she answered, "I never learned to back up." I don't know, to this day, whether or not she was putting me on. [Kim did three film assignments that required her to be behind the wheel before she actually learned to drive.] In any case, she had that wonderful childlike quality and you wanted to shield and protect her. After she'd been shown how, she backed out as though she had done it for years.

Kim wasn't given any special privileges during the shooting of this film and there were no problems or temperament [as reported elsewhere]. She was eager to do the best job she could. Anxious to make good. Afraid not to. There were only twenty-two to twenty-four days' work on the picture and we brought it in on time.

When *Pushover* was completed, both Harry Cohn and Kim were lucky. He had a ready-made replacement to take over for Rita Hayworth; and she was destined to become the Columbia sex symbol. Before the film's release, he decided her name should be changed and she stood up to him and fought like a tigress. She realized she would have to change Marilyn because of Monroe, but she held her ground for Novak, which she liked. [As the story goes, Cohn decided she should be Kit Marlowe, saying "When you were a little girl they called you kitten." Marilyn couldn't see it. On the other hand, when she insisted on keeping Novak, he was just as disturbed. "Who the hell ever heard of a glamour girl named Novak?" An uneasy compromise was effected, Cohn giving in on Novak but not on Kit. Her first act of resistance had gained her some success. She was determined to go after more. She went to publicity director George Lait and told him how much she disliked Kit. His answer was, "I had one helluva time getting Cohn to even keep Novak." But he did arrange a meeting between the two so she could plead her case herself. To Cohn's "What do you mean, you don't like the name we picked for you?" she suggested that she would prefer Kim to Kit—and she emerged from the mogul's office as Kim Novak, smiling because she had won her first point.]

\*     \*

Kim's new name received special "Introducing Kim Novak" billing in *Pushover,* and she could not have had a better vehicle than this one to present her to the moviegoing public. Technically, it was first-rate. Roy Huggins' screenplay was a combination of two similar novels, *The Night Watch* by Thomas Walsh and *Rafferty* by William S. Ballinger. Huggins took the best elements of both and never telegraphed his plot moves in advance. Low-key photography created a

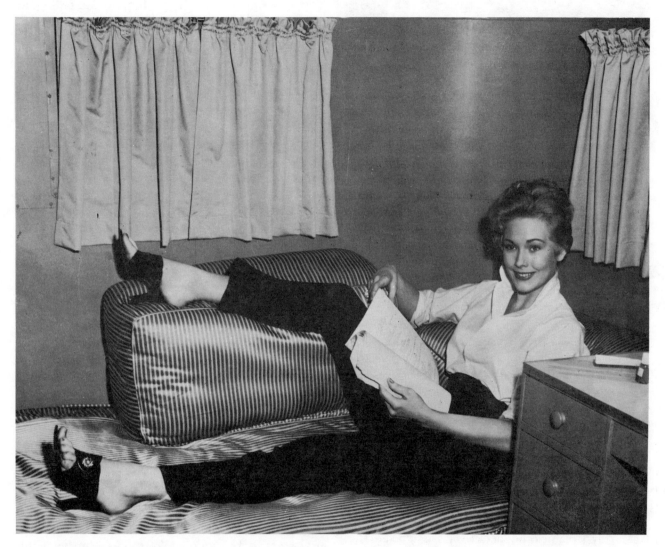

Between scenes on *Pushover*

*Pushover,* with Fred MacMurray on the set

changed, and heads for her car. She gets in, turns on the ignition, and finds it won't start. MacMurray (who has tampered with it beforehand and followed her from the theater) comes up to the car and says, "Need some help? Maybe you've got the motor flooded." Novak looks at him (like a kitten wrapped in mink) and asks, "What do I do about it?"

After trying to start the car himself and failing, he checks under the hood and comes back with, "I don't know, I don't think you're getting any spark." (There may not have been enough to start the automobile but the sparks that she was flashing to MacMurray were enough to ignite both him and the audience.)

Discovering that the auto will require some time to be repaired, she asks him, "Would you like to take me home?" His answer is, "Your place or mine?" And hers is, "Surprise me." Over music and drinks at his place, the dialogue, a series of questions, goes like this:

| | |
|---|---|
| Novak: | Sorry? |
| MacMurray: | Sorry for what? |
| Novak: | Picking me up? |
| MacMurray: | Is that what you call it? |
| Novak: | Don't you? |
| MacMurray: | Do you get picked up often? |
| Novak: | Would you care? |
| MacMurray: | If I said yes, it wouldn't make much sense, would it? |
| Novak: | No, I guess it wouldn't. |
| MacMurray: | The answer's yes. |
| Novak: | Would it make any sense if I told you it's never happened before? |
| MacMurray: | Maybe. |

You know she has him in the palm of her hand and you can see why. Novak is dynamite and looks every inch the femme fatale.

Back at the stakeout, viewing an unsuspecting Novak from across the street, Carey asks MacMurray what makes a dame like that tie up with a guy like Richards, and MacMurray answers, "Money, what else?" He adds: "She's scared—scared of being hungry—scared of being alone. You can wrap up her whole world in that one word—money."

In the meantime, MacMurray has learned from Marshall that there is no record of serial numbers on the money taken in the robbery. With a man on the phone tap and another outside in a lookout car, MacMurray and Carey alternate the around-the-clock watch, observing Novak as she nervously paces her apartment.

Eventually, she finds out that MacMurray is a cop. When she confronts him with this, he says, "I learned

proper mood for the action, and the music was similarly appropriate. Quine's direction was also flawless. He has that rare talent for making his actors seem natural at all times.

Grabbing your interest immediately, *Pushover* opens with an early morning bank robbery (executed by Paul Richards and an accomplice) in which a guard is killed. The action continues as credits are flashed on the screen.

With $200,000 taken in the bank robbery, Fred MacMurray, a plainclothes detective, is assigned to the case. He is to strike up a friendship with the gunman's girlfriend in the hope that she will lead the police to Richards. A police stakeout is started from a building directly across the street from the girl's apartment. E. G. Marshall is in charge, and MacMurray and his partner, Phil Carey, are to observe all of the action at her place.

An air of mystery clings to Novak's presence throughout the film. It is immediately evident in her opening scene. She leaves a movie theater, avoids walking under a ladder where the marquee is being

*Pushover,* with Fred MacMurray

*Pushover,* with Fred MacMurray

everything I wanted to know about you that first night. I went on seeing you because I wanted to, but it's over." Curiosity, however, gets the better of him, and he asks her feelings about Richards. She explains, "He bought me my clothes and my car and a lease on a decent place to live in—things I've never had in my whole life." MacMurray presses: "If you had known where his dough came from, would you still have taken it?" An ice-cold Novak replies, "Money isn't dirty—just people."

Knowing that the police will eventually get Richards, Novak surprises him with, "We could have that money, you and I." She persuades him to kill her boyfriend so they can have each other—and the $200,-000. (There were shades here of one of MacMurray's previous films, the highly acclaimed *Double Indemnity.*)

MacMurray kills Richards when he shows up to see Novak while she's out. He, Novak, and Dorothy Malone (who has spotted his liaison with Novak and, therefore, becomes a hostage) make a hasty exit down the stairs to freedom. First, MacMurray must try to get to Richards's car which still contains the money from the robbery. The police are on to MacMurray's scheme. In a desperate try to get to the car, he is confronted by Carey and shot.

Slowly, Novak comes into view. She walks across the street toward the police, knowing that it's all over. The dying MacMurray, who has told her to leave, thinks she has escaped. She kneels beside him to comfort him and he says, "I thought I told you to go. . . . We really didn't need the money, did we?"

Novak is led to the waiting police car. She looks back at MacMurray for the last time—longing and lost. Somehow, you wish they could have made it.

\*    \*

Jack Moffitt, in the *Hollywood Reporter,* summed up Kim's performance in this way:

> The world now has (and I can think of nothing it needed more) a blonde Ava Gardner. Her name is Kim Novak and I'm pretty sure you'll be hearing much of her. Possessed of a face and figure to set men dreaming and a Jean Harlow-like personality that may set wives seething, she proves in *Pushover* that she is not only a model who can act but something very close to a model actress. She is particularly effective in humid silent scenes where Lester White's camera dwells caressingly on her face and Arthur Morton's musical score strokes the emotional fires of the old Adam in the audience. Miss Novak is a lucky girl to have made her debut in this excellent Jules Schermer production. It isn't a big picture but it's an exceptionally good one.

After the completion of *Pushover,* Kim's old fear took over and the inferiority complex emerged in full force. "I just know I'm terrible. I know the critics will tear me apart, and I'll probably never get to make another movie." But, as it happened, her fears were unfounded. Even the studio was astonished at the ecstatic reviews of her performance. Many critics proclaimed her as their personal choice for future stardom.

Still, the glowing reviews didn't make her feel any more secure. She said:

> I know the reviews were fine, but what will happen if they don't like me as much in my next picture? I just know the next one will turn out much worse. They'll say I'm twice as bad.

Kim's inability to take good luck for granted was to be one of the factors that would insure her a long and successful career. It would act as a built-in worry meter—a sort of brake or anchor that would hold her back and thus enable her to keep her perspective in the

*Pushover*, with Fred MacMurray

*Phffft,* with Jack Lemmon

midst of the dizzying good fortune that was coming her way.

\* \*

The studio was all set to borrow Sheree North from Twentieth Century-Fox for the other-woman role in *Phffft* but cancelled those plans when they saw Kim's footage in *Pushover.* This casting was a wise move on the part of Columbia and provided Kim with one of her rare opportunities to do comedy. Stealing a comedy from Judy Holliday and Jack Lemmon is no easy feat, but that is exactly what she did. In fact, under the expert guidance and direction of Mark Robson, a spark of brilliance was kindled in her.

Jack Lemmon has recalled:

It was a good film—almost a very good film. When I went to the sneak preview of the picture, I couldn't take my eyes off Kim on the screen, even when I was in the scene with her. She was brilliant and the damndest thing—she didn't know she was being funny when she made the movie. I think it's a classic comedy performance.

Walter Winchell was responsible for the film's title. Whenever he stated in his column that a marriage had gone on the rocks, he always said it was "phffft." George Axelrod, who had originally written *Phffft* as a play that was never produced, fashioned the screenplay with the same funny lines and technical brilliance.

Although Kim's role in *Phffft* was not as large as the one she had in *Pushover,* she made every second of it count. Her work is fascinating and perfectly timed, and, as Lemmon says, you can't take your eyes off her on the screen.

\* \*

*Phffft* concerns Judy Holliday and Jack Lemmon, who, after eight years of marriage, come to a parting of the ways. He's a theatrical attorney and she's a writer of television soap opera. They are both ripe for new lives on their own.

The wife turns first to a television actor and then to Jack Carson, already a friend of hers and Lemmon's. Lemmon, who wanted nothing more than a little tranquility, is thrown into the arms of Novak by the well-meaning Carson, who tells Lemmon: "You're in for a ball!" And he is.

When Lemmon first shows up to take Novak to dinner, she is delighted, because, as she says, "I was just about to open a can of spaghetti." Lemmon tells her:

"Well, I'm certainly glad you didn't do that." To which she replies, "Oh, me, too. I hate to cook." A typical dizzy blonde, as dumb as she is beautiful. Next, she floors Lemmon with, "Turn around. I have to finish dressing," and chatters on:

Speaking about spaghetti, you'd be surprised how many fellows you go out on dates with who don't like to buy you any dinner. They'll buy you anything you want to drink, alright, but not to eat. What I think is—they just want to get you plastered.

Seeing someone staring at her in her slip from across the court, Lemmon suggests she pull the curtain. Novak replies:

Oh, no! Don't do that. My girl friend and I—we never pull the curtains. We just have a ball with him. Y'know, that boy must be a nervous wreck. We never let him get any sleep at all. Someday he's going to flip his lid or fall out the window or something. Don't you think he's a scream?

[Lemmon suggests that she call the police.]

No, that would spoil everything. After all, he's been so patient. It only seems fair.

She suggests "a dreamy place" where they can have dinner, and they are on their way.

At the "dreamy place," Novak is in her element. "All the boys here are from Yale," she announces, and their warm greetings show she's on home ground and something of a celebrity with the regulars. Lemmon is far from overjoyed, feeling "kind of old among all these crewcuts."

From the crowded room, one of the guys says, "Get the pompons!" Others shout "Come on, it's your song!" The music begins and we hear "Boola Boola." Novak goes into action with the pom-pons, obviously pleased to be center stage. When her number is over, she joins Lemmon at their table.

| | |
|---|---|
| Novak: | Sometimes, I think I should have gone to college. Y'know, there's so much a person can get outta college—you may not believe this, but they were going to give me a scholarship to this college. But I decided not to take it. I wanted to keep on with my dancing. |
| Lemmon: | That's very interesting. What college was it? |
| Novak: | What? Oh, some little jerkwater college back home.,Here, put your hot one against my cold one and make my cold one hot. That means give me a light. |

A classic line—not on a par with Bette Davis and Paul Henried in *Now, Voyager* or Lauren Bacall and Humphrey Bogart in *To Have And Have Not*—but,

37

*Phffft,* with Jack Lemmon

they will not be disturbed—a lamp named "Sam" with eyes that light up. When Sam is faced to the street, the apartment is occupied. When he's turned around, the coast is clear. Novak aims him toward the street and questions Lemmon about his divorce. She seems genuinely concerned. But, finding the reasons were incompatability and moodiness (nothing juicy), she loses interest.

Lemmon becomes depressed thinking about his marital breakup, so she says, "Y'know, you really ought to try and cheer up. Here—maybe this'll help you." She kisses him, but the situation does not improve. She is puzzled.

Novak: That didn't seem to do any good at all. Hey, what's the matter with you, anyway?
Lemmon: I don't know. I'm sorry but the whole thing is a mistake, that's all. I told Charlie it was, but you know Charlie. I'm still upset and everything. I'm not very good company. You see, I don't even have any ice?

Novak hasn't known rejection before and can't quite figure it out. This is the first time her equipment has failed. Asking if his wife was special, and hearing Lemmon say she was different, Novak quips, "I've got a flash for ya. That much different she couldn't be. Good Night."

Though she struck out on their first meeting, Lemmon doesn't forget her, and, later in the film, he makes another attempt. Summoned by him, an eager Novak rings his doorbell. After some friendly small talk, Lemmon kisses her and, this time, takes her by surprise.

Novak: You seem different, somehow—Y'know, I just wish you'd have called five minutes earlier. I already opened a can of spaghetti so I just stuck it in the icebox. Do ya' think it'll keep?
Lemmon: Forever. (Handing her an orchid corsage) Since this is a party.
Novak: Gee! Gee, thanks. How about that? It's a white orchid! Gee, let's see—where can we pin it? (She is wearing an off-the-shoulder gown.)
Lemmon: Well, I have some scotch tape in the kitchen, maybe—(Novak laughs) Just wear it some other time. Take it with you when you leave—if you leave.
Novak: Okay, I'll keep it in the icebox.
Lemmon: With the spaghetti? It sounds like a popular song, doesn't it? Orchids, spaghetti, and you.
Novak: You're getting cuter every minute.

nevertheless, a classic line.

Lemmon wants to get further into a brain like this and asks her what subject she almost got her scholarship in, to which she answers, "Music." She adds, "I won runner-up in the all-state drum majorette contest."

All this and she's vulnerable too. Wants to please and receive acceptance. Kim's wide-eyed innocence is perfect for the character. Back at Lemmon's apartment, he tells her Carson and he were in the Navy together and that he's been Carson's lawyer for a number of years. Asking if she'd like a drink, Lemmon suggests whiskey.

Novak: I think whiskey'd be dreamy.
Lemmon: (laughing) We don't seem to have any ice. Charlie forgot to put water in the trays.
Novak: Oh, don't worry about it. I'd just as soon have a little straighty.

In the meantime, Novak (who has been to the apartment before in the company of Carson, who shares it with Lemmon) puts a signal in the window so

So far, all is going well. Much better than last time. She's spied a tiger-skin rug and is fascinated by it. The champagne is cold and Novak has paid Lemmon a compliment.

*Phffft*

*Phffft,* with Jack Lemmon

Novak:  Hey, would you mind if I sat on your tiger skin for a minute—I'm just dying to try it?
Lemmon:  Well, that's what it's for!
Novak:  Y'know, this is just wonderful. So glad you asked me. Champagne and the flowers. The tiger skin. Who's all coming?
Lemmon:  Just you and me.

He kisses her passionately.

Novak:  Boooiiing!
Lemmon:  Boing?
Novak:  Yeah, boing. So glad I was free tonight.

Y'know, I had a date with Charlie but he called me up and he broke it—Yeah, he had a call from some girl he knows—a writer up in Westport.
Lemmon:  Huh?
Novak:  Oh, if he hadn't had this call—
Lemmon:  What writer up in Westport?
Novak:  I don't know. She just got a divorce or something. She was married to one of his best friends. So he was going up there to keep her company.
Lemmon:  Why, why—keep her company—
Novak:  Yeah, he was going to play pony express. That's a joke Charlie has. You know what a

*Phffft*, with Jack Lemmon

vein as the latter's in *The Seven Year Itch*, which was also written by Axelrod.

Kim's performance rated well with critics and audiences alike. It did her no harm at Columbia, either. *Variety* reported:

Kim Novak gets across a zesty show as a dizzy, accessible blonde out to cure Lemmon of the post-connubial blues.

Jack Moffitt, in the *Hollywood Reporter*, said:

Kim Novak as the gabby blonde is the big news of the picture. In *Pushover*, Miss Novak proved that mood lighting and careful camera work could make her important star material. But in this comedy role, she really troupes, reading laugh lines with a sureness that reminds you of Jean Harlow at her best in *Platinum Blonde*.

There were many reviewers who remained enchanted with Kim's smoldering "silent star" aura and Columbia beamed with pride.

riot he is? Hey, what's the matter with you anyway?

Lemmon: Look, I'm sorry—I just remembered a previous engagement. I've gotta get up there right away. If you wouldn't mind waiting? I'm sorry. You could go to a movie. I'm sorry.

Novak has struck out again and she doesn't understand any of it. Lemmon gets to Westport in the nick of time to save Holliday from the arms of Carson. They realize old loves are best and the film ends with a reconciliation.

\*　　　　\*

This was a tailor-made role for Kim and she made the most of it. It wasn't surprising that many compared her to Marilyn Monroe. Her vocal inflections were often identical to Monroe's, and she projected a similar childlike innocence. Although Kim never deliberately mimicked Monroe, her performance was in the same

# 3
_____

She was touted as a sex symbol, but Kim Novak wasn't like any of her contemporaries. One movie executive said, "What Marilyn Monroe developed, Kim was born with." Not exactly true. Kim had to learn to use her natural attributes and overcome extreme shyness. Sex was strictly for the cameras. Off screen, she was on the serious side—a home girl, deeply devoted to her family, and far from the femme fatale she would learn to project. "By instinct," she has explained, "I'm the type who prefers full skirts and Peter Pan collars. I had to be told to wear more severe, sophisticated clothes." She did not, however, object to the buildup Columbia had decided upon for her. As she put it, "What girl doesn't like to be considered sexy, even if she herself doesn't believe she is." And so the molding of her image began.

Publicist Muriel Roberts was assigned to teach her how to dress, how to meet the press with poise, and how to handle all the other duties of a star. It was Roberts who hit upon the color that would be associated with Kim far into the future: lavender. She was dressed in various shades of it and subjected to a lavender hair rinse. Soon, everyone linked the color with her. She went along with this, even answering her correspondence on lavender paper with purple ink, but eventually her feelings about the color were profoundly affected. She explains:

I really did like purple, but the studio made such a thing out of it that I grew to hate it. Only recently, after I had cut all the purple out of my life, I realized that the exploitation of it was over and my pure feelings for it had come back, so I said "the hell with it" and got something purple.

Life for Kim was becoming increasingly demanding. Along with press interviews and photographers, there were dancing, singing, and acting lessons, and hours of costume fittings. Requests for still photos kept her in front of the cameras when she wasn't filming, and Bob Coburn, director of still photography at Columbia, was especially pleased with what she had to give. "No matter how you shoot her," he said, "she's beautiful. She's perfect. All the angles are good."

Concentration on her career was a full-time job. It left little room for anything else, including dating. However, Kim was managing to see one person, a young theatre owner and land development investor named Mac Krim. When Harry Cohn learned of this, he didn't approve. Krim was not a celebrated name. Kim resented Cohn's intrusion into her private life and stated:

Mac is a fine friend. Sometimes, when I'm working, I can't possibly get home for dinner by six o'clock. I feel free to call him at the last minute and suggest he take me out. Isn't that a real friend?

Cohn had big plans for Kim, but marriage wasn't one of them. He didn't want a star who was considering wedded bliss that would shatter an image he was busy dreaming up. Actually, Kim wasn't ready for marriage or even thinking of it, but the idea that somebody was telling her what to do annoyed her. So, while Cohn and the publicity department arranged dates for her to attend social functions with name personalities, she continued to see Krim, infuriating Cohn with calling cards that stated "Kim and Krim were here."

She maintained her friendship with him for a number of years and, ultimately, had the last laugh on Cohn. It was during the filming of the bathhouse scene in *Picnic* where Kim, Susan Strasberg, William Holden, and Cliff Robertson are changing on opposite sides of a wall. Before the scene was shot, Kim had printed "MAC & KN" on the men's side of the partition, and circled it for emphasis. Cohn didn't spot this until the scene had been completed and, since it would have been too costly to reshoot, her contribution to the wall's graffiti remained clearly visible in the final print.

*5 Against the House*

\*　　　\*

Her third film assignment from Columbia took Kim on location to Reno, Nevada, for a suspenseful melodrama titled *5 Against the House*. Mary Costa had been signed for the role but, in a last minute switch, the studio set Kim to costar opposite Guy Madison in this love story with an edge-of-the-seat finish.

When it was completed, director Phil Karlson said, "Kim will be a great big star. Nothing can stop her. And she really works."

Actor Alvy Moore recalls:

I remember Kim as a very serious actress. Since this was near the beginning of her career, she spent most of her time thinking about her part and the business at hand. She wanted to be at her best at all times, and I believe this is one of the reasons she sometimes showed temperament and fought the scenes she had to do.

When *5 Against the House* was made, I was recovering from polio. As a matter of fact, it got so cold up in Reno that severe pain was my companion for some time. I remember that Kim borrowed a bathrobe from me and, when she returned it, it became sort of a keepsake. I kept that robe for many years.

I think the picture has held up with the passage of time. If I'm not mistaken, Columbia had originally scheduled it as a "B" movie. In those days, as you undoubtedly know, all films had letters such as A, B, or C. The further down the alphabet—the less money was spent on production. I think *5 Against the House* was a "B" until they started

seeing the dailies and the scenes that were shot in Reno. They decided it was going along better than they'd expected—so they pushed it up to an "A." This meant a little longer shooting schedule, original music, etc.

Kim was really dedicated and worked hard throughout the shooting. I enjoyed being in the film with her very much because she gave her all. I guess that's the best anyone can do.

Since the role required Kim to be a nightclub singer, a professional singer's voice was scheduled for dubbing. Then the overly ambitious Kim started to study with studio music department head Freddie Karger. She was terrified when it came time to record, and so tense that Karger thought she wouldn't be able to sing a note. "But she was terrific," he commented and added, "She has amazing drive. She worked with all her might and her singing comes off fine."

Unfortunately, however, her work was to be in vain. Although the studio issued statements that said, "Novak's voice will surprise everyone and it's her voice you'll hear on the soundtrack," it was Jo Ann Greer who dubbed the two numbers Kim sang in the film.

\*　　　\*

*5 Against the House*

go into her number. Blonde and lovely, she delivers a sultry version of "The Life of the Party," and then comes to their table.

After warm greetings all around, the friends leave discreetly, and Madison tells Novak how he feels about her. Novak's been through it all before and is not sure of anything now. It's clear she isn't taking chances on being hurt again as she says:

> I grew up in this town. I've been dating college boys since I was old enough to be noticed by them. There's something about being away to college that makes for deep and lasting love affairs that are forgotten the minute graduation's over.

Meanwhile, on the terrace outside the club, Keith has become involved in a fight with a former girl-friend's date, and it sends him into a rage. With mounting fury, he beats the boy until Madison interferes and restrains him. Madison realizes that his friend may be in need of a checkup on his old head wound.

As the semester goes on, Keith seems to be back to his normal self and Madison dismisses the problem. Madison's main concern is to convince Novak that his intentions are serious. She doesn't understand the big rush and asks, "What's the matter with being a little sure of ourselves?" With complete honesty, she confesses her love for him, and, though she looks like the blonde bombshell who's been everywhere and done everything, she isn't. Novak continues with:

> I'm not long out of high school and all these big emotions I'm feeling are wonderful. But they sort of scare me, too. I want to get married as much as you do, but then when I think about it, I get so scared I want to turn and run and . . .
>
> [Madison stops her words with a kiss. As long as he knows she loves him, he will wait.]

In the meantime, Mathews has drawn up the master plan to rob Harold's and prove that it can be done. Keith and Moore are intrigued with his foolproof scheme. While Mathews plans the heist strictly as a scientific study, Keith, realizing it could net them over $70,000, begins to take the whole thing seriously.

After a two-day separation from Madison, Novak agrees to go to Reno with him during Thanksgiving vacation and be married. Since Mathews has purchased a new car and a seventeen-foot house trailer (in anticipation of the robbery) to get to Reno, Madison asks for a lift for himself and Novak. Keith, who knows there'll be no chance of carrying out Mathews's plan without an extra man, is delighted and says, "Won't it

*5 Against the House* begins with four college boys (Guy Madison, Kerwin Mathews, Alvy Moore, and Brian Keith) on their way back to Midwestern University after a summer of cowpunching. Madison and Keith were originally war buddies in Korea, where Keith had saved Madison's life and got a head wound in the process. At the university, the two met Mathews and Moore, and all four are now enrolled in law courses.

On a stop-off at the famous Harold's Club in Reno, Mathews becomes intrigued by a guard's comment about a failed robbery attempt that occurred during their visit. After they leave, he begins to formulate a plan to rob the place successfully.

When they arrive back at the university, Madison is eager to see Novak, the girl he's been thinking about all summer. He and his friends go to the Campus Club, where she is employed as a singer, just as she is about to

*5 Against the House,* **with Guy Madison**

*5 Against the House,* **with Guy Madison**

*5 Against the House,* **with Guy Madison**

be grand with just the five of us?"

Eventually, Madison and Novak become aware of the robbery plan. She is aghast and says, "How could you even dream of such a thing?" Madison realizes Keith is sick and that there's no way to discourage him from the robbery. Not only does Keith plan to use Madison on the job, he has also figured out a way to include Novak.

The nightmare begins. Keith covers them with a revolver and orders all but Madison into the trailer. In a last minute change of plans, Novak is to follow them in the car (now unhitched from the trailer) and, exactly three minutes and fifteen seconds after they enter, deliver a money cart that has been duplicated to match the original money carts in Harold's to the back entrance. Then she's to park the car in Harold's garage. Novak is warned by Keith that, if the cart isn't there in exactly three minutes and fifteen seconds on the button, he'll kill Madison. She knows he means what he says. Six minutes later, they are to meet her on the train waiting in the station near Harold's.

As they start off, Madison holds back for a second. Keith pulls the hammer on the gun and Novak screams, "For God's sake, he's insane! Do what he says!" Keith nods his approval as he tosses the car keys to her and the four men move away.

Everything goes exactly as planned. Mathews's idea, so casually conceived and carefully worked out, is a success. While Mathews did the whole thing as a prank, intending to give back the money, he knows Keith will never go along with this. So, when Keith leaves with the money, Mathews takes a chance. With his attention on Madison, Keith is not expecting an attack from any other quarter. As they race down the alley away from the club, Mathews hurls himself at Keith, knocking him against a wall. Still clutching the money sack, Keith breaks away and runs out into the street. Madison races after him. The robbery has been reported and an approaching police siren grows louder.

Police converge on the club and find Mathews and Moore while Keith and Madison are stalking each other in the garage. A bullet ricochets off a metal post near Madison's head. He sees the wild-looking Keith, working his way around the auto toward a fire escape door, and yells his name.

Madison pleads with Keith to come with him. Keith's response is, "I'm going to kill you." Madison reminds his friend of the night in Korea when Keith saved his life. It rings a bell. Keith's body is shaking with sobs and he utters little cries, his mind tortured.

*5 Against the House,* with Brian Keith and Guy Madison

With Madison's arm around his shoulder, they go down to the waiting police.

Moore, Mathews, and Novak are also there. Keith turns over the money sack and holds out his wrists as a policeman snaps on the handcuffs. When they take him away, Novak, clinging to Madison, asks, "What's going to happen to him?" Madison says he'll have to stay in a hospital until he's well. He looks at Novak and adds, "Great start for a marriage." Novak answers, "I just want the marriage to start." Ready to give their statements at headquarters, they get into the police car. It drives off and their future together begins.

\*    \*

Kim's role in *5 Against the House* was unlike those she'd had in either *Pushover* or *Phffft.* The only similarity to what she had done before was that the voltage of her sex appeal remained constant from start to finish.

About the film, *Variety* said:

Guy Madison and Kim Novak . . . should help ticket sales and both do their chores well, as do Brian Keith, Alvy Moore, Kerwin Mathews and other casters. Performances all down the line are excellent, with Phil Karlson's topnotch direction the factor in making the characterizations well valued and the suspense tight.

Jack Moffitt in *The Hollywood Reporter* mentioned that:

The robbery is ingenious, exciting and suspenseful, and I won't spoil it by going into details. Its one fault is that it involves Miss Novak in action more suited to a serial queen. This girl's glamour is such a terrific box-office potential that it should always be backed up by careful lighting and photography (which she gets in most of this picture). The one flaw in Karlson's direction is that he didn't have her wait out events in some shadowy place where the camera could have dwelt lovingly on her troubled face.

\*    \*

Before the release of *5 Against the House,* Kim appeared in *A Kiss for the Lieutenant*—again paired opposite Guy Madison. The episode was on the "Light's Diamond Jubilee" TV special, aired 24 October 1954 on all three networks. In negotiating for this appearance by its star-to-be, Columbia felt it was making a wise move because this would alert viewers to the fact that Novak and Madison could soon be seen together on the big screen.

*     *

Kim's films were beginning to prove that she had potent box-office appeal, and Harry Cohn never argued with an audience. Spurred by this, he shoved aside the misgivings he had had about her possibilities. She'd become a valuable property, and he took her under his protective wing.

Her recollection of that time is realistic but not bitter:

> I don't regret those days even though they were a heavy number, because they helped me grow and gain the kind of freedom I have now. I know I was exploited, but acting at any time is exploiting yourself.

Realizing Kim was ready for the big time, Cohn cast her in one of the studio's most important properties. She was to play the lead opposite William Holden in the film version of the successful stage hit *Picnic.* The character of Madge Owens was a naive girl who had never been out of the small-town environment she'd known all her life. The similarity to Kim's own beginnings would make this a difficult assignment for her.

Joshua Logan, who had directed the play on Broadway, was set to direct the picture. Holden, Rosalind Russell, and Betty Field, all pros, were approved for important roles. Kim tested for Madge and was retested a number of times. Columbia contractee Aldo Ray, who was assisting in the tests, says:

> Josh Logan was losing patience. He knew he wasn't getting what he wanted from the love scene we were doing. He came to me and asked if I would go off with Kim and work with her on my own, saying, "I don't care how you do it but—for Christ's sake—get her to show some emotion any way you can short of rape." We went off by ourselves and began to work on the scene and the problems she was having with it. I liked Kim and there was a good rapport between us. When I felt she was ready, we went back on the set. Kim was prepared to do the scene and she was fine. Logan was pleased and we proceeded.

*Picnic* was probably one of the toughest film assignments Kim could have had so early in her career. Awed

by the long-time professionals in the cast, she was painfully aware of her lack of experience. Similarly, during the early days of shooting, Logan's status as a director also filled her with fear.

One of her most difficult scenes was one that required her to cry. She couldn't. Part of the difficulty may have stemmed from an experience she had had with an English teacher in high school. As the story has been told:

> The teacher objected to Kim's dramatic way of presenting oral book reviews. While other students would get up before the class and discuss the books of their choice, Kim added drama. In reviewing a mystery novel, she imitated the killer "stealthily approaching, step by step"—then acted out the murder and scared the hell out of her classmates.

> Later, in reviewing Pearl Buck's *The Good Earth,* she threw herself down on her knees and wept real, agonizing tears in a poignant scene. After that, the teacher sent word to her parents that Kim "gets carried away and upsets the class." Henceforth, she was told to turn in written book reviews. Kim was crushed and felt guilty because she had been so emotional. And she developed a mental block about crying.

It was this block that Logan had to get through.

Reportedly, the startled, impatient, and slightly disgusted director took her by the arms and shook her until she burst into tears. Then he shot the scene. The force he had grabbed her with was so strong that her arms turned black and blue. Kim later said, "That's when I first started getting a little thick-skinned because he bruised me mentally too. I wasn't so soft from then on."

Kim knew how much depended upon the impression she made in this film. Harry Cohn was gambling on her, and the way she came across would make the difference between whether she was going to be an actress or not. Thus, she worked every minute of her time. On location (in and around Hutchinson, Kansas), the other members of the cast rarely saw her when she wasn't in front of the cameras. She would be by herself, preparing for the ordeal she must face when those cameras turned. Those who worked with her have varied impressions of the experience.

The late Rosalind Russell:

I had very brief scenes with Kim Novak in *Picnic* and never came to know her personally. She worked very hard and more or less remained by herself to study and prepare her work. She had great love and concern for her family in Chicago, and I admired this in her.

Cliff Robertson:

I was less than casual about the firmament of stars around me—including Kim—because *Picnic* was my first film. To me, it was a wonderful, confusing, new, and rather addled experience. Kim was very nice to me and considerate of my "newness" to the medium—having come from the New York stage. I will never forget her kindness.

The late cameraman, James Wong Howe:

Kim Novak could be photographed from any angle. Most beauties have a "favorite" side, but this wasn't so with Kim. I'd certainly have to bracket her among the five most beautiful women I've ever photographed. She had the greatest asset to becoming a star that an actress can possess: she projected from the screen at each male in the darkness of the theatre—as if he alone were the object of her romantic intentions. It's an elusive, intangible thing that either comes out naturally or not at all. It can't be phonied and Miss Novak definitely had it.

The thing that made her so extraordinarily interesting was the combination of her classical beauty with a sensual, lush quality. Her appearance was so breathtaking that it almost defied the camera not to capture it. The one thing most people remember of the film is the dance sequence, and I have been complimented on this more than any one thing I have done. The film was a joyous experience for me and I remember Kim Novak for greatly enhancing what I was trying to capture in my lens.

Susan Strasberg:

*Picnic* was my second film and I was under a great deal of pressure. In looking back, I realize that Kim must have been under equal, if not greater, pressure. I always felt that because she had not formally studied acting—and didn't think of herself as an "actress"—she was especially insecure and did not trust herself.

Joshua Logan:

I'm not sure that Kim Novak wasn't the chief reason for the success of *Picnic,* and I mean that artistically as well as financially.

I don't mean she was necessarily the best actress in the picture, but she was perfect for the part of Madge. I have a feeling that Kim *is* Madge. Her background and Madge's background with the intellectual younger sister were parallel ones.

Also, Kim, being beautiful, was always treated as Madge was treated—"Madge is the pretty one! Isn't Madge beautiful?"—until both of them began to wonder whether they existed beyond their beautiful faces. Kim seemed to understand this almost as if she had written it herself.

Roz Russell was spectacular in the part of Rosemary and Bill Holden in the part of Hal, but it was Kim who took the picture and ran away with it.

There have been remarks made, and I'm afraid by Kim herself, that I did not want her in the part of Madge. This is not true. I am the one who tested her twice to get the proper hairdo and dress, and, from the moment I saw her without her own modern hairstyle (with a slight lavender color), I knew she would be Madge.

[Since Logan didn't like her short haircut or the color of it, Kim's hair was tinted red, and she wore a matching shoulder-length fall throughout the film.]

Of course, there is no denying that I was very moved by the performance of Janice Rule in the New York company of the play, and I tried to make both girls, Kim and Janice, look like what I imagined was the girl on the front of a candy box. Kim and Harry Cohn resisted that a bit, and that was when I put my foot down, saying if I couldn't make her look the way I dreamed of Madge looking, I didn't want her. That remark evidently was twisted to mean something else.

Neither Kim nor Bill Holden were able to do the slow jitterbug dance we had done so successfully on the stage, but, with James Wong Howe's lighting skill and Kim and Bill's concentration, an illusion was created of a romantic, sensual moment that is still hard to top. Kim's entrance onto the platform down the steps, clapping her hands together in rhythm as she joined Holden in the dance, is probably the high moment of the picture. I have had more people point that out as their biggest thrill than any other episode in the film

\*        \*

*Picnic* was acclaimed as one of the year's outstanding motion pictures. Every facet of this splendid rendition of the prize-winning play by William Inge was excellent. When Inge wrote *Picnic* which won a Pulitzer Prize and the Drama Critics Award as the best Broadway play of the year, his dramatic action was, of course, confined to the stage itself. Off-stage action could only be suggested by his dialogue.

In its transformation to the screen, however, with Daniel Taradash's adaptation and under the loving guidance of Joshua Logan, *Picnic* surpassed its initial success. The camera's mobility made it possible to include actual locales, to show rather than imply. Logan was able to present the wheat fields, grain elevators, and spectacular skyscapes—to bring the colorful Kansas town to life.

There was, for instance, no actual picnic on the Broadway stage. It was only talked about. In the film, the picnic sequence became one of the highlights. It served as wholesome counterpoint to the main action and enabled Logan to reveal the stark beauty of American rural life. Technicolor and Cinemascope were additional assets, and all of this enhanced the play's poetic qualities.

While it is frankly a drama about sex, and, as such, has a few ugly moments, *Picnic* has more than its share of beautiful ones to compensate the viewer. The acting by everyone is powerful—the emotions truthful, the characters vivid. And the film's conflicts never cease to be handled with compassion and authority.

\*　　　\*

Set against the vastness of Kansas terrain, *Picnic* tells the story of a stranger in a small town and the havoc he creates in the lives of its people—especially its women. He virtually disrupts the town in twenty-four hours.

The stranger, William Holden, explodes on the scene one summer day after hopping off a freight train. He is a powerfully built young drifter, an ex-college athlete reluctantly aware that he must find himself a job and a place in the world or drift all his life.

Every woman in the vicinity is overwhelmed by him. But Holden isn't having any. He's a simple jock who lost a piece of his soul in childhood and a part of his wits on the football field. All he wants is a job. "I gotta get someplace in this world," he tells his old college chum, Cliff Robertson, "I just gotta."

Robertson, his former roommate at college, does more than find Holden a job. Holden is invited to the annual Labor Day picnic as escort for teen-ager Susan Strasberg, the bookworm kid sister of the town beauty, Novak.

Novak is the fiancee of Robertson. She is a classic beauty, locked to small town life, her mother, Betty Field, and her sister, Strasberg, the latter as plain as Novak is beautiful. Robertson, the richest boy in town, hears Novak lament, "It's no good just to be pretty" but hasn't the slightest idea what is tormenting her.

During Holden and Novak's first meeting, they are unaware of their attraction for each other. The restrained feelings surface later when Holden makes Novak believe she possesses more than just good looks, that she is a real person capable of warmth and giving.

Novak becomes less certain she wants to wed Robertson, even though her mother advises it.

| | |
|---|---|
| Field: | A pretty girl doesn't have long . . . just a few years. Then she's the equal of kings. She can walk out of a shanty like this and live in a palace. If she loses her chance when she's young, she might as well throw all her prettiness away. |
| Novak: | I'm only nineteen. |
| Field: | And next summer you'll be twenty—and then twenty-one—and then forty! |
| Novak: | You don't have to be morbid. |

The memory of what happened to Field (who fell for a handsome ne'er-do-well husband who deserted her years before) has lingered with her, and she doesn't want her daughter to fall into the same trap. Field points out that Robertson offers "comfort, charge accounts, automobile, trips, and the Country Club." Novak says, "Mom, I don't feel right with those people. I get tired of only being looked at."

Novak's sister doesn't make matters any easier. In one of their squabbles, when Novak calls Strasberg a "goon," Strasberg retaliates with "slut." Strasberg clearly resents the fact that Novak "is the pretty one" and bitterly spews out, "She's so dumb they almost had to burn the schoolhouse down to get her out." She further berates Novak for working in a dime store.

With the sisters and their mother, lives a frustrated school teacher, Rosalind Russell, the boarder Field has been forced to take in to supplement the family income. Russell will also be a member of the picnic party, escorted by her unprepossessing shopkeeper boy friend, Arthur O'Connell.

*Picnic,* with Susan Strasberg

Holden affects the women in various ways. Novak becomes more and more interested in him. Russell can't help but compare him to O'Connell, and Strasberg discovers that, with him, she is no longer the shy, awkward "kid sister."

At the picnic itself, with the lusty merriment of the contests, the romantic setting, and the music of a dance band, Novak and Holden realize there is an attraction between them.

As the boat carrying Novak, who is about to be crowned Queen of Neewollah (Halloween spelled backwards), floats to shore and "Ain't She Sweet?" is being sung by townspeople waiting to see their queen, she is calm. It proves once again that she is nothing more than a beautiful face, so there is boredom along with her joy. The scene where she gives her acceptance speech—"Thank you . . . and I'll try hard to be a good queen. I'll try hardest of all not to be conceited."—is one with which Kim could easily identify. (Shortly after she had entered Wright Junior College, she was

*Picnic,* with Susan Strasberg, William Holden, and Cliff Robertson

52

*Picnic,* with Verna Felton, Betty Field, Susan Strasberg, Cliff Robertson, and William Holden

elected Freshman Queen. The *Wright College News* reported that "the queen is friendly, easy to get along with, likes people who are interesting and intelligent, dislikes those who are loud and flashy . . . she prefers considerate fellows with good manners to the Adonis type and has dark thoughts concerning the 'Hiya, babe' variety of male.")

Novak's awakening to the love she bears for Holden creates an impression long remembered. During the dance sequence, one of the highlights of the film, she becomes a true goddess of love to every red-blooded American boy.

To the mounting strains of "Moonglow," intermingled with the "Theme from Picnic," Holden and Novak dance toward each other with what may be the sexiest movements ever choreographed for a film. Novak glides forward on the deserted pavilion. Each movement, each rhythmic clap of the hand, each beat in which she freezes before continuing is executed to perfection. When they reach each other's arms, they continue to dance, moving into another realm. The scene is honest and powerful, its mood skillfully sustained.

The lovers' happiness is shattered later when disaster strikes from all sides. Strasberg has been given booze and is sick, and Russell—who has been spurned by Holden—flies into a vicious tirade against him. He and Novak flee in Robertson's auto, and he tells her, "I'm a bum," that Russell saw through him like an X-ray machine, and "There's no place in the world for a guy like me." Novak sympathizes with "Oh, there's got to be" and points out some of his good qualities:

Novak:  . . . and you're a wonderful dancer.
Holden:  Thanks.
Novak:  Oh, I can tell a lot about a man by dancing with him. You know, some boys, well, when they take a girl in their arms to dance, they, well, they make her feel sort of uncomfortable—but with you, I had the feeling you knew exactly what you were doing. And I could follow you every step of the way. Oh, you've got lots of qualities. [She reassures him with a kiss.]

Afterward, with the police trailing him because of Robertson's jealous reporting of the stolen car, Holden is smuggled in O'Connell's car to Novak's house to see her once more before leaving town.

*Picnic*, with William Holden

Holden:  I just couldn't run out of town and never see ya
           again.
Novak:  Where are you going?
Holden:  Tulsa.

He tells Novak he liked her from the first time he
saw her. Now, he confesses, "I love you . . . [and asks]
do you love me?" He tells Novak he's hopping a freight
and asks her to meet him in Tulsa. He promises they'll
be married, but adds, "It won't be big time." Strasberg,
who's been eavesdropping, says to Novak, "Go with
him . . . for once in your life, do something bright."
Against her mother's warnings, she announces she's
going to Tulsa.

In the final scene, Novak boards a bus for her
destination and the camera pans from the moving bus
to the freight train which is carrying Holden. They are
traveling in the same direction with a new life ahead
for them.

*      *

About her work in the film, Kim said:

The hardest role for me to do up to this point was Madge
Owens in *Picnic*. The only similarity to myself was that

*Picnic*, with William Holden

*Picnic,* with William Holden

with:

*Variety* reported:

And Jack Moffitt, in the *Hollywood Reporter,* said:

my own sister, Arlene, was the bright one in the family who got all the good grades. In the film, Madge wasn't supposed to be very bright. To me, she was childlike. She had never seen New York. She had never been out of that little town. She had never seen men without their shirts on. She had hardly seen men. So there was a conflict within her when she felt sex for the first time.

Everything was the first time for her. It was very difficult to get the feeling of Madge. It wasn't even recalling it. I lived in a small town in a way, since it was the outskirts of Chicago, but still I wasn't Madge. All of a sudden it happened to her—sex, I mean. She wasn't smart, but she had common sense.

She had guts, too. It took guts to leave her home and go into something she knew nothing about. When she stepped into that bus to follow the man she loved, it was like stepping off a cliff into the unknown.

I had to have long red hair for the role, so I wore a wig, and my own hair was dyed to match it. I felt different as a redhead. After the picture, I kept the red hair for a while, but I didn't feel quite the same. Not like myself. I love dark hair, but not on me.

Logan gave Kim a number of exciting scenes and she brought the right quality to the character. Her reviews were good, and Logan said at the time, "She is a sensitive and creative girl, as gifted as she is exquisite, and can handle anything from boredom to terror with impact."

A. H. Weiler in the *New York Times* applauded

It was the first time that audiences had had the chance to see Kim in Technicolor, an asset which greatly enhanced her beauty. Kim attained stardom with *Picnic,* and it became one of the big grossers of the year for Columbia Pictures. Rated both an artistic and commercial success, the picture told an entertaining story that was right for the times. Harry Cohn's reluctant faith had been justified, and his big gamble on the model from Chicago was beginning to pay off.

*Picnic*

# 4

_____

Producer Jerry Wald picked Kim for her role in *The Eddy Duchin Story*. He had watched her progression from the time of *Pushover*. Upon completion of the latter, he had had a script bound in leather and sent it to her with the following inscription: "This is the first in a line of hits and misses. Don't be disturbed about the misses and don't get worked up about the hits." Wald was now about to assist Kim in adding another hit to her list.

Tyrone Power had been cast as Duchin, and Kim was assigned the role of Marjorie Oelrichs, the great love of his life, who would become his first wife. The script showed Marjorie as an unhappy young woman who associated autumn winds, rain, and darkness with impending death. She was a striking contrast to the character Kim had played in *Picnic*, where she'd been a small-town girl—insecure, and torn between the propriety of her environment and the love of a stranger from a more worldly one. As Marjorie, a member of New York's top stratum, Kim would have to be worldly herself, poised, serene, and self-confident. About the assignment, she said:

> The wife I played in *The Eddy Duchin Story* was the character least like me of the roles I have done. She was a society girl: sure of herself, firm, positive, definite in everything she did. Her romance and marriage took place

in the early twenties. I wasn't born until 1933, so everything was strange and new to me.

> I kept a phonograph in my dressing room on the set, and I played music of that era to help me get in the proper mood. [This was a method Kim would rely upon for several future roles.] It was an exciting and dangerous period, and you could feel the people in the music.

*The Eddy Duchin Story* was filmed on location for three weeks in New York City against authentic backgrounds wherever possible. Central Park could never have been duplicated, and the Waldorf-Astoria's Starlight Roof, where Duchin was a top attraction for many years, gave the story added realism.

Playing one of the richest debutantes in New York history, Kim was given twenty-three costume changes. Evening gowns and dresses were topped with mink and sable coats, and, along with the rare jewelry which complimented them, were valued at $125,000. This was a far cry from the three dresses she'd worn in *Picnic,* which totaled roughly $22.50.

Designed by Jean Louis, Kim's gowns were in the style of the twenties. She said, "The styles are so similar to today's that, with a tuck or two, my whole wardrobe in the picture could still go anyplace." She became particularly fond of the clothes and purchased a black broadcloth suit trimmed in white mink and a

*The Eddy Duchin Story*

*The Eddy Duchin Story,* with mother, Blanche Novak, visiting the set

stunning eggshell negligee with matching peignoir for her personal use.

George Sidney directed (he would later guide her through three more assignments) and said at the time:

> She has the facade and the equipment of a bitch in the long shot. Yet when you look in Kim's eyes in a closeup, she's like a baby. There is a fire with the sweetness, a bitchery with the virtue, all in one package.

The "facade and the equipment of a bitch" were noticed by one person *off-camera:* Tyrone Power. His misinterpretation of them led to friction during the filming. This was the first time Kim had not gotten along with her costar. Of his leading lady's behavior Power said: "Confusion between temperament and bad manners is unfortunate." Kim's retort was: "When things are going wrong, it is a waste of time to be calm."

While it appeared that Kim was indulging in bursts of temperament on this film, in reality, she was trying to work out what she felt was right for her and the role. This was a nerve-racking experience because, as she put it:

> When I started getting parts in pictures, I took them seriously and worked hard at them. I went along with the studio, worked at my publicity. I didn't mind. When you're just starting, you don't care. It's when you start thinking for yourself, and try asserting your own personality—not only on the people around you but in the way you feel you should be playing your roles to the best of your ability— that you begin to find yourself moving against the current

and needing to fight every inch of the way. [Ironically, at the beginning of her career, Kim had also given a wrong impression. Her extreme shyness had led some of her coworkers to think she was uncooperative or that she had "gone Hollywood." This was never the case, and, when she curbed that shyness and learned to give (although she would never fully conquer the insecurity and vulnerability that were hampering her), she became one of the most popular persons at Columbia.]

Power obviously did not share the studio's enthusiasm for Kim, but others in the cast of *The Eddy Duchin Story* had different impressions of her. The late Frieda Inescort said:

> Working with Kim Novak was a joy. We really didn't have time to get to know one another very well but I liked what I saw. She was delicate and charming at all times. I saw many of the same qualities in Kim that I noticed in Elizabeth Taylor when we did *A Place in the Sun.* They both became superstars and were both deserving of this status. Kim applied herself to her craft in a dedicated manner and was most perceptive. She was a hard worker and performed her role to the best of her ability. My part in the film was minor but I felt she was instrumental in making the whole thing click.

And Shepperd Strudwick states:

> I remember Kim as a very hard and conscientious worker, easily upset if she thought things weren't going right. I remember seeing her coach, Benno Schneider, on the set from time to time and being told that she had sent for him. [Benno Schneider, the Columbia drama coach, had worked with Kim from the start of her career. He had helped to rid her of self-conscious mannerisms and had taught her to project her voice. In the early days, she had also worked nights with a stage group directed by Batami Schneider, Benno's wife. Benno was a friend, and Kim felt more at ease when she was able to iron out her dramatic shortcomings with him.]
>
> I also recall that she wore me out one day rehearsing a dance we had to do together—and this when she had much more to do than I did. She struck me as being an inexperienced but talented actress, who spared herself nothing in learning to be good at her job.

At this point in her career, as the above indicates, Kim was a mass of contradictions. It was a condition that made her interesting. It also probably made her an actress. Very few successful actresses have uncomplicated, one-track personalities. Her greatest fault was still her lack of self-confidence. As she said, "I'm sure confidence comes only with learning and with improving oneself more and more." This was her constant aim.

Most of Kim's problems could be attributed to the age-old condition of too much too soon. In two short

*The Eddy Duchin Story,* **with Tyrone Power**

years, she had become a star. She was beginning to receive awards, her portraits were appearing on dozens of national magazine covers, and columnists were besieging her for interviews. But the star who was recognized by everyone else was still trying to recognize herself. As she put it:

> Deep inside me, I feel a profound sense of gratitude to the amazing good fortune that has been mine these past two years. The wonderful luck in having everybody at Columbia behind me. Having directors like Joshua Logan on *Picnic,* and George Sidney on *The Eddy Duchin Story;* and stars like William Holden, Rosalind Russell, and Tyrone Power to advise me and give me every consideration. I'm scared, bewildered, thrilled and excited.
>
> I'm sure if I stopped to think about it, I'd faint. I just don't dare stop! It's fantastic and it's not happening to me; that's the way I've worked it out so I can go through this period until I begin to get used to it.

\*         \*

*The Eddy Duchin Story* is a sensitive and human rendering of the life of a man known to millions only by his music. Duchin conquered the golden towers of Manhattan with his fingers on the keys of a piano— and the film mixes stardust and reality to shape a drama rich in love, triumph, loneliness, and despair.

The romance between Power and Novak is presented with heart-warming simplicity. She's a socialite and he's a struggling musician when they meet. One of their most beautiful scenes shows them walking through Central Park in the rain. Because of a strike within the industry, at the time, George Sidney and camerman Harry Stradling were left crewless. The two men with Harry's son Harry, Jr., went out and shot the scene by themselves. Stradling's photography is vital throughout, and the art of the cinematographer has never been more in evidence than in the imaginative and evocative Central Park scenes.

Against the advice of her aunt and uncle, Frieda Inescort and Shepperd Strudwick, Novak marries Power, who, on their wedding night, gives her a gold key, telling her it's "for you . . . to our front door." But all will not be golden. Later that night, a storm blows up and the wind and rain have a strange effect on the new bride. Power gets his first glimpse of an insatiable need for love and protection—a need that will sometimes interfere with his career.

Novak:   Eddy! Eddy!
Power:   Marjorie, what is it? What's wrong?
Novak:   Nothing.
Power:   What do you mean, nothing? Tell me, what is it?
Novak:   No.
Power:   Please, please tell me.
Novak:   Wind frightens me. Oh, I hate the wind. (sobbing)
Power:   Why? Why?
Novak:   A dream I had. I can't seem to fight it off.
Power:   Darling, darling, try to forget it.
Novak:   Try? I try. I tell myself it's only a dream but it keeps coming back. The wind blows between us and I keep trying to reach for you but you're gone.
Power:   It won't be like that.
Novak:   I know. I shouldn't have told you.
Power:   Oh darling, darling, I'm here. It's only a dream.
Novak:   You ought to beat me. I'm . . . I spoiled your wedding night.
Power:   How could you?

Despite the demands of Novak's fragility, however, their marriage brings them happiness. On one outing, as they look forward to parenthood, Power announces from the bandstand with pride: "Ladies and gentlemen—the first appearance of Eddy Duchin and his Central Park Casino Orchestra in front of any special audience." To the strains of "You're My Everything," he continues:

Power:   Mrs. D. Do you dance?
Novak:   Well, I . . . I haven't had time . . . but I'm not the girl I used to be.
Power:   Shall we? Just the three of us.
Novak:   (As they dance) I'm afraid I'm rather keeping you at a distance, Mr. Duchin.

*The Eddy Duchin Story,* **with Tyrone Power**

*The Eddy Duchin Story,* with Tyrone Power

*The Eddy Duchin Story,* **with Tyrone Power**

*The Eddy Duchin Story,* with Tyrone Power

Power:   Yes, you have let someone come between us.
Novak:   Do you mind terribly?
Power:   Not as long as I have you.

Unfortunately, he will not have her for long. Novak dies on Christmas Eve, after giving birth to a son. Her death scene is tragically real. (It was the first for Kim, and she played it flawlessly.) The loss of his wife drives Power out of New York, away from their baby and everything that has been so intimately associated with his happiness.

The rest of the film takes him through years of touring and war and, ultimately, brings him back to New York and his son, Rex Thompson—a lonely boy, with many of his mother's fears of wind and rain, whose love and respect Power must win. A second wife, Victoria Shaw, finally pulls Power out of his protracted grief, but leukemia claims him at the picture's end, putting the final touch to a life dominated by tragedy.

\*          \*

*The Eddy Duchin Story* was a picture for everybody. While melancholy elements prevailed, they were mixed with scenes of gentle and sometimes hilarious comedy which kept the sadness from becoming oppressive. Fictionalized biographies were extremely popular at the time, and this one rated high on filmgoers' lists. Wald's treatment of his subject didn't glorify Duchin. It presented him simply—as a musi-

cian whose life swerved between professional success and personal despair.

Kim was a valuable asset to the movie, romantically at home in the glamour and wealth of Fifth Avenue, and delightful on rain-swept walks through Central Park. The portrait she etched was that of a girl in love, and it was a vivid one, filled with warmth. She was exquisitely photographed, with moments of such great beauty that audiences would remember them long after leaving theatres. In comparison with her other roles, this was a relatively small one, since her character dies midway through the film. However, because Duchin's son suffers from the same fears as his mother, Kim's presence lingers throughout.

The reviews of her performance were all favorable.
*Motion Picture Herald:*

The supremely competent cast assembled by the producer is headed by Tyrone Power as Duchin, Kim Novak as his first wife, James Whitmore as his manager, and Victoria Shaw, a newcomer to American films, as his second wife. The Power performance is his best of recent years; Miss Novak's is totally different from any she's turned in heretofore.

*Variety:*

With Tyrone Power in the title role and Kim Novak as his first wife, the picture is equipped with marquee values that merit top playdates and corresponding boxoffice response . . . Miss Novak continues to enlarge her stature as an actress with her playing of the first wife, Marjorie Oelrichs. It's a distinctive performance that will win her new laurels and added favor with her growing public.

*The Hollywood Reporter:*

[Duchin's] romance with Marjorie Oelrichs, played with restraint and reserve by Kim Novak, is tenderly sketched, and his despair and desolation at her death is believably communicated . . . *The Eddy Duchin Story* should have great appeal to women for many reasons, not the least being that it has two good heroines in Miss Novak and Miss Shaw. The subject of remarriage after the death of one partner in a marriage is always a fascinating one, and it is dealt with here so convincingly that it will be acceptable to everyone.

\*          \*

Kim was now a full-fledged star, and Otto Preminger paid her a supreme compliment. He was about to put *The Man with the Golden Arm* into production, and, as he has described it:

I wanted Kim for the part of the junkie's girl friend. I

thought she was right for it so I went to Harry Cohn at Columbia. He was reluctant to let me have her. We argued back and forth for a while and then he said the loanout price for her would be $100,000. At the time, it was a staggering amount for any young actress but I agreed to it.

The shrewd Cohn, was, of course, happy as a lark. Columbia would realize a substantial profit from Kim's services in the film since her salary, at the time, was still a modest $750 a week. And Kim's career (and, therefore, box-office value) would be considerably advanced by a chance to perform under the guidance of a man as skillful as Preminger.

Of their work together, Preminger said:

Kim had very little confidence in her ability to act and her assurance had not been improved by the directors of her first pictures. They had had her repeat the lines over and over until they were acceptable, and then had dubbed them later. I never believed in that method and didn't work with her in that way.

When we started shooting, Kim was terrified. She had great difficulty delivering her lines believably although she tried very hard. Frank Sinatra was very compassionate about her nervousness. He never complained and never made her feel that he was losing patience through any of it, even when we had to do some scenes again and again.

I was pleased with her performance, and I'm glad I held out for her. I think she is worthy of the praise she received. Because she was not terribly sophisticated, she gave you a feeling of compassion. I think she is full of basic honesty and warmth, and this is the way I remember her.

*        *

Preminger had signed Frank Sinatra for the male lead and Eleanor Parker for the role of his wife. Kim's was the flashier of the two female parts: a world-weary B-Girl, Molly, whose sympathy and encouragement enable Sinatra to finally kick his heroin habit. The supporting roles, also cast to perfection, were played by Darren McGavin, Arnold Stang, John Conte, Robert Strauss, and Doro Merande.

John Conte recalls:

Preminger was in his prime, and some classic confrontations occurred between Otto and Darren McGavin and with Arnold Stang. I was always impressed by Kim's sense of embarrassment for the participants while others in the company were wallowing in enjoyment.

In my work with Kim, I found her to be a most "gentle" person. She was professional, even though she was not a product of an acting "technique." Always prepared and never the cause of any delays in shooting.

There was about her a wonderful quality of childlike innocence and wonder. She had no extensive "formal" education but she did have a natural wisdom about life in terms of her own career and the transience of material things.

About her childlike quality. We were doing a scene together one day sitting in a booth in a bar set. In between takes, I was working a crossword puzzle. Kim confessed that she had never done one and asked me to explain. I did and, after studying it a few minutes, she came up with a word. Her joy was something to see!

Kim and Sinatra were fascinating to watch working together. Both "natural" actors. I enjoyed that film and the opportunity to work with them very much.

*        *

*The Man with the Golden Arm* is an almost flawless picture. From the Saul Bass opening titles to the concluding notes of Elmer Bernstein's exciting jazz score, Preminger filmed it to perfection, embellishing his story with slum characters that were frighteningly real.

However, the movie had its share of problems after completion. The censors refused their Seal of Approval. In spite of the fact that *Man* was a potentially valuable social study which might deter people from drugs, the Hays Office stuck to its ruling that any film about taking and peddling illicit drugs was forbidden.

United Artists, which was distributing, decided to fight the decision; they submitted the picture to state censors. Over one thousand theatre owners elected to show it, with or without the seal, and *The Man with the Golden Arm* subsequently enjoyed healthy grosses, cheered by a public who responded to the boldness of its theme.

*        *

*The Man with the Golden Arm* focuses on a man's struggle against drug addiction. After spending six months at a federal narcotics hospital, Frank Sinatra returns to the Clark Street section of Chicago. He's been cured of the drug habit that sent him away, and he's looking forward to a promised job as a drummer.

Sinatra refuses to take up his old stand as dealer in Robert Strauss's poker games, and, similarly, wants no part of pusher Darren McGavin's attempt to get him back on heroin.

A nagging wife, Eleanor Parker, who uses feigned invalidism to hold him, drives Sinatra to the company of the only real friends he has left: Novak, a B-girl who loves him and wants to see him shake his bad environment, and Arnold Stang, a crafty street person who aids him unselfishly.

Sinatra's reunion with Novak takes place in the hall of their apartment building where he's using the phone. She's glad to see him and expresses her concern. Their next encounter is at the Club Safari where she works.

Sinatra: They tell me you was working here and I was passing by and I thought I'd come in and have a drink.
Novak: Oh, I've been here a while.
Sinatra: Doin' any good?
Novak: Alright . . . small kind of game . . . usual kind of drinks.
Sinatra: Have something!
Novak: You don't have to do that, Frankie . . . I've been hoping you'd come to see me.
Sinatra: You know how it is Molly . . . well, here's to it, Molly-O.
Novak: Molly-O! I ain't heard that since you went away. You're lookin' good, Frankie.
Sinatra: Feel good.

Novak encourages Sinatra. She tells him he has a natural rhythm and that he'll make it as a drummer. Just as they're beginning to get reacquainted, John Conte comes up to her for a buck. Embarrassed, she slips it to him. With a far off gaze, she offers an explanation.

Novak: I got lonely . . . I needed somebody . . . 'n he's a poor beat guy who needs somebody too.
Sinatra: Everybody needs somebody but you can do better than him.
Novak: Can I, Frankie?
Sinatra: Molly, I . . . I thought a lot about you while I was away . . . about you and me and Zosh [his wife] . . . how it'd never work out between you and me as long as she was upstairs sitting in that chair. It'd be different if she didn't love me and she wasn't so helpless. You can't make a fool out of somebody who loves you and they're so helpless. That's why I didn't come around sooner . . . that's why I ain't comin' around no more. You understand?
Novak: Sure . . . sure, I understand.
Sinatra: You're a good girl, Molly.
Novak: Sure . . . real good. Frankie . . . good luck with that fella, tomorrow.

Later, after an argument at home, Parker tells Sinatra to get rid of his drums and "take 'em down to your girlfriend . . . if you gotta practice . . . take them down and give her the headache . . . take them down to that tramp!" Parker has always been jealous and still feels there's something between Novak and Sinatra.

At another of the neighborhood bars, Novak is seated alone in a booth as Sinatra comes up to her. She encourages him to make a phone call about the audition on which he's had no word. Coming back to her after the call, he is beaming. They'd lost his number and couldn't get in touch. Conte comes up to Novak again and, when he leaves, she explains the relationship further.

Novak: I'm all he has in the world . . . don't wanna hurt him . . . a fella like him—sometimes when we're alone . . .
Sinatra: What does he do, cry? He's a lush, Molly. He's a hundred per cent habitual drunk.
Novak: Look, everybody's habitual something . . . with him it's liquor.
Sinatra: Please Molly? Molly-O?
Novak: It ain't just that, Frankie, I don't want it to start with each other again. Look, what you said about us not bein' good—it was the truth. Even before you went away . . . I tried to . . . it just doesn't add up. It never can.
Sinatra: Well, give it a chance. I told you it would, one day.
Novak: All my life has been one day. On and on and on.

In a disturbingly realistic moment, the honesty of her situation and life-style is reflected on Novak's sad weary face. It's a powerful scene.

Sinatra then asks her if he can keep his drums at her place. Not wanting to rekindle the relationship they once had, she is reluctant but tells him, "I guess maybe you could drop in once in a while." He now has a place to use for his practice sessions.

Some time later, after a night of work, an exhausted Novak hears music coming from her room as she returns to it. "I hope the neighbors liked it, too," she comments. Sinatra tells her how well the session went. Wearily, she removes her makeup and washes her face. Then he brings her a glass of milk. She looks at him, suspecting he's back on drugs and in need of a fix. Her concern is strong. "Is it bad?" she asks. As he wipes the tears from her eyes, she tells him he shouldn't have started again. He promises to quit and says that, with the money he will earn as a drummer, he can get his wife into a good hospital so she can walk and thus cease to be a responsibility. Then maybe he and Novak can have a future together. But Novak hasn't heard. She is asleep. He carries her to the bed as he would a child, covers her with a trench coat, and turns out the light. Quietly he settles down for the night in a chair on the other side of the room.

Later, in one of the film's more joyful moments,

*The Man with the Golden Arm*

*The Man with the Golden Arm,* with Frank Sinatra

Novak and Sinatra window shop and dream about what he's proposed. At that point, the future looks great. He really believes he'll be the musician he wants to, and they talk about what their days will be like.

But the odds are against them. Sinatra is coaxed into dealing one more game for Strauss—and needs a fix to help him do it. When he comes to see Novak at work the next night, she knows something is wrong. She asks for a cigarette and, when she sees his eyes and his shaking hand as he lights it for her, realizes he's hooked again. "Why . . . Why?" she asks. After a fight between Sinatra and Conte, she flees across the street to her room and begins to pack her belongings.

Sinatra follows and bangs on her door, begging her to talk to him. But she gives him no chance. Darting past him, she flags down a cab and is off, leaving him alone at the curb. Without her, he heads for his pusher—and another fix.

Persuaded to deal one last game for some big-time gamblers after getting his fix, Sinatra knows this puts the "monkey on his back" again. The game, an all-night one, proves disastrous and he shows up for his drumming audition in bad shape. Needing a fix, he can't control his shaking hands and, knowing this will ruin his performance, he walks out.

Sinatra is now desperate for heroin money, and he returns to his wife briefly in search of it. He rushes out just before his pusher comes looking for him and discovers Sinatra's wife on her feet. When the pusher threatens to expose her ability to walk, she follows and lunges at him and shoves him down the stairs to his

death. Sinatra is blamed and the police begin their search for him.

After Sinatra learns he is wanted for murder, he locates Novak and waits for her to come home. There he pleads with her, telling her he's sick and needs money. Her reply is, "Jump off a roof if you're gonna kill yourself but don't ask me to help ya!" Just then Conte shows up. She opens the door slightly and gets rid of him, but not before he has suspiciously pointed out that she'll be an accessory to the crime if she helps Sinatra.

Sinatra swears he's innocent but can't stand up to the cops in his condition. She suggests he give up drugs "cold turkey"; he doesn't think he can do it. Finally, she relents and offers the money. In one of the most powerful and moving moments Novak has ever had on camera, she says:

Alright. Alright . . . here, take it. Go on and take it all. 'Cause all that you're gonna need after that one shot is another . . . and then another. Take it. Take it! Why should you hurt like other people hurt? Yeah . . . so ya had a dog's life with never a break. Why try to face it like most people do? No . . . just roll up all your pains into one big hurt and then flatten it with a fix. What do you think you'll find just outside that door? Don't ya think that Bednar [the police detective] knows what ya are . . . and what ya need . . . just to get through that next hour? Don't ya know he's just waitin' for ya to come and get it? Go on . . . let him kill ya. Let him kill ya! It'll be quicker and better than doin' it your way.

A sobbing Novak has reached the addict. Sinatra says, "No, I won't let him kill me." He wants to rid himself of the monkey on his back but confesses: "A guy can't do it by himself." Novak says, "I'll help."

Locking him in the apartment, she goes to his wife to plead for the man she loves.

Novak: I thought I'd come to see how ya been, Zosh.
Parker: Alone . . . that's how I been.
Novak: (handing her a package) Somethin' to eat . . . sausage.
Parker: Alone and worried sick. Where is he? Y'know where he is? Did he go to you? What do you want anyway?
Novak: Zosh, what you told Bednar . . . you've seen the papers, you see how bad it makes Frankie look, what ya said.
Parker: I didn't tell Bednar anything. The papers . . . they twist everything all up.
Novak: They wouldn't be able to if you didn't let them.
Parker: I can't help what they do . . . what do ya expect me to do, sittin' here?
Novak: Just tell Bednar that Frankie wasn't here when it happened—and that he didn't do it.
Parker: I never said he did!
Novak: But that's how it sounds if he was the only one

*The Man with the Golden Arm,* **with Eleanor Parker**

around at the time. And you know it was somebody else!

Parker: What do you mean? Who?

Novak: I don't know but maybe Bednar could figure it out if he didn't think it was Frankie.

Parker: What business is it of yours anyway?

Novak: I just wanna help . . . that's all.

Parker: Who you kiddin'? You think I don't know what you really want? You think I don't know what him and you been up to behind my back while I had to sit here all these years? Had to sit here all these years . . .

Novak: Zosh, you got it all wrong.

Parker: No, you got it wrong . . . 'cause you'll never get him. He put me in this chair and as long as I sit here . . . he'll never leave me. He knows he belongs to me.

Novak: No, Zosh, I come here only to help.

Parker: I wouldn't wanna live if he left me. And I'd rather see him dead, too, than have him go to you.

Novak: Zosh, please . . .

Parker: Get out of here! Get out of here you lousy tramp . . . get out! Get out!

Novak leaves a screaming and hysterical Parker. When she returns to her apartment, the hell begins. She is able to convince Sinatra that, if he is to establish his innocence of the murder, he must kick his habit before he gives himself up. He warns her that going through this is torture and that "a junkie will kill." She is afraid—but her compassion predominates and she locks the door and leans against it, knowing there will be no turning back until he's clean.

During the nightmare that follows, Sinatra tries to jump out of the window and, in her struggle with him, slams at her with a chair, threatening to kill her. In desperation, she tricks him and locks him in the closet, torn afterwards by the sobbing she hears on the other side of the door. When the sounds of life cease, she becomes worried and opens it. He falls out, cold and shivering, and begs her to "Make me warm, please." She massages his hands and covers him with blankets. Then, at the sight of the shivering and pathetic creature he has become, she places her body over his for added warmth.

Three days later, when Conte shows up looking for her, he sees the two of them at the window. Sinatra is clean and breathing fresh air. In the hope that, without Sinatra, Novak will return to him, Conte tells the police where they can find their murderer. But when they show up looking for him, he isn't there.

Intending to surrender, Sinatra has gone to see his wife and tell her this. She is so disturbed by the news that she jumps to her feet, forgetting her feigned lameness, just as a detective arrives. Sinatra realizes he's been duped, and the detective realizes who the pusher's killer really is. Parker makes an attempt to escape and falls to her death in the alley below. Sinatra, moving slowly from her side in the alleyway, is followed by Novak as they walk on to a future together.

\*      \*

This was one of the finest dramatic roles Kim Novak was ever permitted to play. She held her own and made each moment count. Even in the confrontation scene with an actress of the calibre of Eleanor Parker, she came out on top. Novak and Sinatra were a good team and worked well together, generating excitement on the screen. Otto Preminger released more of Kim's ability than any other director had taken the time for, and her potential as a dramatic actress was evident. It is also interesting to note another reason for her success as Molly. As she put it:

In every role I play, I try to associate my own feelings with those of the character. I can find a part of myself in almost every one I do. I go on what I feel personally. If you've got heart, you use it.

There have been several parts that I have played that were totally unlike me. The person I felt was most like me was Molly in *The Man with the Golden Arm*. Molly was compassionate. I think I would have acted the same way if I were faced with such a problem in real life. I could understand her feelings.

\*      \*

*The Man with the Golden Arm,* **with Frank Sinatra**

The reviews of the film were all good, and Kim's performance was praised.

*Variety* capsuled:

A downstairs neighbor is Kim Novak, and the [sex appeal] angles are not overlooked by the camera . . . in all cases—stars, featured and semi-featured players—the thesp talent is to be credited with a first-rate job.

And Jack Moffitt, in the *Hollywood Reporter,* stated:

The film is notable for a dozen fine performances, including three arresting and contrasting tours de force of acting by its three stars, Frank Sinatra, Eleanor Parker, and Kim Novak.
Kim Novak, as a warm-hearted street girl, is the one element that sustains the hero in the nightmare world that surrounds him. The film offers a fascinating study in what constitutes movie acting. I am sure that Eleanor Parker is one of the great screen actresses of the day. I really don't know whether Kim Novak in a technical sense, can act at all. I only know that she, like Valentino and Garbo, seems to be one of those rare creatures born with a perfect affinity for the camera. Properly lighted, her face has a poignant emotional quality that carries the audience along with her and makes dialogue seem almost superfluous. She generates a dreamy dramatic magic that cannot be taught or learned. It's what made the movies great in the silent days and apparently you're either born with it or you're not.

The climax comes when Sinatra, suspected of a murder he did not commit, dares not face the cops until he is cured of the drug habit. This means that he must lock himself in her room for three days, during which time she knows he will become crawling and disgusting, violent and murderous. The final moment in which she warms his pitifully shivering body by covering it with her own is an instant of almost unbearable beauty.

Kim's name had been linked with Sinatra's during the filming of *The Man with the Golden Arm.* They were photographed in public on several occasions, but,

*The Man with the Golden Arm*

network television show with Susan Strasberg, where they gave *Picnic* an additional plug.

Kim was a star now, accorded special treatment wherever she went. Some of this was still hard for her to accept. However, if she was uncomfortable about what was expected of her, she carried it off with grace and charm.

There was time for a stopover in Chicago, giving her a chance to spend Christmas at home. In spite of the physical distance between them, Kim and her family had remained close. She would always manage to be with them for the holidays.

Returning to Hollywood, she was anxious to get back to work. It was announced that Columbia would star her opposite Kerwin Mathews in a biblical epic titled *Joseph and His Brethren*. The property had originally been intended for Rita Hayworth but the demands of Hayworth and her husband of the time, Dick Haymes, were more than Harry Cohn would meet. He had, therefore, decided to give the important role of Zuleika to Kim. But this wasn't to be. The film was shelved while still on the planning board (When it was made seven years later, Zuleika had been eliminated from the script.) and Kim played the waiting game in anticipation of what the studio would dictate to her next.

when questioned about a possible romance, she had said, "We're just friends." She and Sinatra enjoyed a pleasant working relationship, and there was no reason for them not to be drawn toward one another. Kim's self-confidence had increased and she thus found herself at ease in his company. She had also learned the importance of being independent.

The year 1955 had been a blockbuster for her. She was the star of what would be three of next season's biggest pictures. Without a moment to catch her breath, she had gone from the filming of *Picnic* in May to that of *The Eddy Duchin Story* in July and *The Man with the Golden Arm* in September. Her career was consuming all of her time.

In December, she was sent to New York for publicity appearances in connection with *Picnic,* which had been rushed into release for Academy Award consideration. It was the Christmas attraction at the famed Radio City Music Hall. Publicist Muriel Roberts accompanied her on the trip. While in New York, Kim appeared on Dave Garroway's early morning television show and played peekaboo with the famed chimp J. Fred Muggs. She also appeared on Ed Sullivan's

*The Man with the Golden Arm,* **with Frank Sinatra**

71

# 5

Kim's fine performances in three top-budget productions now prompted Harry Cohn to try her at carrying a picture on her own. Since reviewers had constantly referred to and been enchanted by her smouldering "silent star" aura, what better idea than to star her as a silent picture actress? *Jeanne Eagels* was the property, and, this time, Kim would be the propelling force and bear the burden of sustaining a film almost single-handedly. It would rise or fall on her merits—a big step forward for her as an actress, and a big responsibility.

In previous efforts, Kim had been surrounded by seasoned pros to whom the studio had wisely given the major share of the acting load. Here, she would be faced with the moment of truth: a test of her ability and of the strength of her growing box-office appeal. After successfully guiding her through *The Eddy Duchin Story,* George Sidney was again in her corner on this production, and, to play opposite her, Jeff Chandler was signed.

\*　　\*

Driving ambition, radiant beauty, brilliant talent, and an unbridled personality that delighted in the unexpected—all these were part of the legend of actress Jeanne Eagels. She flashed across the Broadway horizon like a comet, consumed by the very flame that made her a star. Her story was both triumphant and tragic; her presence as unpredictable as it was beautiful. Such a role was a large order, but Kim felt up to it and was determined to do it justice.

When she began filming, Kim was still seeing Mac Krim, but she soon threw herself into the assignment so enthusiastically that she refrained from dating him for the remainder of the shooting schedule. Recognizing the importance of making good, but still beset by all of her old fears, she devoted her full energies to the exacting task of presenting Jeanne. She read everything she could find on her, learning, for instance, that "Eagels was irrational and sensitive and all the things I sort of am, and she used to eat pickles in school like me."

As she had done on *The Eddy Duchin Story,* Kim played phonograph music of the twenties to get herself into the era's mood. Her dressing room walls were covered with photos of the real Jeanne, and she employed an accordianist for several weeks to play "Poor Butterfly" during the film's sad scenes. Nobody could say she wasn't trying to bring realism to her role.

Designer Jean Louis created one of the largest number of costume changes Columbia Pictures had yet given a single star. Kim had forty-five, taking Jeanne from her beginnings as a carnival perfomer to her arrival on Broadway as a star complete with gowns, furs, and all the trappings of her life both on stage and off.

Most of Kim's off-camera time was spent in her dressing room studying, and coworkers saw little of her between scenes. Once again, the rumors persisted that she was being difficult and had taken her star treatment too seriously. Such was not the case, as remembrances from cast members illustrate.

Charles Drake:

I enjoyed working with Kim very much. She was a quiet friendly girl who came to work prepared in her lines and performed in a professional manner.

Unfortunately, my memories of the picture are not happy ones for many reasons. My good friend, Jeff Chandler, is no longer with us, for one, and my part suffered badly when they cut the film. The drunk scene was much longer and built much better than shown on the screen.

When Kim had a good part and was surrounded by a good cast and director, she always held her own. Take, for example, *Picnic* and *The Man with the Golden Arm*. She was great in both.

Virginia Grey:

As for Kim Novak, I am sorry to say I never got to know her. The only contact we had was in the two scenes we did together. It was a hectic time and there wasn't even an introduction. There was no conversation at all. We were both prepared and just did the job at hand.

Joe DeSantis:

All I remember is that long, long night in Long Beach at that amusement park where we worked. Kim was most kind and respectful towards me. I had a brief moment at the carousel with her, and rode back to town with her father, a dour man who was singularly uncommunicative. *Jeanne Eagels* remains in my memory as an afterglow. Kim was the only star I ever worked with who wrote me a thank-you note after the production.

Larry Gates:

Though I never knew Kim Novak very well, I always liked her, and we had a warm and friendly relationship on the set of *Jeanne Eagels*. She, in retrospect, was the most beautiful woman I think I had ever seen, and seemed to me to be struggling to overcome this wonderful asset.

We did the picture with a loving and very understanding director, George Sidney. Big movie studios in those days often promoted beautiful people, both men and women, because beauty is an important trait for a potential star to

*Jeanne Eagels*

have. Unfortunately, most of the major studio heads, like Harry Cohn at Columbia, had little or no idea of what it takes to make a good performance.

The tackling of a character such as Jeanne Eagels early in one's career would have put an extraordinary burden on Ethel Barrymore who, as a young lady, grew up in a theatrical family and had many opportunities to learn the tricks of the acting trade before she was confronted with major responsibilities in plays or movies.

Kim, at much more of a disadvantage, worked hard and well and always seemed eager for all the help she could get from the rest of us. This she, in large measure, received. But she was still playing over her head.

We who had been around longer in the business were very fond of her and, as I recall, were "pulling for her" as hard as we could. Agnes Moorehead, an old and dear friend, was quite helpful, I believe, to Kim.

On the set, I remember the management, perhaps at Kim's request, had an accordion player who, between takes, played songs of the period for mood. It was very pleasant, indeed.

When we finished the picture, Kim sent me a note on lavender stationery written in purple ink. In it, she was extremely loving and thankful for whatever she perceived I had been in the picture. (Candidly, I always felt I wasn't very good in it!)

It had been my hope, but the years somehow get away from us all, that Kim and I would meet again, but she traveled in a more rarified strain of Hollywood movie society than I have ever been part of. This notwithstanding, I remember her with much fondness and have very high regard for her as a fine, sensitive and caring human being.

\*　　　\*

Amid music and carnival atmosphere, the credits of *Jeanne Eagels* unfold as a smiling and excited Kim Novak, with suitcase in hand, comes into view. There are a number of closeups as she, wide-eyed, looks at her surroundings in awe. She is a small-town girl whose unquenchable thirst to be an actress has led her to a beauty contest staged by carny owner Jeff Chandler.

When she finds out that the contest was rigged (because "the fat one related to the police department" wins), Chandler gives Novak a job with the little troupe, saying, "Maybe in the next town I'll let ya win a contest." (He will and she does.) Chandler lifts her up on the back of the truck taking them to their destination, and there's a look of sheer joy in Novak's closeup as she reflects the hopes and dreams of every aspiring young actress. She's on her way and feels she's getting a start in show business.

Carnival life is not without its problems, but Novak makes the best of them. She fills in at every odd job on the midway—from hula dancer in dark wig and grass skirt to sitting duck who gets knocked into the water in a game concession to live target for Chandler's knife-thrower. She does all of this for money which she saves toward dramatic lessons she will take when they reach New York.

The height of her carnival experience is as a "cooch dancer" in something titled "Dardanella's Secret." (For her cooch routine, more of Kim was revealed than in any of her previous cinema efforts. Wearing a costume of beads, and doing a sensuous and provocative dance in a carnival tent, she was a different person.) A cold and shivering Novak confronts Chandler after he has given the pitch to entice the local yokels in to view her charms. She's chilled and hating every minute of what she's doing.

Novak:     Must ya talk so long? It's cold out there!
Chandler: Don't give me trouble.
Novak:     Sal, I'm sick and tired of playing "Dardanella's Secret."
Chandler: Whatsa' matter? It ain't good enough for ya?
Novak:     All I do is flop around. I want a real play. Sal, I wanna act. I'm not a coochy dancer. I want *Becky Sharp*.

*Jeanne Eagels*

Chandler:  Get out there and shake some Arabian at these people—Becky!

Novak takes her turn on stage in a gold lame cape that she sheds to reveal a costume of beads and little else. While the orchestra plays slinky tunes, she handles pillows and a stuffed tiger skin to excite the audience to fever pitch. Tickling the tiger, she pets and teases it as the yokels howl with laughter. She rises in playful pique and begins throwing pillows at them. The routine was a standard one in carnivals around the country. Suddenly, during her "Arabian" dance, Novak is arrested for obscene conduct. The arrests were also standard, usually bringing nothing worse than an order to get out of town.

When Chandler comes to see Novak behind bars, she is angry and wants a lawyer, but he insists on pleading her case himself. As he compares her to the Venus de Milo to get a point across, a prim and proper Novak looks innocently into the judge's eyes and wins him over with her charm. The case is dismissed. Now that Novak is free from jail, they are ready to move on

*Jeanne Eagels,* **with Jeff Chandler**

fast. The star of a show called *Happy Lady* leaves the cast for a vacation and Novak replaces her. She tells Chandler of her good fortune as they enjoy a roller-coaster ride at the amusement park.

Novak's picture goes up in front of the theatre, and she causes a sensation. But she isn't satisfied, knowing it's only temporary. Chandler suffers too; in her eagerness to make good, she stands him up for a chance to meet the press at a party.

By the time the star returns to her role, Novak is rehearsing in a play of her own. But the play isn't very good, and she knows it. One night in Washington, an exstar on the skids, Virginia Grey, comes backstage with a script she is confident would serve her for a comeback. She begs Novak to get it to producer Larry Gates. Novak reads the play, Somerset Maugham's *Rain,* and instinctively recognizes what it will do for an actress. She wants it herself and, when she learns that Grey's option on it has run out, Novak circumvents her and ties up the rights. She then convinces her producers they should scrap the play they are doing and star her in *Rain.* In spite of her youth, she's learned every trick in the book, and Chandler, aware of it, tells her, "This is a thing you'll regret the rest of your life." But she doesn't want to hear this. Her mind is made up.

On opening night, Grey confronts her backstage and calls her "a monster," telling her the play will "bring you luck—all bad." Novak is shaken but goes on all the same. (Kim's lusty Sadie Thompson, complete with husky voice that matches the coarseness of the character, is an excellent one. If Columbia hadn't already released *Miss Sadie Thompson,* which garnered an Academy Award nomination for Rita Hayworth in 1954, it might have been interested in seeing what Kim could do with the role.)

The reaction to Novak's Sadie is nothing short of brilliant. Cheers and bravos greet her at the end of the second act, and the only thing that mars her happiness is the sight of Chandler leaving his seat during her thank-you bow and walking out before the play is finished.

Critics praise her highly, and she is thrilled to see her name go up on the marquee the next day as a star. But her triumph is dampened by reports that Grey is trying to reach the press to tell them Novak stole the play from her. Taking Moorehead's advice, Novak goes to see Grey and arrives just after Grey has committed suicide by jumping out of a window. Novak's remorse is deep as she looks down on the body. She holds a slipper of Grey's that was on the window sill, and there are breathtaking closeups set to silence as the realiza-

to the next stop, and they ride the merry-go-round back at the carnival grounds in joyful celebration of what lies ahead.

Novak had originally prevailed upon Chandler to give her a job because she knew he was on his way to New York. Looking much like a junior-grade Harlow, she had said, "I just want to be an actress—that's all." She has kept that ambition burning within her and has pestered him to let her do serious plays she wanted him to pirate for her. Now her dream is about to come true.

In New York at last, Novak looks at the Statue of Liberty from the Staten Island ferry and asks Chandler, "Where's Broadway?" Chandler joins his brother, Joe DeSantis, who runs an amusement park and is prepared to offer Novak a permanent job. By now, Chandler is madly in love with her and wants her to settle down with him and start a family. But her sights are higher and she has only one goal: to be a star.

Novak persuades Agnes Moorehead, a famed dramatic coach, to coach her, and, through Moorehead, is soon rewarded with a job in the chorus of a show scheduled to open on Broadway. Now things move

*Jeanne Eagels,* as Sadie Thompson

tion of what has happened registers on her face.

Knowing how she must feel after the incident, Chandler comes to Novak's dressing room to see her. She says, "You're right, Sal. I rob. And I steal. I do everything in the book. You called it . . . I'm a murderer." And she believes it. He tries to comfort her, saying that no matter what he told her before, he still loves her. But it is not enough. Publicity has connected her with Grey's death, and she is now a curiosity. People are coming to the theatre only to see what she looks like, and, driven by guilt feelings, she is drinking heavily. Producer Gates stands by, ready with the understudy, but Novak waves them off.

> I'm going on! They paid their money. They want to know what I look like. I'm not hiding. Whatever I did, I did. Let them look at me. Let them look at me all they want to look at me.

Chandler tries to stop her, saying he still cares for her, and Novak lashes out at him:

> Take your hands off of me. I don't want your help. I don't

want you to wait for me or to take me home. I don't want you to worry about me and I don't want you to love me. I don't want you to do anything at all for me. Now, will you kindly step out of my dressing room, Sal? I have a performance to do and I've got to get ready.

Later, arriving home from the theatre, she finds Charles Drake in her apartment. Drake is a celebrated sports figure from a prominent family. When she met him some time ago at a party, he was married. Now, free from that encumbrance, he tells her, as she reaches for a drink: "You don't need Scotch; what you need is [me]." She decides she does, and they are married, with little regard for Chandler's feelings.

A year later, on the closing night of *Rain,* she addresses the audience: "After two very wonderful years, our show is going on the road. So goodbye, New York, and God bless you." Drake, feeding her habit, waits with a drink for her in the wings. As she is leaving the theatre, one of the cast members asks her to join Actors Equity. Her reply is, "Why? What do I need a union for?" She refuses to join or, ultimately, to abide by any of the rules the union insists actors observe.

Her continual drinking on the road causes performances to be cancelled and earns her the name "Gin" Eagels, the bad girl of Broadway. Union members, angry at her behavior, come to speak to her. A drunken Novak tells Drake to throw them out, saying: "Do you know what I am? I am a star. I don't need Actors Equity. I'm going to Hollywood. I'll be a star there, too."

In Hollywood, Novak makes a silent movie and, when it wraps, is invited to a New Year's Eve party by the director. She declines and spends the evening drinking with Drake. Her subsequent drunk scene is one of the best in the film. On the telephone with Gates, who calls from New York, she turns out a brilliant piece of acting and, after hanging up the receiver, whirls around to wish Drake a Happy New Year. He has passed out. She screams the words in his ear and kisses him passionately, but he remains unaware of her ardor. Novak is pathetically real here, keenly expressing the torture and frustration that are pulling her apart.

Finally, after five years of marriage, she and Drake divorce. He has been reduced to being "Mr. Eagels" and neither has done the other much good. As they wind things up, he says, "Forgive me for messing up your life. I want to thank you for five crazy, wonderful years." Despite their differences, they part friends.

Back in New York, an on-the-wagon Novak is about

*Jeanne Eagels*

*Jeanne Eagels*

*Jeanne Eagels*

*Jeanne Eagels*

to open in a new play titled *Careless Lady.* As she poses for photographers outside the theatre, she is jubilant. Asked to raise her skirt a little higher, she says, "This is as far as I go. You're too young and I'm not that old." And, to questions about the fact that Drake is remarrying, she quips, "I hope his wife appreciates everything I taught him."

Suddenly she sees Chandler in the alleyway and goes up to him. His feelings for her haven't changed, but there is obviously no future for them together. The encounter with Chandler starts Novak drinking again, and she arrives late for her opening night. Explaining her behavior to Moorehead, she says there are "times you feel blue and alone, and everything's dark in front of you. And you get scared." Moorehead scolds her with, "Movies by day—plays by night. Never sleeping. Headaches, pains, pills." But Novak replies, "I faint . . . but I never faint before the show . . . only after."

She seeks a sedative from a disreputable doctor and is particularly effective as she registers the drug-taking effect. It seemed the more difficult the scene, the better

Novak was. While some of the film's simpler moments gave her trouble, here she was strongly convincing. Half dazed, she floats to the stage, makes her entrance, and then begins to crack. Beads of perspiration appear on her face as she tries desperately to remember her lines. She falls and beats the stage with her fists, and the curtain comes down on her screams.

After her recovery, Equity summons her to appear before its Board of Directors who announce that she "may never work on the legitimate stage again." This is a terrible blow, and Moorehead pleads for her, saying, "a long suspension is like a death sentence." The only thing that means anything to her is her work. Without that, she'd rather die.

While photographers await Novak's exit, she goes to the fire escape and looks at the alley below, thinking of Grey. She throws her hat down as she considers suicide. Chandler, who has been listening in on the proceedings, finds her and tells her the suspension has been reduced to eighteen months, and that it's not the end of the world. Novak says simply, "It's the end of my world." Seeing her desperation, he suggests she return to vaudeville where Equity can't stop her. The void is filled as she immediately starts thinking about doing the "high moments of my plays."

However, back in vaudeville, there are long periods between shows. She tries to fill them by seeing Chandler. When she learns he's leaving for Europe to book acts, she is disturbed and proposes marriage. He declines, saying they'd destroy each other. They then plan to have dinner together later that night, and

*Variety* noted:

In the title role, Miss Novak turns in a generally fine performance. There are moments when she appears a little unsure of the characterization, but the portrayal is largely sound and penetrating and is certain to win acclaim.

And James Powers, in the *Hollywood Reporter,* said:

Miss Novak will undoubtedly not be satisfactory to every critic and particularly to some who knew Jeanne Eagels. Miss Eagels died a quarter of a century ago and, in addition to her undoubted brilliance, there is the fact that she has become a source of romantic legend particularly dear to those who saw her in their own youth. The fact remains that Miss Novak, undoubtedly aided by Sidney's persistence, gives a remarkable performance. Especially in the later scenes of drunkenness and despair. she is poignant and most effective . . . George Sidney was faced with an unusual problem in his story and in his leading character. The production is lavish and handsome, as it had to be to convey the period and the peculiar surroundings of his principal protagonist. He was handicapped in conveying the greatness of Jeanne Eagels by the fact that she never appeared in anything great so there could be no recreations of memorable roles such as is usually done in the biographical treatment of a famous personality. He had to suggest this incandescence through her personal life and to do it with a star, Miss Novak, who is relatively inexperienced in tragic roles.

Miss Novak certainly gives a performance that justifies her casting from a popular standpoint and for this Sidney should get credit. *Jeanne Eagels* may not be an unqualified success with some critics, but it should be a rousing success with audiences.

*       *

George Sidney, who had now worked with Kim on *The Eddy Duchin Story* and *Jeanne Eagels,* wanted her for the role of the beautiful chorine, Linda English, in *Pal Joey.* The film did not turn out to be one of Kim's favorites. She stated openly: "I just never cared for the part . . . I can't stand people like that girl Linda—I can't even stand the name." But the studio approved the casting, and Kim went along with it. She plunged into preparation for the role, doubling up on her singing and dancing lessons in order to be convincing as a struggling chorus girl.

Columbia had first acquired the screen rights to *Pal Joey* early in 1941, shortly after the play opened on the Broadway stage. But, for various reasons—some casting, some writing—it was never put into production. Now, the studio felt the timing was right. Rita Hayworth and Frank Sinatra were top-billed, and it would

Novak seems fine—but, in her dressing room, when Murray Hamilton, a cheap vaudevillian on the bill with her, shows up and makes a pass, awareness of her situation hits her. Angry at her rejection of him, Hamilton retaliates by telling her she's just a "drunken tramp they kicked off Broadway." Her suffering is complete and, after he leaves, she mixes sedatives and booze in an attempt to relive the past.

In her final scene, she hallucinates, drifting down a flight of stairs to her death. (In a bit of cinematic hokum, a star falls from the sky at the exact moment of her expiration.) Chandler ends the film, mourning her loss but knowing that, in a way, she still lives. He watches her image on the screen singing "I'll Take Romance" and leaves the theatre with tears in his eyes.

*       *

The reviews for Kim's performance were mixed. Critics either loved it or hated it. Nevertheless, most were captivated by her efforts to bring the character of Jeanne Eagels to the screen.

be Hayworth's last commitment under her studio pact. Although everyone expected a clash between Rita and Kim, there wasn't any. They simply did their jobs.

All three stars sang and danced in the film, but Rita's songs were dubbed by Jo Ann Greer and Kim's by Trudi Erwin. Again, as in *5 Against the House,* after extensive singing training, Kim's voice would be heard only briefly in two numbers where she talk-sang a line or two. ("Don't you know your Mama's got a heart of gold?" in the "I'm A Red Hot Mama" number, and the opening strains of "My Funny Valentine.")

The colorful characters and solid story from John O'Hara's original book, which Dorothy Kingsley adapted for the screen, were built around the Richard Rodgers and Lorenz Hart songs. A total of fourteen tunes was interwoven with the plot. Ten of the numbers (including "Bewitched, Bothered, and Bewildered," "Zip," "What Is a Man?" and "I Could Write a Book") were reprised from the original Broadway hit. Others by the Rodgers and Hart team ("I Didn't Know What Time It Was," "The Lady Is a Tramp," "There's a Small Hotel," and "My Funny Valentine") had originally been written for other Broadway musicals, but they fit in well with this script and, therefore, were used.

In the shaping of the legit hit for the screen, a number of switches were pulled. The role that Kim played was built up from the minor one it had been on the stage to star status. Despite this, however, it remained weak and suffered in comparison with the Hayworth and Sinatra parts.

*Pal Joey* presented Kim in her first screen bath, and marked the debut of the Hollywood helium bath. Special pipes were placed under the tub to feed gas into the water, resulting in an increased volume of suds and a lovely photographic effect.

While there was no feud between Novak and Hayworth, a minor one did brew between Kim and the late Barbara Nichols. Nichols was recreating the wise-cracking Gladys, a role she had played on Broadway in the 1952 revival. Since Kim and Barbara had the same shade of blonde hair, it was suggested that Nichols get herself a new one. She ended up with a brassier hue, while Kim's locks remained intact—and the two girls didn't speak off-camera for the duration of the filming.

Along with Sinatra's compelling singing of the score, Hayworth's make-believe strip and shower bath, and Novak's strip and bathtub scene, the city of San Francisco was thrown in for good measure. Although the original locale of the play had been Chicago, it was felt that the Bay City was more photogenic and would provide better weather conditions. Location filming resulted in shots of Golden Gate's Sausalito Yacht Basin, Fisherman's Wharf, Coit Tower, the St. Francis Yacht Basin, the Oakland-San Francisco ferry, the Spreckels mansion, and Market Street. Ironically, the company was rained out of its fair weather location and had to return to the studio a week earlier than planned.

\*         \*

The fun in *Pal Joey* begins even before the credits as Sinatra is booted out of town over a hotel incident with the Mayor's underage daughter. Given a one-way ticket and escorted onto the train, he heads for his familiar haunts in San Francisco where he talks his way into the singing emcee's spot in a third-rate club owned by Hank Henry.

An old buddy and fellow musician, Bobby Sherwood, also works at the club. He notices Sinatra's interest in Novak who is toiling in the chorus. When Sinatra asks about her, Sherwood tells him, "You gotta lay off. She's a nice kid. Has ambition too. Wants to be a singer." Sherwood says he's helping her with some of her arrangements and Sinatra agrees that she's "pretty well arranged." Novak and Sinatra are introduced backstage, but she is neither interested in nor impressed with his brashness.

A big party on Nob Hill finds Sherwood and the other musicians from the club on the gig. Novak and Sinatra go along as singers. The party, a charity auction, is held by Rita Hayworth, a former stripper who married into money and high society and became a widow in record time. Sinatra incurs Hayworth's wrath when he opens the bidding on her doing one of her old routines to the tune of "Zip."

Sherwood, Sinatra, and Novak ride home via cable car. After he has seen Novak to her door, Sherwood admits he's stuck on her. Sinatra, also interested, manages to rent a room next door to Novak's place. They share a bath, and what better way to get to know your neighbor? For the same reason, he acquires a dog named Snuffy that she falls for when they stop in front of a pet shop. (Snuffy, a terrier with a loveable face and personality, is the biggest scene-stealer in the film. He sleeps in a bureau drawer and prefers his bagels dunked in coffee.)

The talented but egotistical Sinatra is now faced with a problem. All his life, he's been used to charming his way into women's hearts—a heel, but a gilt-edged

*Pal Joey,* with Frank Sinatra and "Snuffy"

*Pal Joey,* with Frank Sinatra and "Snuffy" with Barbara Nichols
in background

heel. As a matter of fact, the entire chorus at the club is smitten with him—willing to do anything he wants from bringing him coffee to laundering his shirts. But, with Novak, he can't seem to get to first base.

To add to his worries, it is soon apparent he doesn't have the "big following" as a performer that he promised club-owner Henry. When confronted with this, he assures Henry he'll soon have the Nob Hill crowd beating a path to the club's door. Hayworth does come in once—slumming. But her purpose is to get even with Sinatra for his treatment of her at the party, and she makes a hasty exit after insulting him. Henry tells Sinatra that, if she doesn't come back, Sinatra will be through at the end of the week.

Sinatra pays a visit to Hayworth at her Nob Hill mansion. He tells her he's through with third-rate clubs and is leaving Henry's at the end of the week. He lays his cards on the table: what interests him now is Hayworth's money. She doesn't react, but Sinatra has an idea she's interested in what he's offering.

As Saturday approaches, he knows his job is finished. When the news is circulated, Novak comes to his dressing room.

Novak: Why didn't you tell me?
Sinatra: Why should I? You don't care what happens to me.
Novak: Of course I do. All the girls do.
Sinatra: I don't care about all the girls, baby, I just care about you.
Novak: Do you mean that, Joey—or is it just an act?
Sinatra: Of course I mean it. We're sure going to miss her, aren't we, Snuffy?
Novak: I'm going to miss you, too. I'm very fond of Snuffy.

He asks her to join him later for a bite to eat, but their rendezvous never materializes. Hayworth appears at the club after closing time "in the mood for a little entertainment" and demands a song. The band is hurried in and Sinatra, Novak no longer on his mind, obliges with "The Lady Is a Tramp" while Henry cringes at his choice of songs. Sinatra knows just what he is doing. Rough treatment is what Hayworth has come for and, to Henry's amazement, Sinatra walks out with her on his arm.

Hayworth and Sinatra set up housekeeping on her yacht, and, although she is making the rules, she does agree to finance a club which will bear his name. His career looks promising, but his interest in Novak will soon interfere. He gives her the top spot in the show that will open the club, and, when Hayworth enters a rehearsal and sees Novak framed in a huge silk and lace

*Pal Joey*

heart and singing "My Funny Valentine," she quickly puts an end to the proceedings. With no intention of sharing her bought-and-paid-for possession with Novak, she tells Sinatra this girl would be better off someplace else. Obediently, Sinatra tries to find a way to make Novak quit on her own.

I've been thinkin'—that you were so good in that number out there—I decided to give ya somethin' better to do . . . a real blockbuster . . . I thought maybe you ought to do the strip.

Novak is shocked and hurt, and she refuses. Later, she heads for the bar where she orders a straight bourbon. Henry wonders if it isn't "a little too early in the day for a girl who doesn't drink at night," and Novak changes the order to a double.

As it happens, Hayworth is giving a dinner party that evening and doesn't think Sinatra will fit in with her guests. She gives him the night off and he spends it on her yacht which is anchored nearby. A drunk Novak appears and slurs, "Aren't you going to pipe me aboard?" She tells him she's decided to take his offer:

To strip. Peel. To take it off and let it lay. You were right, I do have a good shape. Confidentially, I'm stacked. Bet you thought I wouldn't, didn't you? I'll bet you thought I couldn't. I can and I will.

She kisses him and passes out in his arms. He puts her on the bed and says to Snuffy, "If I walk in my sleep—bite me."

The next morning, over a breakfast which she can't eat, Novak is feeling her first hangover:

Novak: Why do people drink when it feels so awful the morning after?
Sinatra: Maybe because it feels so good the night before.
Novak: What did I do last night?
Sinatra: You kissed me.
Novak: I wasn't myself.
Sinatra: Yeah, but whoever you were, you were great.

She tells him she's ashamed of her actions and he asks her where she's from. The answer is Albuquerque.

Sinatra: I'm surprised your mother'd let you come to the big town.
Novak: My mother says, a nice girl's a nice girl wherever she is.
Sinatra: Yeah, and a bummer's a bum!
Novak: She wouldn't say that. Besides, what about last night? I made a fool of myself and you didn't take advantage of me.
Sinatra: Oh, don't pin any medals on me! It just so happens, in my book, it takes two to tango.
Novak: Why are you so ashamed of your good impulses?
Sinatra: Maybe it's because I don't get many.

Before leaving, Novak asks Sinatra if the strip number was his idea or Hayworth's. When he tells her it was his, she agrees to do it and the matter is settled.

Next, the curtain opens on Novak beginning her dress rehearsal for the strip. To a minuet-type version of "I Could Write a Book," she holds an antique hand mirror in milady's chambers, dressed in a gold hoop-skirted affair with a low bodice and transparent puffed sleeves. The music changes to a low-down beat, and she starts to peel. Minus the skirt and its tiered petticoat, she stands in a hoop, then sheds it and her pantaloons as the music gets hotter. Down to panties and a merry-widow, and showing a form divine, she is a surprise to Henry who's been watching from the audience. "I never thought she'd do it," he says. "I've seen them come and I've seen them go, but I thought this one was different."

Suddenly Sinatra stops the number and tells everyone they can "stop droolin'." He orders Novak to "get in the dressing room and put your clothes on" and gives the strip spot to Nichols who says, "A pleasure." To a sobbing Novak, he explains, "A nice girl is a nice girl anywhere. I shouldn't have let you do it." He takes her in his arms and says she'll do the love song instead.

Hayworth, who's been watching from the sidelines, closes the club because Novak has not been fired. She says, "Pay everybody off; the club will not open." Sinatra's dream, a club of his own, has fizzled. Later, when Novak enters his office, he tells her to "beat it and leave me alone."

Seeing his state of mind, she goes to Hayworth to plead for him and for all of the entertainers who will be affected by her decision.

Hayworth: You wanted to see me?
Novak: It's about Joey. I know how you feel and you're right. There's been nothing between us.
Hayworth: Are you sure about that, Miss English?
Novak: I'm quite sure, Mrs. Simpson. Let the club open, please. It's not just Joey. You're hurting a lot of other people.
Hayworth: You're not concerned with other people. It's Joey. You're in love with him.
Novak: Aren't you?
Hayworth: Well, let's say we understand each other. We're alike, Joey and I, the same breed of cat.
Novak: I'm not so sure of that. Joey's better than you think. He's better than he thinks.
Hayworth: Nobody's better than he thinks! This may come as a bit of a surprise, Miss English, but I do believe there's been nothing between you and Joey. That makes you a little more dangerous. He may not know it, but when Joey told you to keep your clothes on today—he played the greatest love scene of his career. I could undress in the lobby of the Fairmont Hotel and he'd never turn a hair. So, you see, Miss English, with you on the scene, I couldn't possibly reopen the club.
Novak: If I wasn't on the scene?
Hayworth: Well, I might give it a serious consideration. After all, I rather enjoyed owning a night club. Of course, it wouldn't do to have our boy know why you're leaving town. He dislikes being under any obligation except financial.

(Kim held her own in this scene with Hayworth. It was one of her best in the film. The reigning queen and her successor were both in fine form and—surprising as it may seem—worked well together.)

With Novak out of the way, Hayworth offers to go through with the club's opening and even proposes marriage to Sinatra. He turns her down. She suggests he tell Novak his true feelings but Sinatra doesn't think he should spoil Novak's life any more than he has.

Before he leaves the shuttered club, there is a dream sequence in which he realizes his ambition: "Chez Joey" opens—as it would have if he hadn't bungled the whole thing. A montage of still photos flashes across the screen showing Novak and Hayworth in glamorous poses. Then, to the tune of "Bewitched, Bothered, and Bewildered," first Novak and then Hayworth share the spotlight with Sinatra in a colorful musical fantasy. (Considering that she was not a trained dancer nor possessed Hayworth's talent in that area, Kim did quite well at keeping up with the dance movements required of her.)

In a contrived ending, Hayworth, after she has bid farewell to Sinatra, brings him and Novak together—literally driving Novak in her car to his departure point.

Novak: Where are we going?
Sinatra: What do ya mean, we?
Novak: Well, we're both out of work, aren't we?
Sinatra: I don't know about you, but I'm on my way to Sacramento.
Novak: Fine, I've always wanted to see the state capitol. Well, look, you asked me to do the love song with you. What are you trying to do, crawl out of it? I thought we were pretty good together.
Sinatra: Are you out of your mind or somethin'? You don't know what you'd be lettin' yourself in for! I'd probably brush you off before we got to the station. Why don't you beat it? Look, I have no desire to be hemmed in. Why don't you beat it? Take the mutt with you. Why don't you get out while you got the chance? What do you think I'm made of? Don't you know I've got a low boiling point? (They kiss) Well, I guess we weren't so bad at that, were we? I could use a girl in the act—give it a little class.
Novak: I could always do a strip.
Sinatra: Don't bring that up again.
Novak: Well, how about my billing?
Sinatra: Your what?
Novak: My name. My picture.
Sinatra: Oh, yes. Well, it'll be Joey Evans and Linda English.
Novak: Oh, well—how about Joey and Linda Evans? It's shorter.
Sinatra: I got a better idea. How about Joey Evans and Company? (He picks up Snuffy) That's shorter still. Let's go.

Sinatra, Novak, and Snuffy walk toward their new life to the tune of "I Could Write a Book" as the chorus sings "How to make two lovers of friends."

\* \*

Kim's performance in this film was not well received by the critics. In fact, she was blasted in print. William K. Zinsser of the *New York Herald-Tribune* said:

[She] has reduced her acting technique to the process of rolling her huge eyes back and forth like pinballs, in the manner of silent film stars, and since she says almost nothing she might as well be in a silent film.

*Pal Joey*

One of the unkindest blows was from *Photoplay* magazine which had previously shouted her praises but now said: "She has no personality beyond a publicity handout, and has outstripped her meagre talent."
And *Variety* stated:

Rita Hayworth, Frank Sinatra and Kim Novak are potent marquee magnets for this racy (not for the kids and grandma) strictly top-money musicalized account of "Beauty Boy" and his conquests as rewritten from the hit legit production. *Pal Joey* is not merely a click, it can't miss being a blockbuster . . . Kim Novak is one of the mice (Joey's pet name for femmes) and rates high as ever in the looks department but her thesping is pallid in contrast with the forceful job done by Sinatra.

Since the early part of the picture gave Kim very little dialogue, there wasn't much she could do except use her eyes. She had nothing else to work with. In addition, although Kim had youth and beauty going for her, Hayworth and Sinatra were a powerful pair to be pitted against. Theirs were the strongest parts, and their experience vastly overshadowed hers.

It was not surprising, after this film, that Kim

*Pal Joey*, with Rita Hayworth and Frank Sinatra

*Pal Joey,* with Frank Sinatra and Rita Hayworth

thought her career might be at an end. As she put it:

> I was good in my first picture and got wonderful reviews. I was afraid I might not be able to live up to them. I felt it could never happen again. Today I'm worried because I didn't enjoy it on the way up, and now maybe I'm on the way down.

The whole incident suggested that Kim could not be really convincing in anything she herself didn't believe. She had not been overjoyed with either the character or the role, and her hunch about them had been right. Seen today, her performance in *Pal Joey* is not one of her best. It almost appears to be two separate performances. During the first half of the film, when there isn't much to say or do, she functions as if she were in a trance; it isn't until the second half that she comes into her own.

It is interesting to note that, in a drunk scene here, she fell flat, while, in a similar one in *Jeanne Eagels,* she was totally right. Same director. Same star. It looked as if she were trying to duplicate the scene in *Pal Joey*—and that may be where the problem started.

Kim's bad reviews in the picture did her no damage. Fans flocked to the theaters anyway and applauded her in the role. *Pal Joey* grossed $4.7 million in domestic rentals alone, and the Columbia stockholders were riding high. With Rita Hayworth's final commitment fulfilled, Kim was acknowledged by a beaming Harry Cohn as the new queen of the studio, and she was given Hayworth's star dressing room to prove it.

# 6

From all outward appearances, the new queen of the lot had everything going for her. She had great beauty, her name was known, and stardom was hers. It looked as if her every desire would be fulfilled whenever she snapped her fingers. But, while all seemed easy and pressure free, such was not the case.

Kim was totally unprepared for the splash she had made, and she was innocent of many of the problems that would accompany it. Conflicts arose between the requirements of her new position and the dictates of her personal beliefs, and, while she was able to reconcile them, it was not without difficulty.

One of the hardest problems for her to face was the question of her image. Important people in the film industry are invariably given tags. Kim was labeled a sex symbol and filed in the love-goddess category. The classification was not one that pleased her. Aware that she would probably never lose it, however, she did manage to accept it professionally as long as she could remain herself personally. Her own individuality was important to her; as she put it, "If I wasn't the way I am, I'd be false."

There have been many myths about Kim Novak. The values she upholds have sometimes given the impression she's too good to be true. She isn't. What she is, is sincere. Abhoring both phonies and pretense, she has accepted glamour trappings only for her image. Privately, she has remained down-to-earth.

As the adherence to her beliefs shows, Kim has never lacked the ability to exercise discipline or self-control. Realizing early the importance of giving her all, she concentrated wholly on her career, closing her eyes to temptation and her ears to gossip. Hers is a story of hard work, study, and humility. She could not have achieved what she has without them.

To function like this, a person must be secure within himself, and a great part of Kim's stability came from the fact that she knew she was loved by her family. She had learned from them how to deal with life, and she was determined to use her knowledge in such a way that they would be proud of her. As she put it:

I was fortunate in that I had a wonderful home and understanding parents. My mother knew that one day my sister and I would have to be on our own so she started preparing us for it early. Each summer she would send us to different camps so we'd be entirely alone. I used to get terribly homesick. In fact, it wasn't until I came to Hollywood and got in pictures that I felt secure enough inside not to become lonely. Soon I was so busy I didn't have time to get lonely, although I still wrote home two or three times a week and called every couple of weeks. I feel it's

93

important for any girl away from home to hold on to her family ties.

My mother and father taught me that I had to work hard for everything. Dad particularly lectured me on the importance of never doing any job half-heartedly. And I never forgot it. Since I loved acting so much, I found it easy to work at my career.

But while she found it easy to work at her career, there were still times when Kim lost belief in herself and literally had to force herself to go on sets with the pros she so admired. "Who am I to go on a set with those people?" she once asked. It was Columbia's drama coach, Benno Schnieder, who gave her the answer.

I met a girl like you in Moscow one time. The great Stanislavsky was directing, and all of us had spent years studying under him. He was the man who originated "The Method" which is taught in the Actors' Studio in New York. We had worked hard, and we knew "The Method," but this girl, she had never acted before in her life. And he gave her the lead. Well, we resented that, so I went up to him and asked why he gave her the lead instead of one of the girls who had worked hard for it for years. He just said, "Wait and see."

The girl was a great hit. She got I don't know how many curtain calls. So again I asked Stanislavsky, "How is it she is such a great success? We study your method for years, but she is better without your lessons than we are." And he said, "You are students, and need all my lessons you can get. But she, well, it could be that she doesn't need lessons. She is an *actress*." Miss Novak, it could be you are exactly like that girl.

Thus reassured, Kim went back to the set and gave a performance that brought forth one of those rare accolades in Hollywood: a spontaneous burst of applause from everyone, including the stagehands.

Benno Schnieder was also responsible, at a later date, for helping Kim out of another difficulty. This time she was looking her best, and walking her best, and she thought she was acting her best, but nothing was happening. No one seemed to know what was wrong, and, after a discouraged director had announced a coffee break, Schnieder took her aside. "You are modeling, not acting," he told her. "But what is the difference?" she asked. His reply was:

Not very much. But a model must be seen, and an actress must see. Beautiful women and beautiful models, they get so accustomed to being looked at, many times they think that is enough, and do not do any looking themselves. But an actress, she must look, and see what she is looking at, and understand it. Now you go back, and look at the other people, and forget about being looked at yourself.

Kim never forgot those words. Many actresses can make a royal entrance in public, be seen by all, and sweep regally on without a glance to one side or the other. When Kim makes an entrance—whether it is a premiere, in a hotel lobby, or in a restaurant—she, too, is seen by everyone. But, with her, there is a friendly difference. She is also seeing.

Such a combination of showmanship and naturalness has allowed her to stage very impressive entrances when the occasion required it. Few actresses since the days of Nazimova, Pola Negri, and Gloria Swanson have been able to get away with anything approaching the purple-tinted hair, mascara, and other accoutrements Kim used. That she succeeded with them is a tribute to her ability to temper the phony with the sincere. The public responded warmly. Even her mother was not disturbed. When informed that Kim had taken to beading her long eyelashes with purple mascara, she merely gave an amused chuckle and said, "That Mickey. What will she think of next?"

\*     \*

Many changes were now occurring in Kim's life, and her mode of living was not the least of them. After

Travel was becoming increasingly important and it was taking a great deal of Kim's time. Between promotional work for her films and location shooting, she was continually en route to one city or another. Attending the premiere of *The Eddy Duchin Story* at Radio City Music Hall, she did guest spots on several New York television shows, including Perry Como's, Steve Allen's, and *What's My Line?*, where she appeared as the mystery celebrity. The studio was pleased with her cooperation and permitted her to make a trip to Europe (her first) to represent them at the Cannes Film Festival and to take a much-needed vacation. (She would subsequently make several trips abroad in rapid succession.) While there, she was introduced to Count Mario Bandini—and wire services flashed the news of her latest "romance."

As a celebrated name, Kim would now learn that any male she was photographed with would be suspected of being the big romance in her life. Her private world would become an open book, presenting some hardships for her with anyone she might actually be drawn toward. She explained Bandini's presence in the following way:

> It was my first trip abroad and Mario asked if he could show me around. We went boating. I like him but, with the kind of publicity I get, there are too many strikes against me. Everyone's out to make a sizzling love affair out of the smallest romance, and consequently nothing develops.

Bandini was one of the most handsome and eligible bachelors around, and, to top it off, he was the millionaire tomato king of Italy. Kim enjoyed his continental manners, and he, in turn, appreciated her beauty. Through him, she was introduced to a way of life that was new and exciting and shown the great cities of Europe, guided by his knowledge and refinement. But there it ended, and, when she returned home, she was once again seen in the company of Mac Krim.

Later the same year, at her home in Chicago, Edward R. Murrow visited with Kim and showed her off to the world in the popular CBS television series, *Person to Person*. The screen's newest sex goddess was surrounded by her family as she chatted, her appearance on this top-rated program an indication of her growing stature in the film industry.

Magazines continued to plaster her likeness on their covers and to feature her in "typical tales of a young star" stories. The results of this publicity were twofold. Superstardom's trappings, no matter how well-de-

three years at the Studio Club, she found herself forced to move, since residency beyond that point was forbidden. She chose a Beverly Hills apartment which the press played up as being "furnished in lavender"—a release aimed at promotion of the lavender-blonde image. (Soon after, she would also rent a beach house in Malibu and commute between the two.) As a result of the move, she needed transportation, and purchased a white, hard-top Corvette.

Her separation from the Studio Club caused her to reflect:

> At first I didn't think I'd like the place at all. I was afraid it would be too crowded and that there wouldn't be enough privacy. But then I really grew to love it and didn't want to live anywhere else. I never had many problems that I might have had to face. I could walk to work so I didn't have to buy a car and meals were served so I had no cooking to worry about. And, above all, I didn't have that pressing problem of loneliness to combat during my newness in the film colony. All of the girls at the club were interested in getting ahead and we always had much to talk about. When I saw others trying to get the big break, it made me appreciate my own good fortune even more. It was a lovely period and a time for growth. In leaving, I couldn't help but have a tinge of sadness—but then one has to learn that life is constant change.

served they may be, are likely to be envied by others; success breeds jealousy, especially from those trying to break into that world. Kim was subjected to her share of this, but, to balance it, there was the satisfaction of knowing her work was being recognized, and, of course, there was the consolation of luxury. Through it all, her perspective remained clear. She realized the unpleasantness was part of the dues she must pay, and that things would balance out in the long run.

One of the nicer rewards of fame for Kim was being able to make life easier for her parents. In addition, she would constantly reassure them that she hadn't changed and was still the same daughter they had known and loved. While they were justly proud of her achievement, they did have doubts about life in Hollywood and how it might affect her. They needn't have worried. Kim would stay in control of both her life and her ideals.

Throughout her career, Kim has remained closer to her parents than has almost any other star. She once said that any man she thought of marrying "will first have to go home, meet my father, then ask him for my hand"—and, over the years, she has taken a number of

prospects home for this reason (although, in some cases, her own feelings have later changed). For Kim, feelings have sometimes been hard to define. They have been even harder to express. This has given her trouble both on the screen and off. As she explains it:

I have always been basically shy. It is not easy for me to show my feelings. Although my physical attributes may be all right, I have found it difficult to be an actress because they have to show life, to portray life. I come from a family that rarely comes out with anything emotional. We feel things but we don't express them. We are just that kind of people and it takes me a long time to adjust myself to expressing emotion outwardly.

To fully understand Kim Novak, one must go back to her origins. Her family, and especially her father, had a great influence upon her idealistic attitude toward life. She has said:

[My father] is a gentle, quiet man with definite personal convictions and beliefs. He taught me the immense importance of strong family ties and family unity. When I was a little girl he used to tell my sister and me the Aesop fables, each with its particular moral. One of his favorites was "The Four Oxen And The Lion," and I liked it, too, because it was all about courage in the face of danger. He always stressed the moral here—United We Stand, Divided We Fall. And he always said that whenever I had any troubles I was to take them back to the family. "We will help you," he would say. "Together we can meet any problems, big or small. Always remember that."

And there would be problems. With all good things come some bad, and, along with all of the glowing tributes, came some barbs. There were those who said that Kim was a great beauty but that she'd never make it as an actress. Others thought she wasn't strong enough to endure under the pressures of the business. And there were a number of critics who would belittle her efforts throughout her career, calling her "emotionless," "mannered," "wooden," and stating that she lacked depth.

Deeply hurt by reviewers who had dipped their pens in acid before applying them to *Jeanne Eagles* and *Pal Joey,* Kim wanted more than anything else to be respected as an actress. She knew neither of these films was going to help her reach this goal but, still, she wished the critics would take into account that her career was in "its adolescent stage," that she was striving to perfect her technique. She hoped it wouldn't be long before she was recognized by her peers as a serious actress with promise.

It didn't help her cause when the *Harvard Lampoon* cited her as the year's worst actress. However, a number of fine actresses have been given this title over the years, and, if Harvard didn't make her its favorite, Liggett and Myers Tobacco Company did when it named her Chesterfield's calendar girl for the year. She was photographed in a seductive pose, seated at a table, a cigarette in her hand, with a vase near her containing a rose. All this for a girl who didn't smoke!

It was at about this time that Kim began attending Los Angeles City College to take art courses. Her talent as a painter would always be a refuge for her, and she would continue to perfect it, along with her acting. As with nature, to which she also turned, it provided the relaxation she needed between films.

Back in Chicago for a brief visit with her family, Kim was welcomed as a star. Regardless of what the critics had said about her performances in *Jeanne Eagles* and *Pal Joey,* audiences were enjoying them. Damn the critics! The public was on her side. During her visit, her mother made one comment that would stay with her: "I hope you never get to be like the character you played in *Jeanne Eagles,* with all those terrible tensions they put on you in Hollywood."

At home in Chicago, with parents

The "tensions" did not make her like Jeanne Eagels but, when she returned to Hollywood, Kim did instigate some changes in her life similar to ones that character might have made. She acquired the William Morris Agency to represent her and to help improve her status at the studio.

Delighted with its new client, the Morris office was well aware that Kim had become one of the most valuable female properties in Hollywood—whether she could or couldn't act—and figured she should be compensated for it. Although her salary was now in the neighborhood of $1,250 weekly, the dickering for more money began.

Kim expressed her views about the situation in this way:

It will have to be a raise that means something, not a little bit. How many more years will I be able to work? *Jeanne Eagels* reminded me I've got to protect my future.

The agents of the Morris office threw themselves into action, adamant in their demands for Kim's welfare. If necessary, she would stage a walk-out on her

97

contractual obligations. Fortunately for all concerned, Columbia came through with an increase which doubled Kim's salary—but not without some groans from Harry Cohn:

> They all believe their publicity after a while. I never met a grateful performer in the picture business. I'm only afraid she'll ask me to make Kim Novak pictures instead of Columbia pictures!

With the aid of the powerful Morris agency, Kim had scored a victory. Now she was more than just a star in name; she was being compensated accordingly. And, if Cohn thought her mercenary, no one who knew the full circumstances of the situation could blame her for the move she had made. Her thirteen weeks' work on *Jeanne Eagels* had earned her only $15,000, while those of her costar, Jeff Chandler, had brought him $200,000.

In striking her first blow for independence, Kim had been encouraged by the fact that *Box Office* magazine had named her the number one ticket seller among all of Hollywood's actresses. She had also been pushed by increasing financial needs. Away from the Studio Club, she had found her personal cost of living rising; and, professionally, she was eager to make changes too. She was tired of borrowing studio dresses and having her hair done by studio personnel for industry parties, and she had reported her plight to the press. An embarrassed Cohn had hastened to scold her for it. "You shouldn't say things like that. It makes me sound cheap." (No doubt, this was a contributing factor in his agreement to pay her more.)

Industry functions were never a favorite of Kim's; she was forced to attend them and gave some of her best performances there, but she would have preferred to stay home. While she recognized the importance of being seen and photographed in order to maintain the glamour image, she was not at ease playing this game, and she resented having her life arranged. Her growing annoyance with the situation eventually led to a resurfacing of the "rebellious Mickey" from her teenage years.

Cohn's orders had been for her to be seen socially— in the right places and with the right people—and to get her name in the columns. She decided that, if this was what he wanted, this was what he would get. The resulting publicity was hardly what Cohn had in mind when Kim's friendship with Sammy Davis, Jr., presented him with a full-blown scandal. Started by blind items from the late columnist Dorothy Kilgallen, the "romance" was quickly picked up by others and blown tantalizingly out of proportion. It became almost a daily item in the papers, and scandal magazines pushed it to the limit with "Kim Novak's new romance is a real shocker to her studio," and speculation about just how serious the whole affair was.

Kim and Davis made no comment. But, before the items were even out of print, Davis had married a Las Vegas show girl named Loray White. The marriage was a short-term one, and many speculated that Cohn had had a serious talk with Davis and ordered him to lay off Columbia's prize package. The truth is known only to those involved, but, regardless of how it happened or why, the friendship between the two celebrities did come to an end. Kim spoke of it only once, when she said:

> People have asked me, "How can you let rumors like this get started?" Everything has a foundation but it takes on a different light, depending on how it's handled. I choose my friends as I see them, not as others see them. Sammy, for example, is such a nice person and we're good friends. I've always admired him as an artist. My parents and I went to see him nearly every time he performed in Chicago. The fuss all started when he came to visit me at my sister's house after Christmas. He brought toys for my two nephews and it's a shame that the whole thing was blown way out of proportion.

Columbia's publicity department immediately came to the rescue, linking Kim's name with a number of other famous ones in hopes that the gossip surrounding her and Davis would die down. It did. Cohn wiped his brow and thanked the powers above that Kim was being a "good girl" about the whole thing—and Columbia continued to map out plans for its number one star.

Before the Davis incident had occurred, Kim had appeared on Frank Sinatra's ABC-TV show along with other guest stars Bob Hope and Peggy Lee. Cohn had not been pleased with this appearance because Kim hadn't seemed at ease. Therefore, it was decided that she would do no further television guest shots. She signed a new contract with the studio and it put all its energies into scouting suitable properties for her. Her next assignment, as it happened, would take her on loan-out to Paramount and provide her with one of the best roles of her career.

In keeping with her newly acquired status, Kim now purchased her first home. The eight-room house was located in Bel Air, and she shared it with her secretary-companion Barbara Mellon, a childhood friend from Chicago, in what proved to be a compatible arrangement. As Kim described it:

> [Barbara] has her own personal life, and it never interferes with mine. The older I get, the more particular I am about privacy. When I study a script or paint, I have to be alone. I can't express my deep feelings in front of a lot of people. I can't let go.

As Kim's career progressed, her publicity settled into a pattern. It dealt constantly with two things: her acting frustrations and her search for love. Regarding the latter, she said:

> I don't feel as though anyone loves me unless I'm in love. Falling in love gives me a kind of reassurance, I guess you'd call it. I think, "There, you see, you are loved, you are attractive!" Maybe I just have to have a lot of men admiring me because when I was a kid, I never even had a date for the high school prom. I was too tall, and I was too shy, and maybe I was too serious.

The fans ate all of this up and the studio continued to dish out what they wanted to hear. But when a woman is so determined to fall in love rather than be in love, what effect does it have on the rest of her life? While most women seek security, one might almost say that Kim sought insecurity. Because she was so terrified of being hurt, she couldn't bring herself to depend on anyone for fear that he might pull the props out from under her. In her heart, at this point, she really didn't believe that the good things of life would be there to stay. A foreshadowing of Kim's fears can be seen in the outlook of the already-concerned 17-year-old Marilyn Novak who, long before she achieved fame and fortune, sat alone in a railway station and wrote this poem:

> *A Train Makes Me Lonely . . .*
> A train makes me lonely
> If you know what I mean—
> I've longed so long for what I've not seen,
> To go and to go and to be oh to be
> The ideal girl but I am not she,
> To travel and learn, to live and to earn,
> To love and be loved when it came my turn.
> So I traveled nay learned,
> I lived and nay earned,
> I loved and got burned
> And I still never learned.
> I long now to go
> To where I know not
> To go and to go
> And to find a fresh plot
> Where all is so new
> All over I'd start.
> But this time I promise
> I play it smart.
> I'd proud board the train
> That's not the express.
> The worth not the price
> Would be more and not less.
> But every stop I'd get out and see
> And maybe I'd find the right home for me.
> And somewhere out there
> He'd hear my plea
> Bring me his love and then marry me.
> Oh marry me, please marry me
> Please bring me your love and then marry me.
> A train makes me lonely,
> Oh now can't you see?
> For I've not the price
> For the trip nor the plea.

A touch of the romantic had always been a part of Kim and it always would be, but, for now, her career was a full-time job that left little time for love of any kind. Similarly, the fact that she was famous presented her with another drawback—the caution of the studio over any involvement she might have. Kim had been groomed as a replacement for Rita Hayworth, whose romantic entanglements had caused the studio people numerous headaches. They were not anxious to have a repeat performance from their current love goddess.

The men in Kim's life up to now had been vastly different from each other. The solid, down-to-earth Mac Krim. The smooth Mario Bandini. Tony Kastner, a skiing instructor. Frank Sinatra. Actor John Ireland. Aly Khan.

A word should be injected here about her relation-

**With Frank Sinatra**

ship with Aly Khan. Eyebrows had been raised over this one, and there'd been those who'd smiled slyly and said that, since Kim had taken Rita Hayworth's place on screen at Columbia, maybe she wanted to take it off the screen as well and be known as Princess Kim. This was totally untrue. Her meeting with Aly Khan was quite accidental. It had occurred while she was attending the Cannes Film Festival where she was subsequently entertained by Aly's father and wife at their villa. In Kim's words:

After the photographers finished their picture-taking of the Aga, the Begum and me, Aly came in from the garden. He wore faded Levis and a soiled shirt. His hands were grimy from working in the earth, and I couldn't take my eyes off them. They were strong, powerful, muddy from working in the rose garden. When we shook hands, he apologized for the dirt, and I told him I loved the earth. He smiled and asked if I wanted to see his garden. We walked around and around the garden, and he asked if I liked horses. We made our first date to go horseback riding.

I loved the quick brisk way he walked. I had to run to keep up with him, but I didn't mind. I liked it. He took deep breaths of air, and I had the feeling of a man enjoying

every minute of life, who wasn't going to waste one precious second of it. Whenever I was with Aly, I felt sorry for all the people around us who seemed half alive.

Despite all these experiences, however, the one man who still impressed Kim the most—and remained closest to her heart—was her father. Her friendship and love for Joseph Novak was perhaps even more poignant because it had been such a long time before she had come to know him. Kim's mother was always the dominant member of the household. Her father was shy and gentle. Easily hurt, solitary, and very much like Kim. The story of these two, father and daughter, finding each other emotionally after so many years, is a heartwarming one. As Kim explained:

It probably happens to other people. It's a matter of seeing a parent one way while you're a child, and then, when you're grown up, seeing him with grown-up eyes; and seeing things you couldn't see before.

Kim's father often spent time with her in California. His railroad pass enabled him to travel easily, and he enjoyed his visits. Between them, Kim would return to Chicago whenever it was convenient, but she was saddened by the fact that home, as she had known it, no longer existed. She put it this way:

I found out what [Thomas Wolfe in *You Can't Go Home Again*] meant when I was home last. Sure, I can go back to Chicago, which I do. I can still baby-sit with my sister's children and help put the laundry in the washing machine. But I can't go shopping without crowds gathering and people saying, "Look, it's Kim Novak!" There's no place I can go, really, where I'm just myself, Marilyn Novak, and there won't be, ever, again.

Kim Novak had learned that privacy was a luxury now denied to her. From here on, there would always be eyes staring when she appeared in public. The beauty she'd been endowed with would become something she'd wish people could forget; she'd prefer it if they'd pay more attention to her dramatic ability instead. Her glamorous clothes she would have neither the time nor the desire to wear; in fact, she'd have no time for anything that was frivolous, that wasn't work or preparing for it. She would be caught up in a feverish drive to earn the fame that was already hers— and in that drive there would, unhappily, be no time to live or to love.

The one luxury she would allow herself was the indulgence of her imagination. Often, she'd let it wander into other people's lives. As a little girl on Chicago's Sayre Street, she had peopled it with make-

Television appearance, with Bob Hope

With Mac Krim

believe inhabitants and had endowed inanimate objects with souls and thoughts of their own. Shy and fearful of strangers, she had not been able to let the real dramas of life touch her, only the drama of living within herself. She could pour out her heart to a rose or weep over the death of a leaf that had fallen from a tree. Perhaps this is the reason that, as an adult, she was able to give so much warmth to make-believe characters.

An example of the strength of Kim's imagination occurred during the making of *The Eddy Duchin Story* when her character was scheduled to die in childbirth. For some reason, she couldn't be sad. As she has described the incident:

I was the despair of director George Sidney. I couldn't bring tears to my eyes. Someone suggested that I try to remember something very sad that had happened in my life. I tried and, as I lay there on the bed in front of all those cameras, nothing seemed sad at all.

Then somebody advised me to think of a sad song. As I ran over the lyrics of one in my mind, I found so much truth in it that I was impressed with hidden meanings I'd never realized about the song before.

I've always believed that life would be incomplete without tears, without a little unhappiness, without a few major problems scattered in between the minor ones. Suddenly, I began to think how sad I would be if I had only one day to live. And I thought of all the things I would want to do.

And I tried to put all my feelings into a poem. I've always liked poetry because it's preserved so many wonderful moments of my life.

And this is what Kim wrote:

If I knew I'd die tomorrow.
I'd ask my lover if he'd sorrow.
I'd ask him not to let me cry.
For silver seconds passing by.
I'd watch a butterfly in flight
And count the stars that dot the night.
I'd walk the streets, I'd walk the shore
To see the world I'd see no more.
These things I'd do, these joys I'd borrow
If I knew I'd die tomorrow.

Along with the poem, there came tears and, ultimately, a performance.

The creator of both the poem and the character was still the romantic little Marilyn Novak. She had wished for a gang to belong to. She'd wished to be popular, to be beautiful, to have pretty clothes. But, most of all, she'd wished to belong—to be accepted by the crowd. Marilyn's star had risen far beyond the heights she'd envisioned in her dreams on Sayre Street. But Kim's star had risen partially without her. And Kim Novak was now consumed with an unrelenting need for Kim, the actress, to catch up with Kim, the star.

"It's now or never," she said. "Things won't wait. I'm not bucking for anything. I'm just trying to do the best job I can." Perhaps the main reason for her impatience was that Kim still felt left out. In her own mind, she didn't belong to the group with which she was associated—the group of talented, able people, the real craftsmen of the movie industry. She was trying desperately to be one of them, and she felt herself at even more of a disadvantage because she hadn't started out as so many of them had. She hadn't been one of the dedicated; movies had fallen into her lap. She explained:

> I never starved to act. I never painted scenery. This wasn't a burning thing from childhood for me, as it has been for so many others. I didn't fight for it. But today, it's in my blood, and I want it to stay.

Kim's close friends saw her determination to succeed as though it were a contest—an inner one: Kim against herself, against her feelings of inferiority, against her fears of never being good enough. They were afraid her standards were too high, that she expected too much. And they saw her becoming ill with fright and anxious with worry over a new role. They were concerned that Kim was driving herself at an inhuman pace.

Perhaps she was, but there was more than one element motivating her. And one of the most powerful

With father, Joseph Novak

was a feeling of impermanence—a certainty that, if she didn't work to prevent it, there would be a decline in her popularity with the public. It did no good to point out *Box Office* magazine's polling which had named her number one star. Her reply was simply, "Do you realize now all I can do is go down?"

While all of the self-doubt was tormenting Kim, director George Sidney said:

> Like Jeanne Eagels, Kim is a natural. She has that golden thing you can't give anybody if it isn't there; she was born with the magic called talent. We wouldn't have made *Jeanne Eagels* without her. No other actress was considered for the role.
>
> Kim is also very much like Eagels. She has depth and, with it, the same kind of spirit; the freedom and abandon; the same latent ability that made Jeanne Eagels the great actress of the American theatre she was.

The most brutal critic of her own performances was Kim herself. In a projection room she would agonize over even a wrist movement that appeared awkward to her. When a reviewer on one of her earlier pictures remarked that she essayed such-and-such a role "and looked beautiful throughout," she was in tears. "Who

With producer/director George Sidney, during filming of
*Jeanne Eagels*

cares about looking beautiful throughout," she said. For Kim, beauty was just one more obstacle in the way of proving she was an actress. Whenever a scene was completed, even when the director thought it was fine, there would still be doubt in her mind, and she'd feel she could do it better if given another chance.

During the making of a film, Kim felt it was extremely important to stay in character. She explained:

I've got to stay in character. I can't be Kim Novak at night and Jeanne Eagels the next morning. [And she added] I believe you keep a part of all the people you portray. Sometimes I think I've left Kim Novak somewhere along the way.

But not too far away. Not too far from the shy little girl who wrote poetry and lived within the world of her imagination, or the girl who used to recite her stories so graphically that the teacher would protest to her mother that Marilyn's "imagination is inflaming the other children."

Not too far away, either, was the Kim Novak who worried when today's pressures closed in so fast that there was no time to share life with those who mattered to her, and who wondered if these people would understand.

Yet, in spite of the long hours, the wearying demands, and the fierce tensions, these times were a

104

to work. This is my happiness now. The only kind of happiness I haven't had is being married, but that will come.

Kim didn't make any predictions about the future. She left that chore to any prophets who cared to do it. She just wanted to get another assignment under her belt—and one that would bring praise for her talent. And it was about to happen.

thrill for Kim. To those who saw her only as a "melancholy blonde," a "bewildered beauty," and the like, she said:

I'm not unhappy. I'm working with emotion all the time. I've always been quick to laugh and cry. When things unhappy happen—and in this business they always seem to be happening—I cry. I'm not good at shrugging it off when somethings goes wrong. I show how I feel. But when it's out and over, I don't go around brooding or boiling under the surface as many others do.

There are all kinds of happiness. And I've had all kinds. But I've never had the work kind, and this is what I want now. Perhaps people think I'm unhappy because I don't do things that spell happiness to them. I've done all that. In college I belonged to a sorority and I went to dances. I've gone out a lot since, and I'm not through. I'm still going to live it up.

But today, my work is my happiness. Believe me, if I were to get dressed up in party clothes—which I hate doing—and go to large parties, this would make me very unhappy. I don't like being out with crowds of people. I have to be with a lot of people all the time in my work.

Just give me a script to read and an open fire and I'm happy. And when I'm happy, nobody could be happier. I'm a moody and impulsive person and I go along with whatever I feel like doing at the time. Right now, I want

Part II

_Acclaim_

# 7

Alfred Hitchcock was responsible for giving Kim one of the greatest opportunities of her career. And it was ironic that she was an alternate choice for *Vertigo,* which was originally titled *From Among the Dead,* when filming began. The director had wanted Vera Miles for the female lead, but pregnancy had forced her withdrawal. Hitchcock then negotiated with Columbia for Kim's services as a replacement, and she added the right touch to what seemed to be inspired casting.

This was the most taxing role that Kim had been called upon to play. To create two different women, within the same character, is a difficult assignment for any actress, but Kim surprised everyone with her ability to make incarnate and project just the right qualities. Utilizing a wide range of emotions, she was totally convincing and climbed to greater heights than anyone would have expected.

*Vertigo* moved and overwhelmed audiences but, at the time of release, was not the critical success it has since become. Since it was ahead of its time, the majority of audiences did not fully understand the hypnotic beauty of the web that Hitchcock wove. However, they were aware of an aura and a dream-like texture that hypnotized the spectator. These were done with the same sensuous and mysterious ease that

Kim used to hypnotize James Stewart on the screen. *Vertigo* is a film that represents Hollywood's romantic tradition while repudiating romanticism. It is a profound film and one of great beauty, today acknowledged as one of Hitchcock's greatest masterpieces.

In her preparation for the role, Kim did all of her homework and did it well. In addition to gearing herself for the dual character she would portray, she improved her driving skill. Since she was required to drive a green Jaguar for a number of scenes, she practiced driving the car in the Hollywood Hills for a few weeks before shooting began. By the time filming commenced, it was as though she had been born in the driver's seat.

*Vertigo* was filmed partly on location. There was some filming in San Francisco and additional shooting in Watsonville, a small town south of the Bay City. During the filming in Watsonville, police had to put a twenty-four hour watch on the hotel where Kim stayed in order to protect her from the curious.

Hitchcock had a home at nearby Santa Cruz, and he invited Kim and her dialogue coach, Luddie Laine, for dinner one Sunday. It was a wet day, and their driver skidded off the road and got stuck in the mud. Kim and Luddie took their shoes off and hiked barefoot over the

With Prince Aly Khan

hill to a nearby farmhouse. Nobody recognized Kim when she asked for permission to phone a garage in town. Then, when she called and identified herself, the garage man flatly refused to believe she was Kim Novak. And he wouldn't come to get her because it was Sunday. Even her superstardom couldn't help her out of this situation, and the girls finally arrived at the Hitchcock home three hours later for dinner.

Gossip columnists had a field day with Kim's romantic life during the filming. She received frequent phone calls from Mario Bandini in Rome and from Aly Khan, who was traveling around Europe. (Before the picture was completed, Aly went to Los Angeles for a visit with his seven-year-old daughter, Princess Yasmin. He also managed to spend some time with Kim. During his two-week vacation, the prince and Kim attended the twenty-third anniversary Thanksgiving party of "The Helpers," a Hollywood charitable organization, on 27 November 1957. Kim wore the dark wig from *Vertigo* and the dress and emerald necklace and earrings that had been so effective on her in the film. The wire services splashed photos throughout the world, and the rumors of her blazing "romance" received maximum coverage.) In addition, she was still dating long-time friend Mac Krim, and, to further confuse the issue, she received red roses daily from a man she never identified.

During the shooting of *Vertigo,* Hitchcock said of Kim's acting ability:

Many things she does in this picture are her own contributions. It isn't an easy picture because she plays two different girls. If I ask her to do certain things, she does them. But she must be made comfortable so that she feels at home doing a scene.

Later, he would speak in a different way of Kim's performance. Their professional relationship was strained because the director couldn't go along with what he has termed "her preconceived notions." Hitchcock is a visual director. He always has a clear picture of exactly what he wants from a screenplay. He has it all on paper and in his head before production ever begins: every color and every costume, down to the smallest detail.

About one of the "preconceived notions" that existed, Edith Head said:

The problem with the gray suit was one of the funniest things. I met Kim in her dressing room. She was charming and said how glad she was to meet me and how much she was going to enjoy working with me.

Then she said, "Now, Miss Head, before we even discuss clothes—there are two things I don't wear—I don't wear suits and I don't wear gray! [A contradiction on Kim's part since she had definitely worn suits both on and off the screen.] Another thing, I never wear black pumps. I always wear nude pumps, the color of my stockings. Outside of that, I'll do anything you want."

The script says she's wearing black pumps. The script says she's wearing a suit. And the script, which obviously she had read, says she's wearing a gray suit.

I think she had certain definite ideas and dislikes, and I think that's her privilege. However, I have always had another point of view. I think an actress is another person from when she is not working. I think, if an actress—if a woman—doesn't want to wear a certain thing in her private life, it's her own business. But if she's told to wear a hoop skirt in *Gone With The Wind*—she'd bloody well better wear it because she is not wearing what she likes. She is wearing what the script says.

I thought it was amusing because I thought she was kidding me at first. And I found out later that it was true—she didn't like gray. But, at the time, she said, "Why can't we make it purple?" I said, "Why don't I ask Mr. Hitchcock?" She wore a gray suit and black pumps in the film.

I found Kim Novak charming and thought our introduction was amusing. She is a beautiful woman with a beautiful figure and a joy for a designer to dress. And I would love to work with her again. I really am very fond of her and enjoyed working with her on *Vertigo.*

The teaming of James Stewart and Kim was one that pleased the public. They would be remembered as one of the all-time romantic duos, and they worked beau-

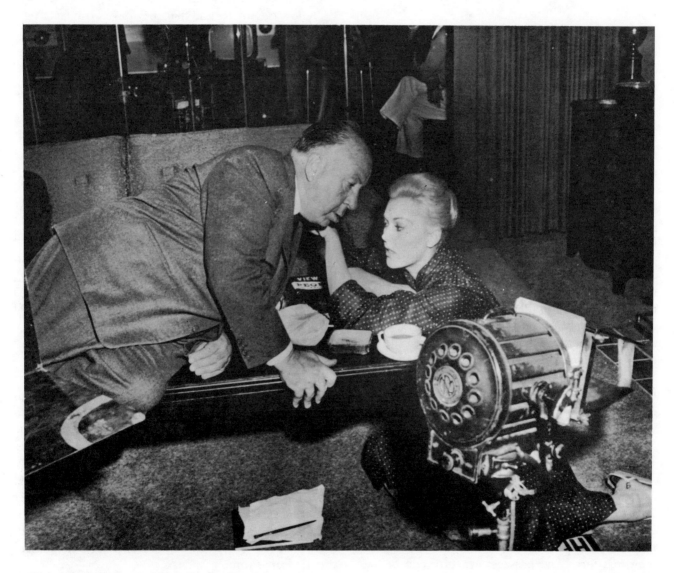

With Alfred Hitchcock during the filming of *Vertigo*

tifully together. About the experience, James Stewart said:

> As far as Kim Novak is concerned, I have nothing but praise. She is a very warm, gentle girl with a kind of electricity about her that certainly comes over to the audience. I found working with her exciting and enjoyable.

\*　　　\*

The haunting beauty of *Vertigo* is established immediately. It is clearly evident in one of the most unique title sequences ever used for a film. While Bernard Herrmann's brilliant prelude is heard, a woman's face is seen in close-up: The left side of the mouth and then the right, the nose, the eyes that glance to the left and then to the right—finally, the camera appears to enter the pupil of the right eye.

Against a black background, psychedelic patterns in a design of multicolored spirals emerge, and, as the credits unfold, brilliant colors invade the screen—red, purple, turquoise, lavender, green, blue, gold and magenta—and then reenter the pupil. This is the first use of color, which Hitchcock employs exquisitely throughout the film. The color green, which so dominates the supernatural and the past, is used effectively and ever so subtly. Contrasted with the reds, yellows, and purples of the real or present sequences, the colors themselves embody the themes of dream and reality. And, throughout the rest of the film, the viewer is mesmerized and held spellbound by the beauty and mystery that unfolds.

\*　　　\*

*Vertigo* grabs the viewer immediately with a chase. A patrolman and James Stewart pursue a suspect across roof tops. When it is time for a leap—across an eight-foot gap between two buildings—the fugitive makes it. The patrolman leaps in pursuit. Then it is Stewart's turn. The passageway, forty feet below, is paved with stone and the opposite roof is sloping and shingled with slate. A loosened slate slides out from under Stewart's foot. He finds himself slipping downward and clawing at the slate. He grabs the gutter and dangles over the passageway. The patrolman reaches for Stewart's hand. There are sheets of falling slate and the patrolman plunges to his death on the stone below.

After the accident, which has left him with acrophobia, a fear of heights, Stewart is recuperating in the company of Barbara Bel Geddes as he visits with her. As a result of his narrow brush with death, he has quit the police force, and, to Bel Geddes, he confesses that he wakes up each night with the memory of what has happened to him. She has always been in love with him, and they were engaged during college days. Remembering this time, Stewart mentions that he has just had a telephone call from Tom Helmore, who was a fellow classmate, and that they have arranged to get together.

As the exterior of the shipbuilding yard that Helmore operates is viewed, Hitchcock makes his customary appearance walking past the camera. Helmore is so successful because he "married into it." His main job is looking after his wife's interests, since her family is gone. Although Helmore knows that Stewart has quit detective work, he asks the latter, as a special favor, to follow his wife. He is happily married but wonders if someone out of the past, someone who is dead, can take possession of a living being. Helmore is referring to his wife's grandmother, who went insane and took her own life. He explains more about his wife:

> She'll be talking to me about something, nothing at all— and suddenly the words fade into silence and a cloud comes into her eyes and they go blank. She is someone I don't know. And then, with a long sigh, she comes back, and looks at me brightly, and doesn't know she's been away.

Helmore confides that his wife makes routine trips regularly and that the speedometer of her car tells him she has driven ninety-four miles. He wants Stewart to find out where she goes and what she does before he gets involved with doctors. He doesn't want a stranger on the case; he needs a friend that he can trust. Helmore further adds that his wife looks so lovely and normal that it will be difficult for Stewart to detect anything when he first sees her. Helmore says he will be taking his wife to Ernie's, the famous old San Francisco restaurant, and Stewart arranges to be there at the same time.

Stewart is seated at the bar where he can observe the wife, Novak, without being detected. She is seated facing Helmore as Stewart stares across the room to the inner dining area. Framed against the plush red walls, Novak's back is to Stewart. She is wearing a strapless gown of black with yards of billowing green satin, in the form of a stole, draped across her chair. (This is Hitchcock's first use of the color green, which will be associated with the supernatural in this charac-

On location for *Vertigo*

ter throughout the film.)

Novak and Helmore rise to leave. She glides through the room as if floating on air. There is an ethereal quality about her, like that of someone from another world or time. And she is aristocratic—very. Waiting, as Helmore stops to speak to someone, she turns to look back at him. She is captured in a timeless moment of beauty, and Stewart is mesmerized by the vision he is seeing. Novak appears unaware of his presence.

The next day Stewart waits for Novak to leave her apartment. When she finally exits, she is driving a green Jaguar, and Stewart tails her, noting all of her stops. First, she goes to a flower shop where she picks up a small bouquet. She enters from the dingy alleyway and Stewart follows. He opens a rear door that reveals Novak amid the brilliantly-colored flowers in the shop. (Hitchcock used a slow wipe from left to right to capture the moment exquisitely.) Next, there is a longer visit at Mission Dolores.

Stewart pauses to study her at the cemetery behind the mission. When she vacates the spot, he goes to look at the inscription on the monument. It reads, "Carlotta Valdes. Born December 3, 1831. Died March 5, 1857." He continues to tail Novak, and she goes to the art gallery in the Palace of the Legion of Honor. She sits quietly, staring at a portrait of a beautiful Spanish woman. It is a painting of Carlotta. An attendant informs Stewart that there is no date and that the portrait is unsigned.

Stewart continues to follow Novak through an old section of San Francisco, where she makes a brief stop at a cheap apartment-hotel. He sees Novak in an upstairs window as she removes the jacket of her gray suit. But, when he questions the manageress, Ellen Corby, he is told that Novak has not been there. After finding the room empty, he looks down to the street where her car had been parked, and it is gone. Later, with Bel Geddes, he goes to a bookseller who tells him Carlotta's tragic story.

The next day the routine is the same. Stewart is one step ahead of Novak at the art gallery. Again, she sits in front of the portrait of Carlotta. Stewart gazes at her intently. He notices that Novak's hair has the same part and the same coil at the back as the woman in the painting.

After leaving the gallery, he continues to follow Novak. She goes to a spot below the Golden Gate Bridge and walks to the water's edge. She is wearing a navy blue dress with a white scarf that is blowing in the breeze as she stands near San Francisco Bay. She is picking the floral bouquet apart and tossing the blossoms among the waves. After discarding the remainder of the bouquet, she jumps into the bay.

Stewart dives in and brings her back to safety. Then he takes her to his apartment. Later, after her clothing has been removed and hung in the kitchen to dry, the sound of the telephone is heard. It awakens Novak. Helmore is on the other end of the line, and Stewart explains briefly what has happened. He terminates the conversation, telling Helmore he'll call him back.

Before the ringing of the telephone, there is a shot of Novak sleeping, covered by a sheet and yellow blanket. The phone awakens her and there is a moment of surprise as she sits up, startled. Stewart hands her a robe to slip into after explaining that she fell into the bay and he fished her out. She remembers none of this.

One of Novak's finest moments evolves at this point. Barefoot, in the red robe, she glides out of the bedroom and moves slowly toward Stewart. Her true beauty is captured via skillful lighting and a minimal use of makeup. She conveys total innocence while still appearing to be in a trance of sorts. Novak was the least self-conscious and most natural that she had ever seemed to be on camera. And there is an open quality that softens her and attracts.

Stewart and Novak sit in front of the fireplace over coffee as he continues to probe. Novak says, "You're terribly direct in your questions." She stuns Stewart by saying that she's never been inside the Palace of the Legion of Honor. During the next moments, she plays many different emotions and never loses sight of the character in this very carefully acted scene. This is the crucial one needed to hook him into her plan (not yet revealed). She must be seductive, but it can't be overdone. And it isn't. She is reaching out to him yet holding back at the same time. The scene is on two-levels.

Novak announces, "I'm married, you know," without the blink of an eye, and further fascinates him while pinning up her hair into a twist. She tells him—with a look—that she's got him. It's a soft-sell seduction scene that works. They are interrupted by the ringing of the telephone, and Stewart goes into the other room to take the call. It is Helmore again wanting to know what has happened. Stewart tells him in detail.

Helmore informs Stewart that Novak is twenty-six years old and that Carlotta Valdes committed suicide when she was the same age—a hundred years ago.

*Vertigo,* **with James Stewart**

*Vertigo*

When he hangs up, Stewart finds the living room empty. Novak is gone. Her Jaguar is also missing from where he had parked it on the street.

The next day, when Novak leaves her place, Stewart continues to follow her. They go round and round in circles. He is totally confused when he finally ends up in front of his own apartment building. He sees Novak get out of her car and watches as she goes to his door with an envelope which she places in the mail slot.

Stewart comes up to her and Novak explains, "It's a formal thank you note and a great big apology." She couldn't mail it because she didn't have the address, but she did have the landmark of Coit Tower. He reads the letter and asks what she intends to do the rest of the day. She answers, "I just thought I'd wander." He asks to join her and she says, "Only one is a wanderer. Two, together, are always going somewhere."

They drive to Muir Woods, the forest of giant redwoods, as the camera lovingly encompasses them in a dream-like haze of soft colors. In the shadows of the huge trees, Stewart asks her what she is thinking about. Her thoughts are of "all the people who have been born and who died while the trees went on living." She says, "I don't like it," and Stewart asks, "Why?" "Knowing I have to die," she answers and she asks him to take her away from the trees and into the light.

The scene dissolves to a hill overlooking the bay, and Stewart says, "I'm responsible for you now. You know the Chinese say that once you've saved a person's life, you're responsible for it forever. So I'm committed." After temporarily forgetting everything else, Novak comes back to reality and begins to describe her recurring dream to him. She tells him it's as though she is walking down a long corridor that once was mirrored. Fragments of that mirror are still hanging there, and, when she comes to the end of the corridor, there's nothing but darkness. She knows she'll die, but she's never come to the final part of the dream.

Remembering more, Novak says, "I sit there alone. Always alone. A grave. An open grave. I stand by the gravestone looking down into it. It's my grave. It's new and clean and waiting." Then she recalls a tower, a bell, and a gondola that seem to be in Spain.

Stewart: If I could just find the key. The beginning, and put it together.
Novak: And explain it away? But there's no way to explain it, you see. If I'm mad, that would explain it, wouldn't it? [Novak runs toward the sea with Stewart in pursuit, following and catching up with her. They embrace as they are framed against the water.] Scottie, I'm not mad. I'm not mad! I don't want to die. There's someone within me says I must die. Scottie, don't let me go!
Stewart: I'm here. I've got you. [There is a long kiss and a fadeout.]

In spite of the age difference between Novak and Stewart (who was twice her age), the viewer is not aware of this gap because of Novak's maturity. The love scenes work and the affair is plausible. She handled herself well in the scenes with Stewart, a testimony to her maturity and Hitchcock's handling of the romanticism of the whole film.

*Vertigo,* **with James Stewart**

It is night when Novak comes back to Stewart's apartment. He opens the door and she is terrified. The dream is back again to haunt her . . . the tower, the bell, and the old Spanish village. As she describes it (and Stewart fills in some of the details)—an old wooden hotel, a saloon, dark, with hanging oil lamps—Stewart recognizes the site she is speaking about. He knows she's seen it all at the mission, but she's unaware of this. He promises to take her there, and tells her that when she sees it, she will be free of her dream.

During the drive to the mission at San Juan Bautista, the camera focuses on Novak's face. The viewer wonders what she is thinking. When they arrive, Stewart gets Novak to try to relive the actual moments when she's been there before. Her madness is totally real. As Stewart kisses her passionately, it confuses her temporarily, and they confess their love for each other. She comes back to reality, and she knows what she must do.

Her eyes go up to the bell tower. She tries to free herself from Stewart's embrace. As an afterthought, Novak says, "It's too late. It wasn't supposed to happen this way. It shouldn't have happened this way. If you lose me, you'll know that I loved you and wanted to go on loving you." Stewart is completely baffled as she makes a dash through the door and up the stairs leading to the tower. She is faster than he is, and he hears her footsteps above him as he desperately tries to follow her up the spiral stairway. Because of his acrophobia, he has to force himself every inch of the way. He is not fast enough. He hears a scream and painfully watches her body fall past the open arch of the mission window and land below.

At the inquest, Stewart is seated next to Helmore. Stewart is blamed only in part because Novak was a woman suffering from delusions and with an inherited suicidal trait. The coroner points out that his vertigo prevented Stewart from saving Novak from death. The case is dismissed as a suicide, but Stewart cannot accept her final words as those of a suicide victim. He knows that a part of himself has died with her. Helmore tries to relieve him of any guilt, but Stewart cannot forget that he let Novak get away from his protection. Helmore confides that he's winding up her affairs and his own and will be going as far away as possible, probably to Europe, for good.

As a result of what he has been through with the death of the patrolman and now Novak, Stewart has a breakdown. Bel Geddes is a daily visitor to the sanitarium where he stays. He is a shadow of his former self, empty of emotions and is unaware of her visits. The doctor advises Bel Geddes that it could take as long as six months or a year for his cure. It all depends on him, and he won't talk. He is suffering from acute melancholia and blames himself. Bel Geddes offers the doctor one clue, "He was in love with her . . . he still is."

Three months later, Stewart returns to life knowing there is something he must do. After his release from the sanitarium, he continues to wander and sees Novak's face, at a distance, in other women; when they come close, he realizes he is mistaken.

One day, Stewart is standing in front of the flower shop, looking in the window, when he spots a shop girl talking with a group of her friends on the street. She has the same figure as Novak. The facial resemblance is uncanny. This person seems to be coarser and her hair is reddish-brown, not blonde, worn long and loose rather than pinned up. Just as Novak was dressed in green when he saw her initially, this Novak is also in green. But, unlike the first Novak, this one's dress is cheap. He watches as she bids her friends good-bye and walks down the street toward the Empire Hotel where she lives. From the street below, he sees her open the window of her room high above where he is standing. He had previously observed the first Novak in a similar setup at the cheap apartment-hotel when she disappeared.

Stewart goes upstairs to the room and knocks at her door. As Novak opens it, there is no recognition on her part. The viewer believes that she thinks he's just a masher who's followed her. He tells her that she reminds him of someone and that he would just like to speak to her. Novak's been around and she isn't buying this line. Finally, she agrees to speak to him and permits him entry after warning him that she can "yell awful loud." Novak lent further credibility as she backed up to the phone while he entered the room, her hands behind her as if to summon help. After she has shown him her driver's license and proved who she is, Stewart is still fascinated by the resemblance and asks her to have dinner with him. Novak finally agrees after informing him she's "been picked up before."

When he leaves, Novak grabs a suitcase and begins to take her clothing from the closet. She spots the gray suit hanging there and pauses. She relives the bell tower scene, and what really happened is revealed to the audience. In flashback, she races up the stairs of the tower to the waiting Helmore. The real wife's body is tossed down as Helmore holds his hand over Novak's mouth to stop her screams, and then they hide in the background of the tower. Anguish is strongly registered by Novak as she relives this painful moment.

She sits at the desk and takes pen and paper to reveal

*Vertigo,* **with James Stewart**

her true feelings. (At this point, Hitchcock has revealed a portion of the mystery and let the viewer know that Novak is the same person Stewart has mistaken her for.) As she writes, and the camera focuses on her in closeup, Novak's voice-over is heard:

Dearest Scottie—
And so you found me. This is the moment that I dreaded, and hoped for, wondering what I would say and do if I ever saw you again. I wanted so to see you again, just once. Now I'll go and you can give up your search. I want you to have peace of mind. You've nothing to blame yourself for—you were the victim. I was the tool and you were the victim of Gavin Elster's plan to murder his wife. He chose me to play the part because I looked like her—dressed me up like her. He was quite safe because she lived in the country and rarely came to town. He chose you to be the witness to a suicide. The Carlotta story was part real, part invented to make you testify that Madeleine wanted to kill herself. He knew of your illness. He knew you'd never get up the stairs at the tower. He planned it so well. He made no mistakes. I made the mistake—I fell in love—that wasn't part of the plan. I'm still in love with you and I want you so to love me. If I had the nerve I'd stay and lie, hoping that I could make you love me again—as I am, for myself—and to forget the other. Forget the past. But—I don't know whether I have the nerve to try.

*Vertigo*

As an afterthought, Novak rises from the chair, rips the letter in pieces and begins putting the clothing back into the closet. She places the telltale gray suit at the far end of the wardrobe rack and grabs a lavender dress with matching sweater to wear on their dinner date. She has decided to see Stewart again.

During dinner at Ernie's, Stewart tells Novak about her predecessor. She studies him in puzzled silence and he confesses that he has spent a number of months in a sanitarium and that his memory is not clear on a number of details. He is beginning to feel comfortable with her and hopes to recreate the woman he knew and loved so briefly. After dinner, they return to Novak's room. She is framed in silhouette in front of the window as the green light from an outside neon sign filters into the room. They agree to see each other the next day and he begins formulating a plan to bring back the original image.

During the next few days, they spend considerable time together. With slight alterations, Stewart can visualize her as the woman he loved. In agreeing to be made over by Stewart, Novak doesn't want to be completely recreated. She doesn't want to be a copy, and would rather be liked for herself this time. There are tortured moments for her as they go to pick out clothing. He buys her a gray suit that is a duplicate of the one Novak wore when the bell tower mishap

occurred. She knows he wants her dressed in the same mode as the original Novak, and it does not please her to be molded into something she is not. Stewart is becoming obsessed with the recreation and Novak says, "Couldn't you like me—just me—the way I am? When we first started out, it was so good, we had fun. And then you started in on clothes. Well, I'll wear the darn clothes if you want me to if you'll just—just like me."

The final point of surrender comes when she agrees to have her hair bleached to the exact shade of the original.

Novak:     If I let you change me—if I do what you tell me—will you love me?
Stewart:   Yes . . . Yes.
Novak:     Alright then, I'll do it because I don't care anymore about me.

In an interview with Alexander Walker in the *Evening Standard,* Alfred Hitchcock said:

That scene in *Vertigo* where James Stewart forces Miss Kim Novak to alter her whole personality by altering her lipstick, hairstyle, even hair-tint—for me it has the compulsion of a striptease in reverse. The woman is made insecure by being forced to make up, not take off.

*Vertigo,* with James Stewart

And this describes it perfectly.

When Novak returns to the hotel from the beauty shop, the likeness is uncanny. However, she is wearing her hair loose rather than in the twist that Stewart had specified.

The viewer now sees another side of the character. Novak really does love Stewart. She goes into the bathroom to put her hair up into the style he has requested. She is dressed in the gray suit that he has chosen. As she returns to the room, she is seen in soft focus through a haze. His original has been resurrected. This is a big acting moment for Novak. She has three different changes of thought to convey to Stewart as she glides slowly toward him. There is no dialogue. She must show them with her expression. And she does it beautifully. First, there is the recognition. *I am her.* They are now together and she sees in his eyes that he recognizes who she is. Second, *I see that you see this.* And third, *Will you love me now?* Perfectly conveyed, Novak's thoughts register strongly. Stewart and Novak lock in a passionate embrace and the camera circles them, completing the high point they have built to.

After this, he suggests dinner and she goes to change. Returning, dressed in black, Novak makes her big mistake. In searching for the right piece of jewelry to wear with her gown, she chooses a necklace. As she asks Stewart to help fasten the chain, his eyes are glued to it as she studies her reflection in the mirror. She is unaware that Stewart recognizes the necklace as a duplicate of the one worn by Carlotta in the painting. Now there is no doubt. Stewart is positive the two women are one. Novak asks him to "muss me a little," and they embrace. She says, "I do have you now, don't I?"

They had originally planned to dine at "our place," Ernie's, but Stewart now suggests they find somewhere down the peninsula. Novak is agreeable. In the car, she is trusting, but uncertainty begins to register when she realizes how far they are going. She questions him, and Stewart says he must do something "and then I'll be free of the past." She looks at him suspiciously, fear taking over. She sees the dark outline of Mission San Juan Bautista in the distance, she knows he realizes who she is.

They reach the familiar site, and Stewart pulls up in front and climbs out of the car. Novak shrinks back against the seat but he forces her out saying, "I need you to be Madeleine awhile. And when it's done, we'll both be free."

Novak panics and says, "I don't want to go in there,"

but Stewart is now possessed by his desire to recreate the scene he experienced. And he talks as if to himself. "We stood here and I kissed her for the last time. And she said, 'If you lose me you'll know that I loved you and wanted to keep on loving you.' And then she turned and ran into the church. When I followed, it was too late."

Novak struggles to break loose from his grasp as he forces her up the stairs to the bell tower. She is now fearful for her life. Her eyes widen with terror. She knows that he is aware of the whole scheme as he commands her to "go up the stairs."

Stewart: We're going up the tower.
Novak: You can't! You're afraid!
Stewart: We'll see . . . we'll see . . . this is my second chance. But you knew that day that I wouldn't be able to follow you, didn't you?

Novak confesses that she did know he couldn't follow, and Stewart begins to put the pieces together. The real wife was the one that died in the planned murder. Novak was the copy, "the counterfeit" to fool him. The real wife was dead before Novak ever got up to the tower. Helmore had broken her neck.

Stewart: Wasn't taking any chances, was he? So when you got up there, he pushed her off the tower. But it was you that screamed. Why did you scream?
Novak: I wanted to stop it, Scottie, I wanted to stop it!
Stewart: You wanted to stop it. Why did you scream? Since you had tricked me so well up to then. You played the wife very well, Judy. He made you over, didn't he? He made you over just as I—only better. Not only the clothes and the hair . . . the looks . . . the manner . . . and the words. And those beautiful phony trances! And you jumped into the bay, didn't you? I'll bet you're a wonderful swimmer, aren't you? Aren't you? [Shaking Novak] Aren't you?
Novak: [Fearfully] Yes.

Stewart has pieced it all together. They picked on him because they knew about his vertigo. He was the setup, the made-to-order witness, the man who couldn't get to the top to see what went on. When he questions Novak as to where Helmore is now, she doesn't know, and Stewart says, "We'll find him."

When they reach the top, Stewart pushes Novak through the door and under the bell, saying, "I made it!" He forces her to look at the scene of the crime. She is heartbreakingly real throughout the final moments as Stewart figures out the rest.

Stewart: This is where it happened. The two of you hid back, back there, and waited for it to clear—

*Vertigo,* **with James Stewart**

and then you sneaked down and drove into town. And then? You were his girl. What happened to you? What happened to you? Did he ditch you? [Novak nods yes.] Oh, Judy! With all of his wife's money and all that freedom and power, and he ditched you. What a shame. But he knew he was safe, he knew you couldn't talk. Did he give you anything?

Novak: Some money.

Stewart: And the necklace! Carlotta's necklace. There was where you made your mistake, Judy. You shouldn't keep souvenirs of a killing. You shouldn't have been . . . you shouldn't have been that sentimental. I loved you so, Madeleine.

Novak: Scottie, I was safe when you found me. There was nothing that you could prove. When I saw you again, I . . . I couldn't run away—I loved you so. I walked into danger, let you change me, because I loved you. I wanted you. Scottie, oh please, you love me . . . keep me safe.

Stewart: It's too late. It's too late. There's no bringing her back!

Novak: Please . . . Please.

Just at this moment, a dark figure looms out of the shadows, and Novak backs up in fear through the archway, screaming, "No . . . No!" She takes one step too many and falls to her death. The dark figure (a nun) says, "God have mercy" and begins tolling the bell. It is all over. Stewart stands on the ledge and looks below.

\*      \*

To conclude the film, Alfred Hitchcock took what would normally be an accident, a weak ordinary device, and made it work. In this case, it is a repetition of what Novak herself did. Although she really did not mean to do it, the character must still pay with her life—divine retribution.

There were those who questioned the ending. Stewart had cured himself of vertigo but did he walk away from it all? Or did he jump and join his love in death? Hitchcock left it up to the viewer to come to his own conclusion.

\*      \*

At last, Kim had a role of substance and she took a step forward. After the reviews of *Jeanne Eagels* and *Pal Joey,* those of *Vertigo* made her believe that it might be possible, after all, for critics to take her seriously.

*Motion Picture Herald:*

Paramount has a big one to crow about in Alfred Hitchcock's newest screen venture into shock, suspense and surprise. Fortified with the marquee name magic of James Stewart and Kim Novak, and the identity of Hitchcock's direction to up the volume of that happy sound at the box office, this entry in the "blockbuster sweepstakes" is an odds on bet . . . Miss Novak finds a new plateau in her career through the expert guidance of the "master of suspense" . . . [in her] enactment of a young woman, bewitched and influenced by the spirit of a long-since dead beauty, who is driving her to suicide.

*Film Daily:*

For marquee material, Hitchcock has James Stewart and Kim Novak, who rank high among the nation's box office attractions and who here do most effective jobs in their roles. While fine performances are standard with Stewart, it is Miss Novak whose work surprises. She scores in her dual role, and under the guidance of Hitchcock emerges as a fine actress. The producer-director makes excellent use of Miss Novak's type of beauty, even to the extent of using her large eyes as part of the main title backgrounds.

Ruth Waterbury, in the *Los Angeles Herald-Examiner:*

There are two vivid stars in *Vertigo* and both of them are displayed at the top of their form. One is Kim Novak, the actress, and the other is Alfred Hitchcock, the director. In their quite different styles, neither of them has ever been more intriguing. Oh, there is, to be sure, a tall and charming gentleman named James Stewart mixed up in this—but Miss Novak and Mr. Hitchcock, as a team, succeed in blanketing him. I don't mean to imply that Mr. Stewart isn't excellent. He is. He always is. There is no such thing as a shabby performance in his repertoire. But as a rather dim-witted detective in *Vertigo* he can't stand up against the vividness of Miss Novak in what proves to be a very complex characterization . . . this proves Miss Novak is an actress, not merely a personality, and that Mr. Hitchcock, behind the camera, has lost none of his cunning. As a team, these two are fine, fine, fine.

*Variety:*

Miss Novak, shopgirl who involves Stewart in love and what turns out to be a clear case of murder, is excellent, too, in her brooding, sexual way—her performance topping those in *Pal Joey* or *Jeanne Eagels,* her most recent releases.

Film's last minute, in which Stewart fights off acrophobia to drag Miss Novak to belltower's top, finds she still loves him and then sees her totter and fall to death through mortal fright of an approaching nun, is spectacular and gorgeously conceived.

Jack Moffitt, in the *Hollywood Reporter:*

Alfred Hitchcock tops his own fabulous record for suspense with *Vertigo,* a super-tale of murder, madness and mysticism that stars James Stewart and Kim Novak. Aside from being big boxoffice, it is a picture no film-maker should miss—if only to observe the pioneering techniques achieved by Hitchcock and his co-workers.

The measure of a great director lies in his ability to inspire his associates to rise above their usual competence and Hitchcock exhibits absolute genius in doing this in *Vertigo.*

Miss Novak has become a fine actress, especially in the latter part of the film where she appears as the love-possessed shop girl. Here, without the support of her ethereal beauty, she does a really fine bit of trouping.

Untapped capabilities were revealed by Kim in *Vertigo,* and it is difficult to imagine how she could ever surpass her quintessential role in this film. She would never cease looking for a script to equal the brilliance this one had given her. No actress comes to mind who would have been better in the role, and Kim's performance in *Vertigo* remains one of her finest.

*Vertigo,* with James Stewart, and both characters Kim portrayed
via camera trickery

# 8

Returning to her home lot, Columbia, Kim was handed the script of *Bell, Book and Candle*. The Broadway comedy by John Van Druten had enjoyed a long and successful run starring Rex Harrison and Lilli Palmer in the leading roles. The plot dealt with a witch searching for love. And, in case mere mortals didn't know, witches can't express human emotions. They can't feel love. They can't blush and they can't cry. It required Kim to be beautiful, bewitching and enchanting. Needless to say, she filled the bill on all counts.

While Kim was pleased with the assignment, she had secretly hoped for something stronger as a follow-up to *Vertigo*. James Stewart was again paired opposite her in their second screen teaming. In agreeing to Kim's loanout to Paramount for Alfred Hitchock's film, Columbia had negotiated with Stewart to do two additional films for them as part of the package deal.

There was comfort in the fact that Kim was not among strangers on this production. In addition to being reunited with Stewart, Jack Lemmon was also costarred. James Wong Howe, who had captured Kim's beauty so vividly in *Picnic,* was again behind the camera, and Richard Quine was directing. Added insurance was provided with a cast that included Ernie

Kovacs, Hermione Gingold, Elsa Lanchester, and Janice Rule.

While immersed in glamorous witchery, during the making of this film, Kim learned that Harry Cohn had died of heart failure at the age of sixty-six. The man who ran Columbia Pictures with an iron fist was gone. Although they had clashed on numerous occasions during their contractual relationship, Kim was visibly shaken by the news.

Cohn had opened many doors for Kim and, in an odd way, was a type of father figure. He had master-minded and built an image that had done much for the career of the blonde model from Chicago. Her feelings about the man remained private, and, with due respect, she attended the services for Cohn in the company of Norma Kasell. She returned to work on the set later that same day.

It was also during the making of this film that Kim met General Rafael Trujillo of the Dominican Republic and set the wire services ablaze with the "hottest romance" in Hollywood. Ramfis, as he was known to intimates, had confessed that he had a crush on Kim even before meeting her. It was Zsa Zsa Gabor who was instrumental in their introduction at a party given

Attending services for Harry Cohn with Norma Kasell and publicity director Al Horwitz

Prince Rainier did for Monaco when he married Grace Kelly. And it prompted producer Julian Blaustein to quip:

> This is great for the United States. With Grace Kelly in Monaco and Kim Novak in the Dominican Republic, we'll have a pincers movement on the whole world.

But *Life* magazine blew the lid off the whole keg of dynamite with a photo layout of the Gabor party showing Kim and Ramfis enjoying themselves—and a second grouping of pictures showing Ramfis's wife and six children. Once again, Kim received a public spanking in print. Since the Dominican Republic was receiving foreign aid, the Congress of the United States became involved, and the incident received added coverage.

One of Ramfis's aides offered the following statement:

> The General is known to be one of the wealthiest young men in the world and he has always believed that any man, wealthy or not, should have the right to spend his money as he sees fit. It's ridiculous to believe there's any connection between the money he spends on his personal life and any funds given to his country.

Representative Wayne Hays of Ohio (who would, many years later, be involved in headlines of his own, the Elizabeth Ray/Washington scandal) was the person in Congress who was most critical. He was taking pot shots at Gabor, and newspapers were full of the entire incident.

Kim's public image was in danger, but, when she was asked to comment about the fact that she had been chastised by the press for her involvement with a married man, she honestly commented:

> It was a fine relationship until all those stories started. I liked Ramfis. He was very sweet and a fine gentleman. I'm sure he didn't tell me he had a wife because he is shy and probably was afraid I wouldn't go out with a married man.

in his honor to introduce him to the movie set. The guest list read like *Who's Who of Hollywood* and included such beauties as Rhonda Fleming, Ginger Rogers, Shirley MacLaine, Jeanne Crain, Maureen O'Hara, Kathryn Grayson, and Ann Miller.

Once again, Kim's latest "romance" was reported daily in the various columns in publications throughout the world. And Kim openly admitted, "He's the most attractive man I've met in years." Kim and Ramfis saw more and more of each other, and he gifted her with jewelry and a Mercedes 220-S convertible. When reporters questioned the gifts, Kim said, "When Ramfis gives you a Mercedes-Benz, it's like another man sending you flowers." It was figured by many that he wanted to marry Kim and do for his country what

And this did not please Columbia at all! The studio called Kim on the carpet, ordered her not to see Trujillo again, and insisted that she return the Mercedes-Benz to him. She was also forbidden to talk to reporters.

The studio assigned round-the-clock publicity people to Kim's home in order to prevent any further encounters with Trujillo, but the "rebellious Mickey" eluded her guards and defied the studio edict. When

With Pyewacket

I was warned before I did the film that I would find Miss Novak very difficult to work with and that she wasn't very professional. I found her to be quite the opposite. And she was the only actress I've worked with who sent me a letter in her own writing when the film was finished, telling me how much she enjoyed working with me, which I thought was pretty nice.

Elsa Lanchester recalled:

I really liked Kim Novak and wish I had known her better. I felt she was too vulnerable a person to hold the course in show business and that maybe her choice was a more peaceful life. I sincerely hope she has found it.

And producer Julian Blaustein noted:

It's astonishing to me that I can recall very few on-the-set remembrances, but I liked Kim, found her a serious and diligent actress—and I thoroughly enjoyed working with her.

Perhaps the most important fringe benefit connected with this assignment was the fact that Kim was introduced to one more member of the cast, someone who would enrich and become a most significant part of her life. It was the feline character known as "Pyewacket," who indeed played an important role in the film proceedings. The Siamese charmer stole a number of scenes, but Kim didn't mind. The rapport between them was beautiful, and, upon completion of the film, they could not be separated. The cat remained with Kim. Pye, for short, became a member of Kim's family (the first of many pets she would adopt) and was delighted with his new mistress. Both were independents and they accepted each other on their own terms.

Kim was able to play most of the role barefoot, which delighted her. Off screen, she had always preferred walking without shoes. The studio, however, had to resort to heroic measures to keep her from getting chilled in a number of scenes where she ran barefoot through the snow. They provided an attendant with a blanket in which to wrap Kim's feet and keep them warm between takes.

Jean Louis designed an exotic wardrobe in keeping with the story. Among the knockout numbers that he created for Kim, the topper was a full-length burgundy velvet cape lined in begal red satin with gloves and shoes to match the lining. Under the cape, Kim wore a burgundy velvet gown backless, with a high-necked front, and with long sleeves encrusted with jewels. It was a stunner.

Ramfis left town, Kim met him in his private railway car for a tender good-bye. As always, Kim had a mind of her own. Later, Trujillo wrote Kim apologizing "for any trouble I caused you." And although he later divorced his wife and anchored his private yacht off the Southern California coast in the hope of renewing their friendship, Kim did not see him again. All of this only whetted the appetites of the movie fans who rushed to the boxoffice to view Kim in *Bell, Book and Candle* when it was released.

As the beautiful, Bohemian-type blonde with "strange" powers, Kim had her first opportunity since *Phffft* to display her light comedy talents. Jimmy Stewart felt the picture had class and said:

When you do a domestic comedy and it comes out right, there's a tremendous sense of achievement because it's about the most difficult kind of of thing to do. Comedy is no laughing matter. It's tough to write, tough to direct, and tough to act. So when it's a success—you really feel good about it.

About working with Kim, Hermione Gingold said:

*Bell, Book and Candle*, with director Richard Quine

To lend authenticity, a valuable collection of native primitive art, valued at $75,000 and consisting of more than eighty pieces assembled from Africa and the South Sea islands, was used in the film. Producer Julian Blaustein arranged for the collection to be loaned by the famous Carlebach Gallery in New York, and the collection was used to stock the art gallery that was run by Kim. The masks, dolls, statues, and other objets d'art were some of the most expensive props in screen annals.

\*     \*

*Bell, Book and Candle* begins on Christmas Eve. Novak is closing her African art objects shop for the night. With her is her Siamese cat, Pyewacket, who purrs contentedly as Novak asks:

Oh Pye, Pye—Pyewacket. What's the matter with me? Why do I feel this way? It's such a rut. Same old thing day after day—same old people. Oh, I know I'm feeling sorry for myself but it's true. Why don't you give me something for Christmas, Pye? Hmmm. What would I like? I'd like to do something different. I'd like to meet someone different. [As she looks out the window, she sees James

Stewart, a book publisher, who lives in an apartment above the shop and whom she had never met, enter the building. And she confides to Pyewacket:] Look, there's that man upstairs! He's different. Why don't I ever know people like that? Hmmm? Why don't you give me him for Christmas, Pye? Why don't you give me him?

And Pyewacket answers his mistress with loud purring sounds of approval.

Novak's aunt, Elsa Lanchester, lives in another apartment in the same building. When Lanchester puts a hex on Stewart's phone, he goes downstairs to make a call from Novak's place. Stewart becomes interested in Novak and she is attracted to him. Lanchester arrives to invite her niece to a party at the Zodiac Club and Stewart says he'll try to be there too.

After he leaves, Lanchester confesses to hexing Stewart's phone. She's a practicing witch, as is Novak. Lanchester has also pried into Stewart's correspondence in his apartment and learned that he will be married shortly. "I think you like him," Lanchester remarks to Novak who readily responds with, "Yes I do. Very much." Lanchester is all set to hex the romance between Stewart and his fiancee, but Novak exacts a promise from her to stop practicing witchcraft in their building.

At the Zodiac, a "dive with personality," Novak's brother Jack Lemmon—who is a warlock (the male version of a witch)—is playing bongos. Presiding over one of the tables is Hermione Gingold, one of the high priestesses of witchcraft.

Novak is despondent on this Christmas Eve, and, seated at a table with Lanchester, she confesses, "I wish I could just spend some time with some everyday people for a change." When her aunt says she'd soon tire of the humdrum routine of everyday life, Novak says, "It might be pleasant to be humdrum once in a while."

Stewart, intrigued by Lanchester's earlier description of the Zodiac, arrives with his intended, Janice Rule, who is a beautiful but cold type. Novak recognizes Rule as a college classmate, but they were never friends. Rule had written poison-pen letters to the dean about Novak. In return, knowing of Rule's passionate dislike of thunder showers, Novak had put her hex on the weather so it rained and thundered for long periods of time.

To get even with her catty rival now, Novak signals Lemmon to give out with the loudest version of "Stormy Weather" ever heard. It sends Rule running from the club. Stewart, of course, follows her. After

*Bell, Book and Candle,* **with Elsa Lanchester and Jack Lemmon**

they have gone, Novak ponders the question, "I wonder if I could get him without tricks?" She then confesses to her aunt that she will not use her witch's power to lure him.

Back at her place, Novak exchanges Christmas presents with Lemmon and Lanchester. Lemmon gives Novak a vial of liquid with which she may summon anyone by painting the liquid on a photograph and then setting fire to it. Novak tests it with a picture of Ernie Kovacs, author of a book on witchcraft, who is now in Mexico. But it is Stewart who arrives, thinking the place is on fire. Lemmon and Lanchester leave.

Stewart tells Novak that he and Rule are to elope the next day. Despite her previous resolution, Novak puts a spell on him and the two end up in a wild embrace. He falls in love with her and knows he can't go through with his marriage plans. The next day, he tells a furious Rule that he cannot marry her.

In response to Novak's "summons," Kovacs arrives at Stewart's office the day after Christmas. He discusses a new book he is writing on witchcraft and tells an uncomprehending Stewart that New York is full of witches and that the Zodiac is their headquarters.

Stewart takes Kovacs to meet Novak, Lemmon, and Lanchester, and then agrees to publish Kovacs's book. Lemmon and the author leave, and Lemmon persuades Kovacs to allow him to collaborate on the book.

Novak and Stewart continue their courtship and the thoroughly bewitched Stewart proposes marriage. Disturbed and uncertain—but hoping for the best—Novak acquiesces. She learns of Lemmon's collaboration with the author and demands he stop, telling her brother that she has renounced witchcraft and will marry Stewart. Lemmon refuses and Novak promises to hex the book, whereupon Lemmon threatens to expose her as a witch to Stewart.

In an effort to "come clean," Novak tells Stewart that she lives by magic and is a witch. He, of course, refuses to believe her. Lanchester clumsily tries to tell him the same thing, and the bewildered Stewart has a showdown with Novak. When he angrily tries to leave, convinced that whatever has motivated Novak hasn't been love, he is finally convinced of her powers when she uses them to prevent him from going.

A distraught Stewart, accompanied by Lemmon and Kovacs, visits Gingold who exorcises Novak's spell by feeding him a disgusting witch's brew. He then confronts Novak and tells her he intends to marry Rule. Novak tries to cast a spell on Rule with Pyewacket's help but the feline deserts her and goes to live with

*Bell, Book and Candle*

Lanchester. Rule refuses to take Stewart back and treats him so abominably he isn't at all sorry.

Novak is heartbroken over the status of her romance. She confesses to her aunt that she is truly in love, something of which no real witch is capable. Pyewacket is then sent to Stewart's office by the well-meaning Lanchester. Thinking the cat still belongs to Novak, Stewart takes it back to her.

It's a different Novak. She has changed the name of her shop, and she now deals in flowers and sea shells. The transition (since losing her powers of witchery) is evident at first glance, and Novak registers this feeling strongly. Whereas she has worn dark colors or red during most of the film, she is now attired in white chiffon and yellow.

After engaging in conversation, Stewart sees Novak blush and cry and he realizes love has turned her into a

*Bell, Book and Candle,* with Elsa Lanchester, Jack Lemmon, Ernie
Kovacs, and James Stewart

human being since a witch can do neither. When he takes Novak in his arms, there is no longer any doubt that this happy transformation has occurred. The lovers are reunited.

\*　　　\*

Kim was largely responsible for bringing what life there was to *Bell, Book and Candle*. The film itself was simple in plot and lavish with costumes. It was a heavy load to carry, but Kim tried valiantly to do what she could with the characterization and make it effective. Her extraordinary beauty was again captured through the ingenious camera technique of James Wong Howe, and she displayed an excellent sense of timing throughout.

During her telephone scene, Kim was particularly effective, as she had been previously during the phone sequence in *Jeanne Eagels*. Phone conversations can be disastrous for actors, but Kim excels at them, probably because, as a loner, she need not depend upon the reaction of a costar. She is on her own.

Lavishly costumed in the burgundy velvet cape and walking through the snow-lined streets, Kim evoked a sense of timelessness and ethereal beauty. One could hope that she might some day have the opportunity to play a costumed heroine like *Anna Karenina*, but such has not yet been Kim's fate.

Though the role was unrewarding, Kim gave to it her very best and got whatever mileage could be mustered from the property. Reviewers enjoyed her part in the proceedings.

The *Hollywood Reporter* said:

In teaming Jimmy Stewart and Kim Novak in a vehicle reminiscent of *Vertigo* (in which they did blockbuster business), producer Julian Blaustein should find preopening recruited crowds waiting at the boxoffice.

Miss Novak, imparting a fey and other-worldly tone to her characterization of a pretty witch who longs to know love, as humans know it, does much, in the early sequences, to get this concept off the ground.

*Variety* noted:

*Bell, Book and Candle* has a dream cast and a story that might have been taken from a dream book. It's a whimsical, novelty comedy about witches in modern Manhattan. With James Stewart and Kim Novak toplined, and Jack Lemmon and Ernie Kovacs co-starred, the Julian Blaustein production for Columbia, directed by Richard Quine, has hilarity and romance in about equal portions. It should bring hefty box office returns.

These are some of the plus factors, and it has others. On the minus side, however, the light mood of comedy occasionally becomes as heavy as a witch's curse. One reason is that the screen's treatment of John van Druten's play sometimes overdoes the physical aspects of witchery. Another is Miss Novak. She does probably the best acting of her career, or at any rate, the most, but she doesn't seem equipped for light comedy. Miss Novak's casting is obviously for boxoffice reasons, and it will pay off there.

And *Motion Picture Herald* applauded with:

Polish up that S.R.O. sign. Here comes Entertainment with a capital E. It is elegant, enchanting escapism in a modern story of witches and witchcraft, with Love having the guile to steal a sorcerer's heart and transform it into one capable of responding to human emotion. James Stewart and Kim Novak are nothing less than superb in their respective delineations as a book publisher who falls in love with a beautiful, bewitching owner of a Greenwich Village shop specializing in weird masks and African objets d'art.

This is easily Miss Novak's best effort, in a role demanding the same sly, graceful movements displayed by her accomplice, a Siamese cat.

\*　　　\*

*Bell, Book and Candle* wasn't the hit everyone expected it to be, but it did fairly well at the box office and was entertaining. It provided a role Kim could identify with, since both the character of Gillian Holroyd and Kim herself (in her private life) were searching for love. Perhaps, though, even more than love, Kim was longing now for a role that would give proper vent to her acting desires.

Her next film seemed as if it might supply one. *Middle of the Night* by Paddy Chayefsky was a successful dramatic play that had run for more than two years on Broadway, with Edward G. Robinson winning high praise in the male starring role. In the film version, Fredric March was cast in the Robinson role, and it was a joint decision on the part of Chayefsky, producer George Justin, and director Delbert Mann to cast Kim in the role that Gena Rowlands had created on the stage. The decision was made to produce the film entirely in New York City, because many of the exteriors called for the typically changeable weather to be found in the New York area.

Rehearsals were held at the Palladium Ballroom, noted for being the home of mambo night, on Broadway at Fifty-Third Street. This seemingly unlikely place was used by Chayefsky and Mann partly because of superstition. It was there that the old "Philco Play-

*Bell, Book and Candle,* **with James Stewart and Pyewacket**

136

house" television series, in which both had won their first recognition, had rehearsed. Their most noted TV plays (*Marty, The Bachelor Party, The Catered Affair,* and *Middle of the Night*) had also rehearsed there and the men thus felt at home.

Filming on *Middle of the Night* began on Monday, 5 January 1959 at the newly-titled Gold Medal Studios in New York City's East Bronx. Previously, this big building had been known as the Biograph Studios and it was there that D. W. Griffith made his first films. Mann, Chayefsky, and March were all impressed with the natural acting ability of their feminine star.

About working with Kim, Delbert Mann said:

I have always felt great affection for Kim and great admiration for her courage. When she agreed to do *Middle of the Night* she was setting out into uncharted and frightening waters. She was to be working in New York, away from the security of her Hollywood studio base, with a cast of theatre-trained, stage-oriented actors, and playing a terribly demanding role opposite Fredric March—one of the greatest actors in the world. She knew that we planned to rehearse like a stage production or as if for a live television performance, and this was a method of working, I believe, she had never experienced. There would be no well-known Hollywood cameraman to take the pains to make her look good. She would be working with a writer-director team known to favor a kind of grubby realism rather than studio-type glamour. She would be doing a script which demanded a level of emotional highs and lows she knew she had never achieved—and which she had the gravest doubts about ever being able to achieve. Everything was against her, yet she accepted the challenge.

Kim, I always felt, had a terrible insecurity and an open vulnerability. Her fear was palpable. She simply didn't know how to handle the two weeks rehearsal, especially faced with the example set by Freddy March, working so meticulously to set every detail in advance so that he could then forget that aspect and concentrate on the emotion of the scene. Kim was pretty much at sea as we rehearsed with such consummate actors as Lee Grant, Martin Balsam, Lee Philips, Edith Meiser and all the others. It was all intimidating to her.

I think she was especially intimidated by Freddy's reputation, but what he did for her and for me! It was my greatest experience of working with a creative actor—his openness to directorial suggestions, his kindness, his warmth and understanding—and it was extended into his relationship to Kim. He was ever gentle and helpful, always aware of her feelings and fears.

Paddy was also understanding and helpful to her. But probably the greatest contributor was Everett Chambers who is now a producer. At that time, he was our Casting Director, then became my Dialogue Coach. He took Kim under his wing, coaching, teasing, jollying her along. I remember his story of their rehearsal of one particularly difficult scene. We had rehearsed as long as time permitted but she still had an inability to let her emotions go fully. Ev and I had discussed in detail what was still needed

*Middle of the Night,* with director Delbert Mann

and I asked him to work further with her in a more informal atmosphere.

They went back to her apartment and started to work on the scene. The more they worked the more depressed and frustrated she became, convinced that she could never do it. She just couldn't find the way to turn her emotions loose. She cried, he yelled, according to his story. Suddenly, in frustration and anger, she smashed one of the balls off the Christmas tree which was standing in the corner. He yelled for her to do it again and again. Increasing the level of tension and release higher and higher, together they smashed every ornament on the tree and she collapsed in tears on the sofa. Ev then talked quietly to her for a few moments about how to recapture the memory and use those emotions in playing the scene the next day, and then he departed.

Her performance the following day was extraordinary. Fuller and more real than she had ever achieved before. It was startling.

It was not an easy, comfortable picture physically. We were shooting in the old Gold Medal Studios in the Bronx which were cold and depressing in the dead of winter. It was miserable shooting on the New York streets at night in the freezing cold. We were lacking in the amenities which help make an actress comfortable and keep her happy, but Kim never complained. She was a real trouper. The veteran New York crew began by being somewhat suspicious of her, then very quickly adopted her. She became one of the gang. George Justin, the Producer-Production Manager led the way in kidding her unmercifully. She loved it and responded in kind. We ended the shooting with a tremendous feeling of family of which Kim and Freddy were the essential elements.

Seen today, her performance, for me, stands the test of time. It is full of truth, heart, and deep feeling. She truly projects the vulnerable, confused creature Paddy created. I have always felt that had she not been a "star," if audiences had never seen her in any other role, her performance would have been acclaimed as sensationally interesting and real.

It was a most satisfying experience for me and Kim retains a very warm spot in my heart.

Paddy Chayefsky recalls:

I remember Kim Novak very well and very fondly. I felt she had a natural acting ability, and, at the time, I wished she wasn't so intelligent about the role. Every time she asked a question, it was a penetrating one, and one I found tough to answer. And more often than not, when she had a comment to make, she was right. I think she was a very underrated actress.

And Martin Balsam observed:

I had very little to do with Miss Novak—only one brief scene in which we exchanged no dialogue. But my recalled impression of Kim Novak was that she had more talent to offer than was ever required of her. But that would lead into the "SYSTEM" and we could go on and on about that.

Kim had put her heart and soul into this characterization and she tried to break the mold that had been hers in previous efforts. This was a role that called for a real acting job. Kim realized some of her shortcomings and was trying her damndest to make good with this difficult and very different assignment. As she put it:

I have only been in pictures five years. Before that I had no dramatic training—so different from most actors who first learn their craft and then perform. So up until my present project—I've always been tense and unnatural on camera, trying so hard to do just what the director told me to do but never contributing anything of my own personality.

When I did *Picnic,* for instance, Josh Logan told me never to use my own mannerisms before the camera—little things I do like touching my eyes when I talk, or, when I hold a glass in my hand, fussing with ice cubes. So I never adjusted to having a free face while withholding my mannerisms. That's why I have seemed so expressionless. At last, in *Middle of the Night,* Delbert Mann has given me a good deal of dramatic freedom. I hope, if my performance turns out well, that my parts from now on will be deeper.

Thoroughly enjoying the filming experience in New York, Kim also fell in love with the city. For a time, she considered maintaining an apartment there. She spent much of her free time as an observer at the famed Actor's Studio. After all the years under Harry Cohn's strict domination, she was also trying to find herself as a person and recognize her own identity. In a way, she was being liberated. Kim was learning how to be a human being again and wanted to climb down from the pedestal that she had been forced to ascend.

New York was opening many new doors. During Kim's off-duty hours, she wandered through the streets (sometimes under the cover of a dark wig) and observed the people, visited art and book shops in the Village, and went to off-Broadway plays and out-of-the-way bistros to listen to jazz. Kim enjoyed the whole New York experience and the freedom of expression—and she was thrilled to know that people were willing to listen to her and consider her opinion. She remained in New York, after filming on *Middle of the Night* was completed, for a while longer. She knew, eventually, she'd have to return to Hollywood but, before doing so, she flew to Cannes and attended the Film Festival where *Middle of the Night* was being screened.

\*     \*

The action of *Middle of the Night* takes place mainly in the garment firm of Lock-Lee, Incorporated. It is co-owned by Albert Dekker, a middle-aged lecher, and Fredric March, who is a lonely widower. One of the girls in the small office is Novak, who acts as receptionist, typist, and also as an occasional model for the buyers. She's lonely, confused, and frightened as a result of her recent divorce. She receives little companionship from her mother and younger sister, with whom she lives. March's life is equally lonely, since the death of his wife, and he lives with his spinster sister, Edith Meiser, a domineering matriarch.

One day, when she just cannot seem to cope, Novak develops a blinding headache and decides to leave the office early. She takes home with her a union contract to type. Later that day, March discovers that he needs the contract and goes to Novak's home to retrieve it.

When March arrives at Novak's place, he finds her depressed from the unhappiness that she has dammed up inside. She seems on the verge of a breakdown and is in need of a friend. March, exactly the kind of companion to help, shows her the warmth and understanding that are lacking in her life. For the entire afternoon, Novak pours out her heart to him in a torrent of pent-up confidences as he discreetly listens to her troubles.

Novak is seated on a sofa with her feet tucked under her skirt, and March sits in a chair opposite. She

*Middle of the Night*, with Fredric March

discusses her marriage to Lee Philips. He is a jazz musician who reduced the experience to a sheer animal level. Novak tells March of the lonely, aching void that has been hers since the divorce:

> Everybody else that we knew was getting married—so we got married. I guess we just got tired of necking in the back of the car. We used to eat in restaurants all the time. When we'd come home, we'd watch television and around eleven o'clock we'd both march into the bedroom like it was the gas chamber. I used to wonder if everyone was like this. I . . . I must have been unbearable the last years of our marriage . . . I mean I'd go into silences that . . . that lasted for days. Poor Georgie, he'd plead with me, "What did I do?"—but when he'd put his arm around me at night . . . I . . . I'd turn my back on him and I could just feel him getting furious lying there beside me. One thing that we always had . . . was our . . . our mutual attraction for each other and now we didn't even have that. We'd just lie there hating each other and waiting for sleep. Then finally . . . he got a job playing in a band out in Las Vegas . . . a piano player . . . I think I told you that. And I said to him, "Well, George, as long as you're going to Nevada anyway—we might as well get a divorce. So, I . . . I went to Hawaii . . . that was it. Now, I'm more miserable . . . living at my mother's. Y'know, it's so funny . . . couldn't stand living with him the three years I was married to him and now I . . . I just sit here aching for him . . . just aching for him. Calls me on the phone last night and he says he wants to get married again, but I just don't know if I can do it.

After sobbing and relieving herself of some of the pain, Novak feels better. Later, in a happier mood, after March has made her smile, she tells him something of her childhood and her teenage years:

> So, anyway, we used to cut school, see, and we'd hang around downtown. Well, there were four of us and we were wearing a pound of lipstick, see, and we had high heels and we were sashaying around like we were women of the world. Fifteen years old . . . I don't know what we were looking for . . . sailors, I think. Anyway, the one time that a couple of men did try to pick us up we began giggling like we were babies and we ran all the way home. [And Novak laughs about the incident.] I was a wild kid. Y'know . . . I used to go out every night and neck in Central Park with any boy who'd asked me. Everyone thought I was going to turn out to be a real bad type. Then, I'd come home . . . we used to live on 89th Street, only a couple of blocks away from here . . . Everybody was always sleeping in my house, y'know, that's the one thing I'll always remember about my house. Everybody was always sleeping. So I'd get undressed. I'd lie in bed and listen to my kid sister sleep. I'd always get the same feeling . . . I'm all alone. I used to dream about getting married and having a home. Everything would be so wonderful, y'know? What's wrong with me? I can't seem to make peace with anything.

March talks to her like a father, and Novak realizes that the qualities lacking in both her mother and former husband are those tendered her by March. Novak confesses that she doesn't want to go back to her husband and March advises her to start dating again, adding, "You're a young girl, and you're so pretty." When March leaves her, feeling better, he goes home and discusses the young twenty-four-year-old with his sister. He describes her as an unhappy girl, "intelligent but emotionally immature."

Novak and March are drawn together and they begin dating. Novak is honest and direct in her feelings. While seated across from March in a restaurant, she says:

> If you weren't such a decent man, you'd probably make out a lot better with me . . . I mean if you were just on the make. I . . . I'd probably be saying to myself, "Well, I'm pretty lonely and he's a gentleman." The way I've been feeling lately, who cares anyway? I think what really scares me to death about you is that you might really fall in love with me.

March admits he is "really in love" with her now. But she doesn't even know what "really in love" means. She doubts that she's ever been in love in her life and doesn't think she could do it.

March: Do what?
Novak: To really love somebody. I mean, I . . . I couldn't give it back to you. Do you know what I mean?

They continue to see each other and finally spend a weekend together at Lake George. He is deeply in love, but it's a difficult and involved relationship, and its progress is not smooth. Their families, friends, and backgrounds do everything to pull them apart. Neither family approves of their association. March's sister, his possessive daughter, Joan Copeland, and son-in-law, Martin Balsam, continually harp on the obvious. The girl he's planning on marrying is younger than his own daughter and her family background is a poor one.

Novak is under constant attack from her mother, Glenda Farrell, and her best friend, Lee Grant, who also focus on the obvious surface points—basing their main attack on the age difference. In a very good scene with Grant, Novak says, "he gives me kindness with both hands," after Grant has pointed out some of the problems she will have to face. But most damaging are the inner doubts and jealousies with which Novak and March torment themselves.

One night, after an argument with March, a distraught Novak returns to her mother's apartment to find that her ex-husband has returned from Las Vegas and is waiting to see her. After small talk, she tells

*Middle of the Night,* **with Fredric March**

Philips she's getting married, and he tries everything in the book to "get it on" with his ex-wife. He's testing to see how sure his ground is—but it's not firm. He desperately tries to convince her that she still has "a thing" for him. Novak projects the inner torment of the character and the needs of a woman on the verge of a breakdown. Shaken and confused, Novak submits, and she pleads, "Why don't you help me?"

The following day, against the snow-filled background of the New York skyline, Novak meets March in a deserted Central Park playground. She admits her affair with Philips the night before. Her confusion is still obvious.

> Novak: I let him make love to me. Even with his hands on me, all I could think about was you and that I'd let you down.
> March: What? [and furiously.] You want too much from me. You'd break my heart every day of my life. I don't want to see you anymore.

She confesses her love for him but he says it's a "lousy kind of love." She answers, "It's the only kind of love I know." She promises him that she'll be a good wife but March doesn't believe her. He leaves her alone in the park and slowly walks away.

Returning home, a broken and aged man, March tells his sister that it's all over between himself and Novak. And he confesses his weakness of being "drunk with vanity." His tragic mood is broken by a phone call telling him that his partner, the loveless Dekker, has tried to commit suicide and is in a New York hotel room dying. Seeing the condition of his friend, March realizes that love—no matter how shabby or wrong it may seem to others—is still a beautiful thing. And love is what makes life worth living.

March goes to Novak's apartment. She opens the door and he simply says, "I love you." They embrace and the fade-out shows him with a strong determination to live as he holds her gently in his arms.

\*          \*

*Middle of the Night* is a fine film. Fredric March is brilliant in his role, and this characterization is one of his finest. The picture also bared new and compelling resources in Kim as an actress. Her classic features and her character appeared to be more youthful-looking and of a softer and more vulnerable nature. In spite of the age difference (as in the case of Kim and James Stewart in *Vertigo,* which also worked), the two stars made their relationship seem very real and true-to-life. The only difference was that this time the age factor was an integral part of the story, and audiences could empathize with the characters in terms of it.

The loving looks between the two were timed exactly right. In one scene in the garment firm, Kim gives March a fast kiss on the cheek—as if she's put something over on him—then looks back at him in childlike fashion to detect his reaction. Such bits of interplay do much to endear her character to the audience. Another pleasant acting moment for Kim comes after their romance is in progress. She enters the office with a tray full of coffee containers to pass out among the staff. As she holds the container meant for herself, the office life she has been a part of for so long is contrasted with her present state of well-being and elation. She is seeing her position in a different light because she now has something within her that removes her from her humdrum surroundings. As she lifts the lid from the container, we see that she has a secret, and we know what it is.

One of March's lines in the film perfectly described

*Middle of the Night,* with Jan Norris and Lee Philips

Kim's character and what she projected on the screen. He said, "This girl needs an older man . . . she's that kind of kid. She's so hungry for love—like an orphan—like a baby—there's such a delight in her." And this is what audiences saw in her interpretation of the role.

Some of the credit for Kim's performance had to be the result of the rehearsals she was subjected to before production began. Although she had always studied each role diligently before any production started, rehearsing as though for a stage play was an entirely new and gratifying experience for her.

About this setup, Paddy Chayefsky said:

She was great in the role and she enjoyed those rehearsals more than anyone else. She was the first one there in the morning and the last one to leave at night and she showed a tremendously keen intelligence of both the script and character delineation.

And Kim put it this way:

I am not the surest person in the world. I am sort of insecure. It takes me time to feel at ease and be myself. I never saw the scripts of my first two movies in Hollywood. They would say, "Don't bother with that, just get out there and do as you're told." Alfred Hitchcock wouldn't even discuss the part [in *Vertigo*] with me. So if I couldn't even feel myself, how could I play somebody else?

But for *Middle of the Night,* I've had weeks of rehearsal until I understand what this girl is going through. I never had that before. Not that I'm criticising Hollywood. That isn't the point. I still want to make films there. It's just that I love working here, in this way. Everyone's so excited. We all pitch in—sometimes even on the other person's job. Sometimes you freeze a little [she was referring to the temperature], sometimes you perspire a little. Mostly, it's that I'm so grateful for the chance to act.

*Middle of the Night*

Fredric March plays the lonely widower who is a half-owner of a garment firm. Through his characterization comes that glimpse of the heart and mind which is the quiet feat of the finest acting. Kim Novak is a pretty adornment to the film as the frightened and confused secretary who falls in love with her boss. The story is primarily a closeup of their emotions, explored from many angles.

John L. Scott in the *Los Angeles Herald-Examiner:*

I thought director Mann extracted the maximum from both March and Miss Novak . . . Miss Novak's characterization of an unsettled divorcee is designed to emerge as erratic but believable, and does just that, which attests to her determination to "understand" the nervous, immature secretary and, to be sure, Mann's painstaking direction.

About Mann's "painstaking direction" and what he extracted from her, Kim said:

*Middle of the Night* was one of the most satisfactory pictures I've ever done and Delbert Mann, our director, was largely responsible for everything going so well.

Ever since I'd been in the business, I had been regarded as a baby, studying and learning. Now, for the first time,

Most critics approved of her work in the film and enjoyed her performance.

Jack Moffitt in the *Hollywood Reporter* said:

*Middle of the Night* may be a box office hit, but it's far from a certainty. The popularity of its star, Kim Novak, is a great asset. And the fact that the public accepted drab and downbeat screen artistry in *Separate Tables* also makes one hopeful . . . Miss Novak has the youth and beauty to keep the story going but her interpretation of the neurotic heroine relies heavily on actor's tricks, and, through most of it, you feel her pressing for effect.

Philip K. Scheuer in the *Los Angeles Times:*

It is a new, nervous, unsure but understandably desirable Miss Novak that Mann has created, and I found her performance fascinating. Also, I hasten to add, there is nothing "unsure" about the actress; that is the part she is playing. This Betty Preisser has had affection neither from parents nor the cocksure jazz musician (Lee Philips) she married and divorced, and she is one mixed-up kid.

The *Film Daily* noted:

Paddy Chayefsky again examines the heart and thought of little people. Splendid performances. Marvelous story-telling. A hypnotically entertaining film for the discriminating.

*Middle of the Night*

someone asked my opinion, and I was able to express myself, able to give something of myself, instead of just saying, "Yes, Sir." Right or wrong, if my ideas aren't going to be used, don't put me in the part.

You read a script, you get stimulated, and you know just how you want to "paint" this person in the script. Then you get up before the camera, and, before you have a chance to say one single word about what you think, they say, "Do it this way!"

Delbert Mann gave me the chance to speak my mind and a marvelous director he is—he likes actors and this is very important for an actor to know.

Certainly, directors like Joshua Logan, Otto Preminger, and Alfred Hitchcock had gotten top performances out of Kim by saying, "Do it this way," but Kim preferred Mann's method and the fact that he was willing to listen to her opinion.

The film was not a blockbuster hit, but *Middle of the Night* had a special appeal to art house patrons and it offered valued artistry to those who cared for a large slice of reality. Everyone connected with this property contributed to a first-rate production.

And to Kim's growing list of memorable performances—including *Picnic, The Man with the Golden Arm,* and *Vertigo*—was added *Middle of the Night.* To echo Delbert Mann's astute observation, "Seen today, her performance . . . stands the test of time. It is full of truth, heart and deep feeling."

*Middle of the Night,* with Fredric March

145

# 9

Although she had enjoyed the time she'd spent in New York and the new way of life she had experienced, eventually it was time for Kim to climb back atop her love-goddess pedestal. Her temporary liberation was about to end. Columbia arranged for her to fly to Cannes for the Film Festival showing of *Middle of the Night* and allowed Kim's parents to accompany her.

In Europe, Kim was able to show Joe and Blanche Novak the sights of Paris and Rome. The elder Novaks also had the opportunity to visit relatives in Czechoslovakia. Cannes was a whirlwind of personal appearances for Kim and she was treated royally everywhere. Once again, the photographers and gossip columnists had a field day with her latest "romance." This time, the man was suave and sophisticated Cary Grant who, at fifty-five, was at his handsomest. Kim informed the press, "I adore him."

Since she had just completed a film in which the central topic was her romance with a middle-aged man, the publicity department was delighted. Kim and Cary danced until dawn and photographers recorded the event, as well as their attendance at all of the galas. However, nothing more came of it, and soon it was time for each of them to go their separate ways, with Kim returning to Hollywood.

Back in filmland, Kim's next screen venture was *Strangers When We Meet,* and, once again, she was directed by Richard Quine. Rumors continued to persist that Kim and Quine were headed for the altar, and it was expected that they would marry as soon as his divorce became final. Photographed together during the making of this film, both on the set and at public appearances in their off-duty hours, they looked very much in love and provided additional fuel for the columnists' fires.

When questioned by writer Joe Hyams as to whether or not she and Quine were romantically involved, Kim answered, "I'm not saying we aren't having a romance . . . but marriage is another question." And she added:

I think when I'm ready for marriage, I'll elope. I've had enough of the newspapers planning my marriage. When I marry—it'll be on the spur of the moment and to someone I know very well.

I think I'll have to know the man I marry a little better than I know Richard. During all the time we've been together, there has always been an undercurrent of work. I'd like to get to know him when we aren't working on a picture together.

This was a sensible explanation of Kim's reasoning.

The plot of *Strangers When We Meet* concerned an architect building an ultramodern house. A real house was built on a lofty perch midway up a Bel Air canyon during the course of the filming. The two-story structure cost Columbia $250,000, and people wondered why the studio would invest this amount rather than rent or borrow one at a fraction of the cost. Later, it was reported that Kim and Quine had okayed the floor plans and the studio presented the house to them as a wedding present. But, when shooting was completed, the house was never occupied by Kim. Quine did move into it—but alone.

Later, when questioned, Kim said:

I'm going to England for a Command Performance, [and] since Richard is there making a picture, of course I'll see him. But I don't know if we'll get married there as everyone seems to think.

The statement was honest and direct. The marriage never took place, and, to the names of Mac Krim, Mario Bandini, Aly Khan, Frank Sinatra, and Cary Grant, was added Richard Quine. Kim remained a free spirit and she was not about to give up her independence. At least, not yet.

All did not run smoothly during the making of *Strangers When We Meet,* and the late columnist Mike Connolly suggested that a more appropriate title for the film would have been *Stranglers When We Meet.* Kim's costar, Kirk Douglas, was not amused by the whole situation. He lost patience with Kim's constant probing into her character, and, according to rumor, didn't take kindly to her suggestions when she attempted to tell him how to play certain scenes.

Regardless of what took place off camera, on camera Kim and Kirk were a winning team and the chemistry between them was stimulating and real. Watching Kim on this set, one could see that she knew more than just her lines. She knew the position of every light, and she knew her face better than anyone. To some, that might have suggested she was difficult, but, actually, Kim exhibited some of the same perfectionism that characterized the great actresses of the thirties.

Kim possessed that throbbing quality which radiated from the screen to make her a logical successor to the long line of Hollywood glamour girls, starting with Theda Bara and Nazimova and progressing to such red-hot personalities as Clara Bow, Jean Harlow, Marlene Dietrich, and Rita Hayworth. But about this condition she said:

Those girls radiated sex and magnetism in a basic, earthy way. I'm just an actress trying to become a better actress. Any comparisons to any of the other ladies is ridiculous.

Although Kim still remained by herself most of the time between set-ups, she had learned by now that the mood on a sound stage is very important and she tried to keep it light. She realized that part of an actor's job is to create this mood—that, when she was performing, the people working with her were her audience—and, since she disliked disharmony, she never deliberately set out to cause any. As always, too, her thirst for knowledge was evident. As Walter Matthau put it:

Kim was constantly discussing the intricate possibilities inherent in the interpretation of a role. She gave me many an interesting tip. I think she has helped me more as an actor than anyone else in the field.

There was no doubt that *Strangers When We Meet* should have been a box-office success and a money-maker. For those who considered film content as the prime box-office requisite, this was an intimate, emotion-charged portrayal of love and morals in modern suburbia. The locale was Bel Air, but it could have been anywhere in the United States.

This was the love story of a man and a woman, each married to another, their passions, strengths, and weaknesses, and their final decision at the moment of crisis. Evan Hunter, best remembered for the explosive force of *Blackboard Jungle,* fashioned for this production an equally stirring and provocative screenplay from his best-selling novel. Its earthy dialogue enlivened it and made it the perfect woman's picture.

Filmed in CinemaScope and Eastman Color, Novak and Douglas were ably supported by Ernie Kovacs, Barbara Rush, and Walter Matthau.

\*　　　\*

*Strangers When We Meet* begins with two different parents taking their sons to the school bus stop. One of them is Novak and the other is Kirk Douglas. He looks at her with her child as the credits flash on the screen.

Douglas is an idealistic architect and has scheduled a meeting with a commercially successful and easy-living novelist, Ernie Kovacs, about building a home overlooking Bel Air, a Los Angeles suburb. Kovacs has been attracted by magazine illustrations depicting Douglas's individualistic style, and he commissions Douglas to design his modern house. Kovacs has two best-sellers and a movie adaptation to his credit, and has, as well, an adoring coterie of amorous females. The new house will give Kovacs and his new-found importance a chance to branch out and flourish in this rather plush environment.

After his meeting with Kovacs, Douglas meets Novak again at the local super market more than ably supervised by Walter Matthau, the owner. Novak has mistakenly walked off with Douglas's shopping basket. She is new to the neighborhood, and he has been an inhabitant for some time. They engage in brief conversation on the way to the check-out stand.

At home, Novak is terrified by a phone call she receives from a man she has been involved with in the past. She is married to John Bryant, who does not respond to her warmth. She feels neglected and alone but will not admit this fact to her mother, Virginia Bruce. There is a very good scene between Novak and Bruce in which Bruce explains to her daughter the reason for her past infidelity towards her husband, Novak's father. It is obvious that Novak has never forgiven the indiscretion and took her father's side rather than her mother's.

Bruce: Don't judge me . . . I'm not to be judged by you. I'm still your mother, you know . . . and I know a little more about life and living than you might imagine.
Novak: I imagine you know a great deal about life and living, Mother.

Their bitchiness comes through, and you're aware that mother and daughter have never been able to speak to each other openly. Bruce concludes with, "I'm not a tramp . . . what happened to me could happen to any woman." After the phone call from the man in Novak's past, Bruce suspects that her daughter is facing a similar situation in her own life.

Alone with Bryant one evening, Novak appears at her most seductive. Their son is away with her mother. "Do you think of making love to me?" Novak asks. Bryant answers, "I don't know!" Novak later tells him, "I'm no different from anyone else . . . I've got the same feelings, the same flesh, the same passion . . . 'Passion' isn't a dirty word." However, Bryant doesn't seem to get the message.

Douglas, who is married to Barbara Rush, continues to find Novak attractive, and their next encounter is also at the familiar bus stop. It starts out innocently enough although Novak has second thoughts about the whole thing and what she is getting into. He offers to drive her to the location site of the home he's building for Kovacs. At first, she refuses to accompany him until he says, "Change your mind," and she does.

Novak: Is this something you do all the time?
Douglas: . . . What do you mean?
Novak: I don't know . . . ask a perfect stranger to . . . I just feel odd sitting here with someone I don't even know.

Midway during the drive, Novak does not feel right about the whole thing and asks him to turn back. Douglas says, "Look, this is silly . . . you don't really want to go back, do you?" She doesn't. They continue on to the location site where the house is to be built and Novak and Douglas have a thoroughly enjoyable time as she helps him with some measurements for the future "dream" house.

At home, Novak is still being taken for granted by her husband and leading a most barren and unhappy existence. When Douglas catches up with her in a parking lot, he tells her he'd like to see her again. And he is persistent.

Douglas: . . . I want to see you again.
Novak: Why? You don't even know me.
Douglas: I want to know you. When can you get away?
Novak: No, I can't. I couldn't.
Douglas: When?
Novak: Don't ask me . . . I don't want to.
Douglas: When? Tomorrow night?
Novak: No.

Finally, she relents, and they make a date. Before keeping the appointment, Novak makes one last attempt to get her husband's attention. But Bryant insists that she keep her date with "the girls," and she's out of the house and on her way to meet Douglas.

At an out-of-the-way restaurant near the beach, Novak and Douglas sip martinis as they look out at the giant waves. She says, "I feel very guilty, don't you?" It is evident Novak is nervous during the beginning of the affair. Her conscience is bothering her, and she has to leave their table when Douglas says, "I want to make love to you."

Douglas catches up with her outside the restaurant. She is standing with her back to him as he joins her away from the bright lights. They move over a short distance, giving Novak a chance to display her seductiveness. She wants him, yet holds back. He takes her in

*Strangers When We Meet,* with Kirk Douglas

his arms and they embrace. His hand slides sensually down her body while the camera follows every movement. Although her words say no, her body says yes. (Bad editing ruined what might otherwise have been a beautiful moment. During the early part of this scene, Novak was posed artificially and the interjection of a shot of her like this, alone, killed the scene's momentum. Had the concentration stayed on what the lovers were building, the scene would have been a powerful one.)

Their passionate and forbidden love sweeps Novak and Douglas to secret meetings on deserted roads and beaches and in roadside motels. There are moments of great beauty between them as they climb along rocks with waves splashing at their feet. She is fascinated by the cleft in his chin, and they are enjoying every moment of each other. A particularly lovely moment occurs when they lie on the sand and she gently massages his back.

It is during one of these clandestine meetings at a roadhouse when trouble begins for them. Novak goes to a phone booth to make a call and is accosted by the same man that had disturbed her earlier on the telephone during her mother's visit, a man with whom she has had a previous affair. A fight ensues when Douglas sees the man annoying Novak. She is noticeably upset after the encounter. "What did he want?" Douglas asks. "The same thing they all want," Novak answers wearily. But he continues to probe. "Is the truth so terrible?" he wants to know. Finally, she tells him the sordid story of her meeting with the man.

Novak:    Alright. It was this last summer. July . . . Ken [her husband] was away on a business trip . . . Patrick [her son] was staying with my mother. I was alone.

Douglas:    Forget it, Maggie, I have no right to know.

Novak:    But you have to know, don't you? . . . It was very hot that evening. I was sitting out in front when the truck went by. The driver waved and he smiled at me and I smiled back . . . he came back the next night. I was ironing and he rang the doorbell and asked for a glass of water. He said he was thirsty. I didn't see any harm in it so he came in and he stayed a while. I was so grateful to have someone to talk to. So we talked. He said he was driving the truck for his father; they had a rug cleaning business or something.

Douglas:    So what happened?

Novak:    He kissed me. We were standing at the door saying good night. Suddenly he grabbed me. He was trembling all over like a baby.

Douglas:    What was he making such a fuss about?

Novak:    . . . There's more, Larry. I got ready for bed after he left. I was in bed when the phone rang. It was him. He said he was coming over. I told him he was crazy . . . that I was in bed, that I'd call the police, but he said he was coming over.

Douglas:    Why didn't you call the police?

Novak:    I have a young son. I locked all the doors instead and I took some sleeping pills and I . . .

Douglas:    Sleeping pills! When you knew he was on his way—you took sleeping pills?

Novak:    I wanted to sleep . . . I wanted to hide.

Douglas:    Go ahead.

Novak:    I was almost asleep when I heard his car pull up. He rang the front doorbell . . . I didn't answer it. The pills were beginning to work. I couldn't have gotten out of bed if I wanted to. Then I heard him trying the kitchen door. Then I heard the door open.

*Strangers When We Meet*, with Kirk Douglas

*Strangers When We Meet,* with Kirk Douglas

| Douglas: | You said you locked it! |
| Novak: | I did but somehow he was in the house. He called, "Margaret" from the kitchen. I lay there half drugged—unable to move. Then I heard his footsteps in my room . . . and I couldn't move. I tried to fight him, Larry. I tried. Can you understand that? |
| Douglas: | No, I can't. Why'd you take those sleeping pills? |
| Novak: | I wanted to sleep . . . I wanted to hide. |
| Douglas: | Why'd you leave the door open? |
| Novak: | I thought it was locked. |
| Douglas: | Door's either open or it isn't. You wanted him inside that house, Maggie, you didn't want to hide or sleep. You wanted him to find you. You took those pills to make it easy for yourself. You wanted what happened. |
| Novak: | Alright, Larry. I wanted him. That's what you really want to hear, isn't it? I wanted him. |

Douglas continues the inquisition until she admits, "I enjoyed it." She asks, "Is that what you wanted to hear? . . . Alright, yes, yes, yes!" Douglas says, "You! . . ." in disgust, and is shattered and unforgiving. Novak drives off. (This was one of Kim's finest moments in the film, and she was able to project totally the vulnerability and heartbreak of this lonely woman's desperate plight.

This past indiscretion was a strange story point that Kim, as an actress, must have found difficult to accept.)

Douglas stops seeing her, but his desires soon overcome his judgment. Rush suspects that something is wrong, but assumes it is overwork. Finally, not being able to stand the separation any longer and not seeing Novak at the bus stop that morning, Douglas slowly walks to her house to see her. Novak is ill, so her mother answers the door. Douglas gives Bruce the excuse that his wife missed Novak at the bus stop that morning. Novak is in the bedroom and Bruce brings Douglas in to see her. After her mother leaves the room to get them coffee, the lovers have a moment alone.

| Novak: | Larry, you have to know. You have to understand. |
| Douglas: | I don't have to know anything! I love you. |
| Novak: | I love you. |

He promises to call soon. After Douglas leaves, Novak's mother is aware that they are more than friends and says, "So it happened to you . . ." Novak answers, "Yes, Mother, it happened."

Still aware of a problem, but not knowing what it is, Rush decides to give a party to try to relax her husband. When she calls to invite Novak to the party, Novak has a moment of shock as she speaks to her lover's wife and accepts the invitation.

At the party, Novak and her husband mingle with other guests. Douglas and Novak have not acknowledged each other in any special way until finally they get a moment alone together. Novak goes into Douglas's office and says, "This is where you work?" He answers, "Yes, this is where I miss you most." Matthau, who is also at the party, has been observing the two and enters the room after Douglas has scrawled "I love you" on a piece of paper. As Matthau interrupts their conversation, Douglas crumbles the paper and tosses it in the waste basket.

As Novak prepares to leave the party, she has to go to Douglas's bedroom (that he shares with Rush) to pick up her coat. (There is a nice moment for Novak as her image is reflected in a mirror.) She studies the room carefully before exiting. In the hall, she sees Douglas's son and stoops down to speak to him. The child says, "You're pretty." The incident is more than Novak can bear.

At the evening's end, Matthau snidely reveals to Douglas that he knows of the affair between him and

*Strangers When We Meet*, **with Kirk Douglas**

*Strangers When We Meet*, with Kirk Douglas

*Strangers When We Meet,* with Kirk Douglas

*Strangers When We Meet,* with Kirk Douglas

Novak. It is Matthau's contention that "Any place you've got a housewife—you've got a potential mistress". When Douglas tries to deny the accusation of the affair, Matthau refers to the piece of paper that he has fished out of the wastebasket. Later shots, of that same evening, of Novak restless and crying into her pillow, and of Douglas with Rush at home trying to get their problems into the open, reveal the tortures that both are experiencing.

On an afternoon outing at a children's playground, Novak and Douglas meet amid the carnival setting. They are both there with their respective children, and, after putting them on a ride, the two have a moment alone. Douglas tells her that Matthau is on to them, and Novak says, "We'll have to be more careful, won't we?" Neither of them wants to hurt anybody else but they are both suffering. Novak wants things to stay as they are. As the children's merry-go-round revolves, it is similar to their love affair: It goes round and round with no beginning and no end. When Douglas says he feels "like I'm talking to a stranger," Novak answers, "Maybe you are." They decide to stay away from each other for a while.

Douglas appeals to Kovacs for guidance, but all the worldly novelist can tell him is to keep his head. From Kovacs, Douglas realizes there is a lot to be said for marriage. "You didn't invent infidelity," Kovacs offers. Still fearing exposure by Matthau, Douglas is suddenly offered a job in Hawaii. It's his dream come true and

the chance to build a city. He is faced with a significant decision about his life.

Meanwhile, Matthau, taking advantage of Douglas's infidelity and Rush's growing frustration, attempts to seduce her, but is repulsed. Douglas finds out and beats up Matthau. Matthau flings the charge—the architect is no different from himself—in Douglas's face. Stunned, Douglas returns to his wife. Rush accuses him of infidelity, but, after the initial outburst, pleads her love and begs him to remain with his family.

Douglas phones Novak and asks her to meet him at the location site where the "dream" home has been completed. On the telephone, in closeup, Novak registers strongly in projecting her sadness, happiness, and self-doubt. They've both missed each other. After agreeing to meet him on the following day, Novak hangs up the receiver and then says, "I love you."

Novak arrives at the site before Douglas. She looks at the completed house and wanders about peeking in through the windows. Douglas drives up and joins her. They look at each other lovingly and embrace. Douglas tells her that he is taking his family to Hawaii. She accepts the finality of his decision without question. He tells her, "I do love you," and Novak answers, "I know

155

that, and I love you". The foreman comes into the house to check out some last-minute detail and assumes Novak is Douglas's wife. He says, "You've got quite a husband." A look comes over her face in which Novak beautifully projects the wish that it were true.

She walks out of Douglas's life, alone again, and gets into her car. She drives down the way leading to the road. At the roadway, a workman gives her the eye and a knowing smile. Tears fall from her eyes, and she knows her future is questionable. Novak drives on as the theme music is played, and the camera holds on her car moving away in the distance.

\*         \*

The picture was not the rocketing commercial success it was expected to be. Nevertheless, it did well at the box office in spite of the "soap suds" connected with the script. *Strangers When We Meet* attracted a great many customers because of the talents involved, and the picture pleased most audiences. Thrill seekers found it pictorially attractive but dramatically vacuous; this study of modern-style infidelity was easy on the eyes but hard on the intellect.

While it was a rather pointless, slow-moving story, it was brought to the screen with photographic and atmospheric skill and charmed the spectator into an attitude of relaxed enjoyment. During the course of the story, *Strangers When We Meet* managed to break five of the Ten Commandments—three, five, seven, nine, and ten—and to chip away at six and eight by implication. At the time of release, it was not recommended film fare for adolescents, but, today, it's as tame as Mother Goose rhymes.

Kim did what was possible with the role and came through with a convincing performance. Unlike *Middle of the Night, Strangers* did not offer her the dramatic freedom to expand her range beyond the written word. Kim was believable and she was also likeable, but it was difficult for audiences to fathom a husband as distant as the one portrayed in this script. Kim's charms were too apparent to be so totally ignored.

Her reviews were generally favorable, but there were some who found fault. *Time* Magazine observed the following:

Like the scholiasts of old, two U.S. intellectuals sternly debated the question of whether Cinemactress Kim Novak can dance on the head of a pin. Reviewing her latest movie, *Strangers When We Meet,* critic Stanley Kauffmann announced in the *New Republic* that Kim's diction struck him as an "unvaried strangulated hush." Charging to her defense, gallant young Author John Updike first of all pointed out in a letter to the editors that "she is a terrific-looking woman." Lectured Updike: "To criticize Miss Novak because her tone of voice is always the same is as absurd as criticizing a Byzantine ikon because it is static and badly drawn." Sniffed Kauffmann, in what undoubtedly is not the last word: to "intellectuals" like Updike, "a film theater is a kind of steam bath or opium den to which one goes for a faintly wicked and figuratively supine little debauch . . . Presumably Miss Novak as Medea would raise him to the heights of Kimiolatry."

"Kimiolatry" or not, there was more to be said for Kim's performance and James Powers in the *Hollywood Reporter* said:

*Strangers When We Meet* will undoubtedly be a rocketing commercial success, a big boxoffice attraction, even though it will be a disappointment considering the talents involved . . . The actors deliver with authority and force . . . Miss Novak, while always more of a personality than an actress, conveys more naturalness than she ever has before, and achieves persuasion.

*Variety* noted:

Douglas does well by his role, and Miss Novak brings to hers that cool, up-to-date, style-setting attitude that has become her trademark.

Philip K. Scheuer in the *Los Angeles Times:*

The characterizations are excellent—Misses Novak and Rush; Ernie Kovacs as a best-selling author who loathes his success; the returning Virginia Bruce as Miss Novak's mother; Kent Smith, Helen Gallagher, [Walter] Matthau, even Douglas.

The *New Yorker* reported:

Kim Novak is as beautiful as they come, and Kirk Douglas has a handsome head of teeth and hair, but because they are depicting "nice" people the affair between them is doomed from the start, and, having read the script, these two diligent actors know it and show it.

Kay Proctor in the *Los Angeles Examiner* said:

Aside from its story and flagrantly sensational passages of dialogue (such as wives frankly discussing the sexual appetites of their husbands, or lines like "Every housewife is a potential mistress") *Strangers When We Meet* has much to applaud.

It has for instance, forceful and fine performances by Kirk Douglas, Barbara Rush, and Virginia Bruce, and the beauteous, sexy Kim Novak proving she can be a persuasive actress as well as an eye-filling figure.

And, once again, *Time* Magazine got its point across:

*Strangers When We Meet* . . . discusses adultery, but instead of probing to the heart of the matter, it settles for pure tripe. Its outlook is expressed in the observation: "Anyplace you've got a housewife, you've got a potential mistress. We're slobs in our pajamas—shaving at home—but next door we're heroes."

In the pajamas is Kirk Douglas and the suburban woman more or less next door is Kim Novak. He meets her in a supermarket, and his love, at first sight, is framed against a pyramid of oranges. She is fresh and not too seedy, but at home no one is squeezing her. She even leaves her blouse open to attract her husband when he returns from work, but the husband's reaction is: "Why don't you get dressed?" Any man who says that to Kim Novak isn't even a slob.

\*      \*

Kim next did box-office duty for Columbia's colorful grab-bag of make believe, *Pepe,* when she appeared in a brief cameo role in this George Sidney production. It starred Cantinflas, the great Mexican and Latin American star, and was designed as a showcase for his many and varied talents. After his success in *Around the World in 80 Days,* it was expected that Cantinflas's name would become a household word with motion picture audiences throughout the world. To further promote him, the studio wisely added thirty-five top stars to the film to increase its box-office appeal but, unfortunately, even this did not help, and the picture fell short of expectations.

Cantinflas was a lovable and wholly appealing comedian, and his versatile genius was touted as being the greatest talent of its kind since Charlie Chaplin made his indelible mark upon the entertainment industry. And there *was* a Chaplin-like appeal in the little man with the droopy trousers, the sad and expressive eyes, and the remarkable skill at drawing a tear or a laugh, almost at will.

*Pepe* was selected to display the endless talent of the star in a dramatic story with variety turns in which he could shine in high comedy with touches of low. Dan Dailey and Shirley Jones shared the spotlight in costarring roles, and, among the guest stars, in addition to Kim, were Maurice Chevalier, Bing Crosby, Sammy Davis, Jr., Jimmy Durante, Zsa Zsa Gabor, Greer Garson, Janet Leigh, Jack Lemmon, Donna Reed, Deb-

*Pepe,* with Cantinflas

bie Reynolds, Edward G. Robinson, and Frank Sinatra. There was even the voice of Judy Garland. However, the guest stars contributed more to the promotional values of the film than to the cause of entertainment.

\*      \*

The story had Cantinflas playing a little Mexican who handled and adored a fine horse. When it is bought by a movie director, Dan Dailey, who is down on his luck, the distraught Cantinflas follows the pair to Hollywood. He meets a beatnik actress, Shirley Jones, who is also down on her luck. After a series of trials and tribulations, Jones ends up in Dailey's arms (and as the star of the movie he is directing), and Cantinflas winds up with the horse.

During the course of the story, Cantinflas has mistaken Jones's friendship for love and goes to Mexico City to make arrangements for the wedding and to pick out a ring. Kim's part in the proceedings is playing a customer in a jewelry store. She steps in to lend a helping hand when Cantinflas is having difficulty with a clerk, and she ends up helping him pick out an engagement ring. She says, "Now, if I was your girl—

*Pepe,* with Cantinflas

I'd pick this one." And Cantinflas agrees with her selection. He describes his girl as the most beautiful girl in the world. After taking a closer look, he tells Novak, "You are very pretty, too."

When he is 2,000 pesos short in his piggy bank, Kim gets the clerk's eye and makes good the balance—as the clerk says he must have misread the price tag. Cantinflas is elated and says, "Thank you very much . . . muchas gracias . . . you are very kind . . . you are so sweet . . . I never forget you help Pepe very much."

Novak:      You're welcome, Pepe, and you tell your Suzie for me—I think she's getting a wonderful guy.
Cantinflas: Thank you very much. I tell her and . . . Who are you?
Novak:      My name's Kim Novak.
Cantinflas: I try to remember, Miss Kim Novak. Goodbye, Miss Kim Novak.

Kim finds him instantly loveable, and the catch of it all is that her name and fame mean nothing to him. He's just a friendly little fellow who reacts to her in a trusting way. Their accidental meeting and parting was incidental to the general plot, and, in her one scene, Kim wore a chiffon dress similar to the one she had worn in the final scene of *Bell, Book and Candle*.

Reviews for the film were luke-warm. *Newsweek* magazine described the film as "Cold Chili," said that it was an "overlong potpourri," and summed it up as having "Too many stars".

*Variety* said:

Hardly any theatre, except the Radio City Music Hall, would have enough marquee space to post the pic's array of "guest" personalities . . . In summation, *Pepe* is generous entertainment, but excessive length works against fullest enjoyment of its many very excellent parts. Yet it's the stuff of which dreams are made, and the screen can use more pix that afford such relaxation.

There were rumors that a sequel, *Pepe in Paris*, would be forthcoming, but it never materialized. What could be said of *Pepe* was that it was wholly free from violence, horror, and rampant sex, which made it a much-wanted picture as well as a much-needed one by audiences. And at three hours and fifteen minutes, it gave the viewers their money's worth as well as a sore backside.

*Pepe* didn't require Kim to do anything other than be decorative, and this she could manage with her eyes closed. During the course of filming, she and Cantinflas became friends, and he jokingly offered to teach

**With Cantinflas in Mexico City**

her bullfighting if she was ever in Mexico City. Months later, when the studio pursuaded her to go to Mexico to help exploit the film, she took a surprised Cantinflas up on his offer. The event was photographed for posterity, and Kim managed to survive the Moment of Truth.

\*          \*

Still in a traveling mood, Kim moved on to Rio de Janeiro to participate in the excitement and spectacle of carnival time. The city was alive with music and singing in the streets. Kim lost her sex-symbol image and, in a jovial and exuberant mood, became one of the merry-making participants. Although her face and figure were known worldwide, with the disguise of a dark wig, an old shirt, and jeans, she managed to go unnoticed among the natives and had the time of her life singing and dancing in the streets. As she put it:

I was nobody, a girl without a name, without a background. This is what I call living! I long to participate in

The Moment of Truth

everything, not to detach myself and observe but to jump in and be part of it.

Next, Kim traveled to England for a Royal Command Performance of *The Last Angry Man*, which starred Paul Muni. The studio had selected Kim to represent them in spite of the fact that she had no other connection with the film. She caught up with Dick Quine and they attended the Command Performance and were seen together constantly. Quine was in London filming a portion of *The World of Suzie Wong* before moving on to Hong Kong for location scenes.

After her farewell to Quine, Kim returned to New York City and was immediately rushed to Doctors Hospital. After a series of tests and examinations, it was discovered that she had a liver infection—a mild case of hepatitis caused partially by overwork and overexertion. Although she had not felt well for about a month, she had no idea she was suffering from fatigue. The wire services photographed the event, and pictures of Kim playing solitaire in her hospital bed and holding a white rose were distributed to newspapers throughout the world.

Kim's first bout with ill health became big news for the wire services, and it also taught her to take things easy for a while and follow the doctor's orders. Returning to California she could not be pressured into working for the remainder of the year. She regained her health and devoted most of her leisure time to painting. In a way, it was another taste of freedom permitting her to enjoy this period and the time it gave her to think for herself. It also afforded her the opportunity to be selective in choosing her next screen property.

# 10

Success, fame, and a worldwide reputation as one of the loveliest women in the world were hers, but, inwardly, Kim continued her quest for a more peaceful existence. Her recent bout with illness had given her a much needed breathing spell and considerable time to think about the future. There had been numerous occasions when Kim wished to escape the rigors of picture-making altogether, and she considered the possibility more than once. However, inwardly, she loved the motion picture industry and was never serious about trading in the celluloid mystique she was so proficient in creating—mainly because she really didn't want to give it up completely. So what she finally settled for was the best of both worlds.

Away from the spotlight, Kim enjoyed a more secluded life in the company of Pyewacket and Warlock, her beloved Great Dane. These were the first two of the many animals she would grow to love in the ensuing years. Pye and Warlock accompanied her whenever and wherever possible. They were frequently seen boarding trains with their mistress during Kim's many cross-country trips. She still favored railroads (partly because of her father's long-standing employment), and trains were her favorite mode of transportation. Warlock remained at her side while

Pye was mainly confined to a traveling cage.

For whatever length of time she would enjoy "away from it all" during her "back to nature" periods, the day always came when the cameras turned once more, and she became Kim Novak, forcing Marilyn Novak, the very private person, to take a back seat temporarily.

A turning point in Kim's life happened during the filming of her next screen assignment. *The Notorious Landlady* changed the course of her life style completely. This comedy-suspense melodrama called for many coastline scenes, making it necessary for the company to locate in and around beautiful Monterey. Before filming was completed, Kim fell madly in love with the rural area and, even more, with a house of stone she found perched on a rocky pinnacle high above the sea. As she described it:

> It's the peaceful haven I've always wanted and the most romantic place in the world. You can almost hear music as you approach. I'll live here, look at the ocean, and paint.

This was the home she would buy and name "Gull House." Although the asking price was far beyond her reach, Kim acted as her own real estate agent, finalizing the deal on her own terms. Immediately, she made plans to convert a turret with a breath-taking view of

Traveling with Warlock and Pyewacket

the ocean into a studio for her painting.

During the filming of *The Notorious Landlady,* Kim maneuvered some of the most unique casting ever done for a film when she secured a part for her mother who was visiting her at the time. Not to be outdone, costar Jack Lemmon agented for his father, John V. Lemmon, who made his film debut. It was becoming a family affair by the time director Richard Quine found an unbilled spot for his son, Tim. The lone holdout, in this family casting, was Fred Astaire (playing the third starring part, a straight dramatic role with no dancing involved) whose daughter, Ava, came up to visit him. When asked if she wanted to play a bit part, the young Miss Astaire started packing.

For the story—which was set in England—Producer Fred Kohlmar and director Quine wisely avoided the

unpredictable weather of London. Instead, they brought London to Burbank, California, where the Columbia Ranch was located. At a cost of a quarter-million dollars, they constructed a replica—complete with fog machines and rain gadgets—of famed Grosvenor Square. This way, they could turn the weather on and off at their convenience. The supporting cast, which consisted of Lionel Jeffries, Estelle Winwood, Maxwell Reed, and Philippa Bevans, only saw California's famous sunshine during their lunch hours. Working in all that artificial fog and rain made them feel as if they had never left home.

Kim performed double duty on this film, as an actress and—for the first time—as designer of her own wardrobe. Her fifteen separate costume changes (executed by Elizabeth Courtney) were such a challenge that Kim closeted herself in her $7,000 lavender-and-white cottage-dressing room on Saturdays when the studio was closed, and there, undisturbed, sketched from nine to five. About the experience, she said:

> The studio promised to give me screen credit as fashion designer, so if I didn't come off looking like an American-born London landlady, no one would be blamed but myself. But at least I didn't have to worry about my wardrobe in one scene. That was the one where I took my bath.

Although the studio publicized the fact that she would be seen in her first movie bath, Kim had previously done the soap 'n' suds bit in *Jeanne Eagels* and *Pal Joey*—showered in the first and tubbed in the second.

The exciting, climactic chase scene was the high spot of the picture. The action called for Jack Lemmon to rescue Estelle Winwood who, in a wheelchair, was flying down a hill and approaching a dangerously steep cliff while Kim and the others were racing behind on foot to catch up. The scenes took four weeks to plan and construct and two weeks to film, for only three minutes of action on the screen. A track had to be laid on the rocky terrain and was controlled by 1,800 feet of carefully-laid cable under the earth and 1,000 feet of plywood board under the chair.

About working with Kim, Estelle Winwood remembered:

> I saw very little of Kim Novak, and only between takes, as our scenes were never together—but I had great admiration for her. Not only was she a superb actress and a beauty but she was so well bred and gracious in her manners. I found this very refreshing and so unusual in this profession.

On location for *The Notorious Landlady,* with mother, Jack
Lemmon, and his father

Sister Arlene and her husband Bill Malmborg, with their children, were set visitors

Kim's image as a seductive temptress with every hair in place was completely shattered in this film venture. The comic knockdown slugging match, a climactic high point in *The Notorious Landlady,* definitely showed a different Novak image. Kim, accused of murder, pursued the real villainess, played by oversized Philippa Bevans, in a wild chase near perilous cliffs. About her first big movie fight, a new experience she thoroughly savored, Kim said:

This sequence even has crazy background music like an old *Our Gang* comedy. I love physical scenes like this, into which I can throw myself without any self-consciousness. It's great not to care how your hair and face are looking every minute. This wasn't just an ordinary hair-pulling and scratching match, either. We fought like men, with our fists. A woman fight is much dirtier, without any rules. When I did this fight scene, I actually thought of myself as a charging bull I'd seen in Mexico, where I once fought two young bulls just for the fun of it.

During the filming, Kim lunged at her murderous target, missed and fell. The villainess grabbed Kim and hurled her to the ground. Kim said, "I got up instantly and started fighting again." With the melee completed, Kim emerged as the bedraggled and exhausted victor—as the script required. Her preparation—zealous training with a stunt man and faithful practicing on a punching bag in the gym—had paid off handsomely.

The big fight scene was filmed on location in the Big Sur country on an old estate where the exteriors of *Rebecca* were filmed in 1939. It was also near the stone castle "Gull House" that Kim purchased.

*The Notorious Landlady* was Kim's final picture for Columbia, and she was paid $600,000 for her services. Her contractual obligations ended with the completion of this film. Although negotiations for additional films were in the talking stage, they never materialized.

\*      \*

Music to the tune of "A Foggy Day" sets the mood and begins *The Notorious Landlady.* Estelle Winwood, in a wheelchair, is being pushed down the street by her nurse. Suddenly, a shot is heard from Thirty-Three Gray Square. A man's body is being dragged into a garage. A motor swiftly roars to life, the door of the garage crashes open, and tires screech on the cobblestones. The credits flash on the screen while the music continues.

The garage belongs to Novak and her husband, and this is the beginning of her troubles. With her husband missing, she is charged with murdering him, but, because no body can be found, there is no proof that a murder has been committed. Novak is released but her passport is held by the authorities so she cannot escape and flee to America.

Pressed for ready cash and with her picture in all of the newspapers, Novak finds she can't get a job. As a means of bringing in some money, she decides to rent her second floor as an apartment. Prospective tenants flee in horror when they realize who the landlady is. Then Jack Lemmon arrives. He works for the American Embassy, is just back from Arabia, and has never heard of the case.

Novak answers the door with her hair concealed by a dust cap and her figure covered by a maid's apron. Lemmon thinks she is the maid when he inquires about the apartment, and Novak answers him in a rich Cockney accent. Realizing that the neighbors are gossiping about her enough already, she tries to avoid what taking in a single man will bring about. "You are

*The Notorious Landlady,* **bedraggled and exhausted after fight scene**

*The Notorious Landlady*

a couple, aren't you?" she asks. "I mean, you 'ave a Missus?" Lemmon says that the ad reads, "Couple preferred," which indicates an open mind.

With this, Novak says, "Come on now, be a sport and beat it". Her accent is beginning to slip and Lemmon picks up on it immediately with "Where are you from?" "Chicago," she admits. Finally after much pleading, Novak succumbs to his inspired pitch and he is so impressed with her that he is willing "to sign a hundred-year lease". "I have a dubious reputation," she warns and slyly adds, after agreeing to rent the flat, "It's your funeral." Novak's words almost turn out to be a prophecy of things to come.

Even when Lemmon's embassy chief, Fred Astaire, recognizes Novak as the woman involved in the recent sensational newspaper headlines, Lemmon remains smitten and refuses to do the sensible thing by getting another apartment. Novak, still suspected of her husband's murder, is kept under strict surveillance by Scotland Yard.

In no time at all, Novak and Lemmon are in love. On their first date together, they do a mambo and thoroughly enjoy the evening. Lemmon is a little uncertain

when a dark figure emerges from the shadows and asks to speak to Novak as they leave the night spot. Saying good night to Novak, Lemmon says, "Certainly is convenient living in the same house," and promptly makes a date for the following evening. Novak says, "Why don't you wait and see what happens tomorrow?"

In the middle of the night, Lemmon hears the sound of organ music and goes downstairs to investigate. He finds Novak playing it.

Lemmon: Do you do this very often . . . at night?
Novak:  No, not often.
Lemmon: I wouldn't mind . . . I love organ music.
Novak:  To me, there's something about the tone that's . . . almost like the sound of eternity.
Lemmon: Yeah. Do you know "My Funny Valentine"?
Novak:  Better go upstairs now, Bill, I was just saying good-bye to an old friend.

What Lemmon does not know is that Novak plans to sell the organ to the man who stopped her outside the restaurant.

Lemmon is so sure of Novak's innocence that he continues living in her flat to prove to Scotland Yard that he can dig up enough evidence to absolve her from the case. He continues to insist she is not capable of the murder. After another case has been explained to Lemmon about a beautiful murderess who also seemed incapable of the crime, Lemmon is informed that Novak has purchased a large amount of arsenic. Suspicion begins to mount in his mind when, arriving home before Novak, he investigates her quarters and finds a gun in the nightstand drawer in her bedroom. When she arrives home, he is further unnerved by a part of her telephone conversation which he overhears: "I'd say about one hundred and sixty pounds . . . the problem is getting it out of the house . . . you'd better send two men".

Arsenic. A gun. And now something that weighs one hundred and sixty pounds that has to be removed. He visualizes himself as the next victim just as Novak announces "I'm going to provide dinner for you tonight," and adds that she has a surprise for him. He's sure he is doomed. But, soon, he is relieved to find that his drink hasn't been spiked with arsenic and that Novak plans to fix plain steaks on an outdoor barbecue rather than some dish with exotic sauces.

Lighting the barbecue turns out to be a riotous affair. An awning catches fire as the two are drenched with hoses, and Novak gets a pail of water doused on her from a "friendly neighbor" who aims it right at her head. Eventually, the fire department arrives and the situation is put under control. Their quiet evening alone has been ruined, but they spend time in front of the fireplace which provides a romantic setting.

After the fire incident, which has made the front pages of the newspapers because of Novak's previous notoriety, she pays Astaire a visit to intercede for Lemmon when he has been called on the carpet for his behavior. After she states her case in Lemmon's behalf, she says she has been "hounded by the police, slandered by the press, and humiliated by my neighbors" Astaire is impressed with her honesty and her beauty, and he really believes that she is innocent of the entire charge.

Astaire: And you know your photographs don't really do you justice.
Novak: Well, the lighting is not terribly good in police stations.

Over lunch, which Astaire insists she have with him, Novak saves Lemmon's job.

Later, Astaire describes Novak's "hazel eyes like an innocent little child" and he's convinced "that she couldn't possibly have done it!" He's even fired up enough courage to tackle the files of the entire case in an effort to establish her innocence.

When Novak comes home, she promptly packs up Lemmon's belongings and has them waiting at the door when he arrives. She's also refunding his rental money. (The suspicious "one hundred-and-sixty-pound" thing was the organ; she sold it in order to get the amount necessary.) But Lemmon doesn't want to move.

Novak: Why do you want to stay here? Don't you know . . . I murdered my husband?
Lemmon: I don't care whether you killed him or not.
Novak: Well, I . . . you don't?
Lemmon: No, I don't. I knew about that the day after I moved in here.

He continues with, "If you killed three husbands—I'd still love you." Novak confesses, "I didn't do it!" Lemmon believes her and is more in love with her than ever.

One night, Lemmon hears sounds of a scuffle from Novak's room, then a shot. Rushing down, he finds her holding a revolver in her hand, and bending over the lifeless body of her husband, Maxwell Reed.

At the trial, Novak's testimony reveals that her supposedly dead husband materialized in her room, drunk and violent, said he had stolen some valuable, illegal cargo from his employer, killed a man sent to retrieve it, and now needed money to get out of the country. When she refused to aid him, Reed pulled a gun, and, in the ensuing struggle, he was accidentally killed—this time without any shadow of a doubt. It seems obvious that Novak's story of the accidental shooting is a fabrication, in view of Lemmon's testimony on the stand and the virtual admission that they are in love. But, at the trial, Novak becomes furious with Lemmon when it is revealed that he has been working with Scotland Yard to solve the case.

It is almost certain that Novak will be convicted of the crime when suddenly a kindly looking woman among the spectators in the courtroom, Philippa Bevans, gets to her feet and testifies that she saw it all and verifies that it was an accident. Bevans said she heard the argument before the shooting, rushed to her window, and witnessed everything. She is the private nurse caring for the crippled and elderly Winwood next door. Novak is acquitted when the nurse swears it happened exactly as Novak said.

Later, Lemmon forces Novak to speak to him after

*The Notorious Landlady,* with Jack Lemmon

*The Notorious Landlady*, with Jack Lemmon

she has given him half an hour to get his things out of her house. Novak confesses that she left out some vital testimony at the trial: the fact that the illegal cargo her husband was talking about was a half million dollars in stolen jewels that he had left in a candelabra in the house before he disappeared. Novak, in need of money, had pawned the candelabra, and, when she refused to give her husband the ticket, he pulled the gun. She didn't mention this at the inquest because she was afraid the police would think she was involved with the jewels. Bevans, not such a sweet little lady after all, had forced Novak to give her the pawn ticket after threatening blackmail.

Suddenly, Novak realizes that Bevans had been away from the house on the day of the killing—she had seen her leave—but Winwood had been home. Someone had to tell Bevans what happened, and that someone couldn't have been anyone other than Winwood, her employer, who is spending the rest of her days at a senior citizens' resort spa near the ocean.

Lemmon and Novak rush to the pawnshop to check on the jewels and find the pawnbroker lying murdered on the floor, with the candelabra, broken open and lying beside the body. Obviously, he had known what was inside, refused to redeem the ticket, and had been killed by Bevans, who, at that precise moment, is eavesdropping in an adjoining room. Bevans overhears Lemmon and Novak making plans to go to see Winwood at the spa and realizes what will happen when the whole story is unfolded.

The cunning nurse, Lemmon with Novak, Astaire, and a Scotland Yard inspector arrive at the resort almost simultaneously. The spa, which caters to elderly guests, is providing a musical concert for the residents. Because of the sun, all of the chairs have built-in umbrellas covering the faces, and Novak and Lemmon race from wheelchair to wheelchair, peering under the umbrellas and scaring most of the elderly guests. (It is during this sequence that Novak looks under one umbrella to find her real mother, Blanche Novak, just about to sip a drink before she is scared out of her wits. Lemmon looks in on his real-life father in the same manner.) They continue their search for Winwood, but Bevans gets to her first and attempts to run her wheelchair off a steep cliff. Lemmon and Novak arrive just as Bevans is wheeling the cowering old lady to the edge of the precipice. The nurse lets go and the chair races downhill toward destruction with Lemmon in pursuit. He catches it seconds before it is to go over the cliff.

Novak disposes of Bevans (after topping it all off with a well-aimed right to the jaw) but not before taking some mean whacks herself from the powerful woman. Finally Novak, with her head bowed low in the fashion of a charging bull, butts Bevans in the stomach. At that instant the investigators arrive. Winwood assures them that she had seen everything on the night of the shooting, and that she had told Bevans of the experience. The ruthless woman, in turn, utilized the information to get the jewels for herself.

With Novak's innocence established, Astaire offers Lemmon an assignment in the States, and Lemmon announces he will marry Novak and take her back with him. Astaire shakes Lemmon's hand, the one holding the wheelchair, and Winwood starts rolling down the cliff again. They all start running after her.

*       *

*The Notorious Landlady* did satisfactory box-office business, but most of the praise went to Lemmon for his excellent comedy timing. Kim handled her role in fine fashion, like the professional she is, and showed herself to definite advantage in a number of scenes. Her bath scene (a moment within the context of the story) was one of the highlights of the film and it gave audiences their money's worth in case they didn't enjoy the rest of the picture. Reviews for the film were lukewarm and some critics were brutal.

*Time* Magazine capsuled the film in this way:

"Oyme jus' the parlor mide," says Kim Novak in her best Berlitz cockney. "Are you a sleep-in maid?" asks arch Jack Lemmon, with his eyes doing a twist. "Coo, yew Yanks do kum raht aout wiv it, don't yew?" wuffles the new Eliza Doolittle. "Well, most of it, anyway," says Lemmon, a film comedian who knows how to throw away a line before it deserts him.

Kim pretends to be a cockney slavey only to get this beguiling if hokey mystery-comedy off to a start . . . the plot gets almost as impenetrable as a London fog . . . but whenever the script gets draggy, Director Richard Quine perks things up with a sight gag—like Kim Novak tubbing with the nude serenity of the White Rock girl while the intruding Lemmon clicks his eyes open and shut at the speed of a navy signal light. In a berserk finale, Novak trades punches with a lady nurse the size of a Japanese *Sumo* wrestler, and Lemmon goes on a piston-legged, cliffside pursuit of an old lady's runaway wheelchair, with the old lady in it, while a brass band spiritedly renders *I Am the Very Model of a Modern Major-General.*

Kim Novak has never been more opulently Kim Novak. Since she will never be an actress, the best time to enjoy her is now.

*The Notorious Landlady*

*Boxoffice* Magazine stated:

Once again the beautiful Kim Novak receives top billing but it is her costars, the talented comedian Jack Lemmon and the engaging Fred Astaire, who carry this Fred Kohlmar comedy with mystery undertones to hilarious heights . . . Miss Novak, as a woman suspected of murdering her husband, remains enigmatic during most of the film, wears striking clothes to interest the woman fans and includes a bath interlude to intrigue the men.

*Variety* noted:

*Landlady* is fortunate to have in its employ Jack Lemmon, thanks to whose comic perception the picture has some scattered moments of notable comedy. These and the potent marquee trio of Lemmon-Kim Novak-Fred Astaire insure the Columbia release of a healthy boxoffice response . . . Miss Novak's latitude of expression remains narrow, but she utilizes her emotional resources to what appears maximum advantage on this outing. Coupled with her sexy attitude and natural physical endowments, it gets her by in the role.

And the *Hollywood Reporter* said:

Mystery, romance, comedy, these are the elements of *The Notorious Landlady*, Richard Kohlmar's production for Columbia. The mystery and romance are expertly handled, and the comedy is often very good, although it sometimes gets muted in the shift of moods. Whatever its faults, however, *The Notorious Landlady* is a light-hearted spoof, if not always light-handed, and will be a good commercial prospect.

Miss Novak, who seems to be developing as an actress these days, gives a light-textured performance that is engaging and convincing.

\*     \*

Immediately after completing *The Notorious Landlady*, Kim was about to take one of the biggest steps of her life. During seven years in pictures she had come a long way. Now, pursuing increased independence, she negotiated with Filmways, in association with her own recently formed company, Kimco Pictures Corporation, to jointly produce three films. She had finally decided, as Harry Cohn once predicted, to make "Kim Novak pictures." The first—and only—film to materialize from this deal was *Boys' Night Out*.

Regarding the bow of Kimco, Kim said:

You'll be hearing from Kimco again as my company will be co-producing two other films with Martin Ransohoff, the producer of *Boys' Night Out*. I wouldn't be a bit surprised if they both didn't turn out to be comedies [and although several things were on the planning board,

nothing materialized beyond this production], because I firmly believe that audiences want to be entertained, to be taken completely away from the problems of the world as well as their own. Of course, I wouldn't think of turning down drama if the script is worthwhile, but frankly I'd rather laugh than cry.

Many performers consider comedy to be the most precarious form of expression, but Kim describes her feelings about it in another way:

With comedy, I feel on top of the world. So well that life becomes a breeze. I look forward to going to the studio each morning because I know the spirit will be wholeheartedly light on the set. When I'm busy on a picture, it takes me over completely. Everything else becomes secondary in importance. How my work progresses colors my attitude, even when I'm away from the sound stage. But comedy, like *Boys' Night Out*, doesn't worry me as much as drama because of the happy mood I'm in while performing.

*Boys' Night Out* was scripted by Ira Wallach from an adaptation by Marion Hargrove, and was a spoof on suburban malaise and its effects on the American male. It revolved around a bachelor and his three "restless" married pals who are seeking some diversion on the one night out when they attempt to escape from their homes and spouses. The idea of sharing an elegant New York apartment with a built-in blonde seems to be the perfect answer to a glorious evening for them all.

This cynical and lighthearted farce had all the necessary ingredients to please audiences, including a duo consisting of James Garner and Tony Randall in costarring roles, with able support by Howard Duff, Janet Blair, Patti Page, Jessie Royce Landis, Oscar Homolka, Howard Morris, and Anne Jeffreys, plus guest appearances by Zsa Zsa Gabor, William Bendix, and Jim Backus. Michael Gordon, fresh from his *Pillow Talk* success, was the director and the film was produced by Martin Ransohoff. Cinemascope and Metrocolor added to it visually, and, as in the case of *Landlady*, Kim again had a hand in designing her wardrobe which she did with Bill Thomas. She chose a number of casual things including bulky sweaters and pants which she enjoyed wearing off screen.

Kim proved to be as luscious as ever and her talents as a comedienne were touted as equal to her physical adornments. She was the perfect "femme fatale" to James Garner and the other male members of the cast.

Jim Backus had an interesting observation regarding Kim and put it in this way:

*Boys' Night Out*, with Oscar Homolka

Kim and I (unfortunately for me) didn't have any scenes together, but the thing I remember most were those magic eyes. To this day, I have no idea what color they are. I remember that Kim was a very private person. Never could figure out whether it was shyness or vulnerability. The one thing I remember most clearly is that she always reminded me of "That girl from High School you wish you had married."

And Patti Page said:

As you know, it's rare for performers to really get to know each other on a movie set. In *Boys' Night Out* I had only two or three scenes where Miss Novak and I appeared together and there were always three or more actors or actresses in the same scene.

I only have my impression of her professionalism. She knew instinctively where the cameras, lights, etc. were, and she was always prepared for what was expected of her. She was also a perfectionist, which everyone appreciated.

I really didn't get to see or observe Kim or any of the other stars on the picture as much as I would have liked, but working with her, even briefly, was a very enjoyable experience for me.

\* \* .

*Boys' Night Out* begins with bachelor, James Garner, and his three married pals, Tony Randall, Howard Duff, and Howard Morris, realizing that their nightly get-together once a week has turned into a complete bust and that they are in a rut. They hit upon what they believe will be the happy solution to this problem when they see a successful operator, Garner's boss, with an elegant beauty that he keeps on the side without his wife's knowlege. As they ride the commuter train home, they decide they will share the expense of a seductive hideaway and a blonde to go with it.

Garner discovers a sumptuous apartment in New York's posh east side and begins looking for a blonde. Out of the blue, comes Novak. She is really interested in renting the apartment, but Garner mistakes her for the femme fatale applicant he has advertised for in the paper. When he tells her that she would be the perfect answer to a four-way dream, she can't believe her ears.

| Novak: | Boys? Are there more than just one? |
| Garner: | In a manner of speaking, yes. |
| Novak: | Two? |
| Garner: | Almost. |
| Novak: | What's almost two? |
| Garner: | Three. There's Doug and George and Howie. |
| Novak: | And you. That makes four. |
| Garner: | Me? Oh no, I'm not part of this deal. |
| Novak: | What are you—the house mother? |

She finds out Garner isn't married but the others are, and her reaction is: "Four aces chasing one queen. This I really gotta see."

To Garner's bewilderment, Novak accepts the position and says, "It isn't every day a girl gets a chance to meet men who know how to share—I mean really share." After the other men arrive at the apartment, to the strains of some Greek music playing on the phonograph, Novak says, "Hello, boys," and, to Garner, "When would you like me to start?"

Novak actually has an ulterior motive for this move, as she later explains to a professor, Oscar Homolka. It will provide the perfect opportunity for her to gather information for a thesis on sex habits of suburban males. She tells him, "It's exactly what I need—four men—I can use all four. It's a gold mine, Doctor, and it fell right into my lap." Homolka thinks the "whole idea is insane." Novak contends that "when it comes to sex, men don't even tell themselves the truth," and she intends to get the facts.

Homolka warns Novak, a student and sociologist, of the dangers involved, and forbids the whole experiment. Novak is just as forceful in her beliefs and argues the point.

| Novak: | Why, they're wide-eyed kids who dream of being locked in a candy store and eating their way out. |
| Homolka: | Scientifically speaking, a love nest is not a candy bar. |
| Novak: | . . . It's a modern pipe dream . . . and the whole thing is a fantasy . . . they don't really want this adventure—they've been told they're supposed to want it. |

The boys tell their wives, Janet Blair, Anne Jeffreys, and Patti Page, that they are breaking up the night out and each is now taking a course (on a different night) at a school in the city. Garner is annoyed about the arrangements. He likes Novak and begs her to change her mind.

| Garner: | Do you know where all this is going to lead? You're going to end up in some dingy third-rate hotel room trying to squeeze some comfort out of a bottle. Please, Cathy, there's still time. Pack your things and get out of this place. |
| Novak: | Why? I'm comfortable. The apartment is lovely and the boys are all aces. |
| Garner: | Facts are facts, Cathy—without a home and family, what . . . |
| Novak: | Fred, did anyone ever tell you? You talk too much. |

175

They kiss, and she says, "Anything else you want to keep me from?" Then she reminds him it's Sunday, and everyone should have a day off. She also pins his day down to Thursday after he admits he does not have a day. Novak is willing to continue all for the sake of science.

Through Novak's skillful curbing, the boys all behave like innocent lambs. She gets them to open up and conducts her research with the aid of a trusty tape recorder. Randall talks endlessly about himself. Duff describes his do-it-yourself antics and Morris, who has been forced to share his wife's starvation diet, stuffs himself with delicious food.

Not wanting the others to get the wrong idea, each man lies to the others about his "torrid night" with Novak, and Garner finds himself wild with jealousy. He's becoming more and more interested in Novak. Overcome with remorse at their "cheating," each husband has sent his wife a loving gift as the girls become suspicious. The wives are convinced the boys must have guilty consciences, and they hire a detective, Fred Clark, to follow them.

In the meantime, Novak, in line with her scientific research, has paid a visit to see all of the wives, trying to learn something about their home life. On the pretext that she is doing a door-to-door survey, similar to the Kinsey Report, Novak gains entry, and all three wives open up, telling her everything she wants to know.

Garner eventually falls in love with Novak. They attend a Little League ball game for which Garner is the coach. Blair, Page, and Jeffreys see Novak in the company of Garner and know she's the same person who was at their homes for her report. When the husbands learn of Novak's visits, they figure she is going to blackmail them.

At the game, which has been rained out, Novak and Garner head for shelter.

Novak:    Don't you think we ought to get in out of the rain?
Garner:   Why? This is the most romantic spot in town.
Novak:    How about the dugout?
Garner:   No, it leaks like a sieve.
Novak:    And the car?
Garner:   What are we—a couple of teenagers?
Novak:    (laughing) Did you know it was going to rain today?
Garner:   Uh—sort of—of course when I knew you were coming, I didn't think it would dare.
Novak:    The game doesn't count, does it?
Garner:   No, the rain washed everything out.

*Boys' Night Out*

Novak:    Next time, they can start all over?
Garner:   With no score.
Novak:    Pretty good break for you.
Garner:   Good break for both of us. That's what we're going to do.
Novak:    What do you mean?
Garner:   Start all over—with no score.

Garner is still under the impression that she "dates" men for a living, but he is definitely in love with her, and she feels the same way about him. He asks her to marry him, and Novak says, "Everything you think you know about me—you still want to marry me?" Garner only says, "I told you it's all rained out." They agree to marry, but he will not permit Novak to explain her evenings with the boys and the fact that nothing happened on any of these dates.

When the detective—who has been following the boys—makes his report to the wives and tells them about the apartment with the blonde temptress, Blair, Page, and Jeffreys (with the help of Garner's mother, Jessie Royce Landis) proceed to have a few drinks too

*Boys' Night Out,* **with James Garner**

*Boys' Night Out,* with Howard Morris, Tony Randall, and
Howard Duff

many. They finally decide to confront Novak and offer one of the men for her very own if she will give back the rest.

When the boys learn that Garner plans to marry Novak, they still think she intends blackmail, and Randall, Duff, and Morris march in on her to force her to reveal her purpose. Novak admits the truth about the thesis, but when Garner, who has also dropped in, thinks he has been used as a guinea pig in the experiment, he feels "it's about as low as you can get." His pals are relieved and rib one another about their exploits and the fact that none of them "scored" with Novak.

Garner stomps out in a rage but is promptly dragged back by the invading group of "crocked" women, led by his mother. Novak refuses to accept Duff as a consolation prize and the ladies are again furious. Havoc breaks loose and the day of retribution has indeed arrived. All the wives are on a rampage as they head for Novak.

Novak pursues the departing Garner, pushing Homolka (who has just entered) out of her way. "Does she want to end up like all these screaming married people?" Homolka demands to know. "Exactly," is Novak's reply as she hurries to corner Garner in the elevator. By the time they reach the lobby, they have kissed and reconciled. At the end, all four couples have settled for the "routine" life.

*     *

*Boys' Night Out* didn't demand anything from Kim that she wasn't adept at delivering, but the breezy romantic comedy fell short of expectations. In this outing, Kim acted with warmth, intelligence, and an easy naturalness that was beguiling, and she proved to be a creditable comedienne. *Boys' Night Out* was released just before *The Notorious Landlady* (which was filmed first) and did so-so business.

Kim attended the glittering preview of her first and only Kimco production at Loew's Capitol theatre in New York and participated in a series of press interviews and television appearances in order to hype business. She appeared on such high-rated network television shows as CBS's "I've Got a Secret" and "To Tell the Truth," NBC's "Today," and WBC's "PM." Her schedule included interviews with the New York newspapers and syndicated columnists; color-cover sittings and interviews for the *Sunday News* and *This*

*Week* Magazine; and interviews with *Holiday, Glamour, Show, Newsweek,* and other magazines.

Critics generally accepted her performance in *Boys' Night Out* as pleasing, but there were those who blasted her work. Archer Winsten, in the *New York Post,* wrote: "Kim Novak ambles along, content to affect mankind without straining but simply being." And Bosley Crowther, in the *New York Times,* said:

> But then it must be said that Kim Novak is not a glowing inspiration as the girl. Her inclination to ardor appears no more powerful than her passion for a doctor's degree. She wears leotards and bulky sweaters with a certain awareness of dash, but she does not seem to have the same awareness in performing the gyrations of a comedienne.

These estimations of her ability were par for the course with these two hardened deans of the drama pages, and, even if she literally set fire to her hair in an effort to impress, it wouldn't have helped her with them. She would continue to be underrated in their eyes. Fortunately, all critics didn't agree.

Dorothy Masters, in the *New York Daily News,* noted:

> *Boys' Night Out* careens merrily on the premise that a man's vanity is more potent than his libido. As for the female; all she does is look like "yes" and avoid having to say "no."
>
> Simple? With Kim Novak it works out fine, though not without a big assist from a zany script loaded with improbables. Her escape from dishonor is a farce of intriguing contrivance embellished with professionally polished patter. The bons mots are dillies.

*Motion Picture Daily* said:

> With top flight names bracketing both glamour and comedy, a fast-moving story, and well-paced and liberally spiced gags, this roistering and slightly bawdy comedy of manners makes top summer program material. Heading the glamour cast are Kim Novak, never looking better, James Garner and Tony Randall ... All of the cast, down to the bit parts by Ruth McDevitt and Larry Keating, are excellent, but Miss Novak and Garner earn extra credit for carrying the burden of the comedy.

*Variety* opined:

> Kim Novak slinks and purrs through the role of the object of all this extra-marital monkeyshine, an upstanding young post-grad sociology student who is secretly compiling data for a thesis on "Adolescent Sexual Fantasies in the Adult Suburban Male." James Garner seems comfortable in the part of the number one son-of-a-gun who wins her heart.

*Boys' Night Out,*with James Garner

And James Powers, in the *Hollywood Reporter,* said:

Miss Novak, who has not always been a notably supple actress, displays an appealing light touch under Gordon's direction. Although the part itself is not the best one she's ever had, it is possibly her best performance, altogether charming and delightful.

After getting out and "selling" the film, Kim returned to her secluded fortress in Big Sur and enjoyed the freedom she now possessed after her years of being trapped in contractual obligations. She was free to be herself and roam barefooted, to paint, to sculpt, to write, and to join the other inhabitants of the artists colony away from the bright lights of Hollywood and the prying lens of the cameras. The unconfident child was growing into a secure, reliant adult who knew what she wanted from life and how to go about getting it.

# *11*

Her peaceful existence was interrupted when Kim was assigned the lead in the third version of the W. Somerset Maugham classic *Of Human Bondage.* The role of Mildred, the coarse, but appealing woman with weak morals, with whom a young medical student is hopelessly and passionately in love in this powerful story was the bait that lured Kim back in front of the cameras.

In describing the character, a beautiful but heartless guttersnipe from the slums of London, Maugham said:

> She had a horrible fascination for every man who ever met her. We were all her victims and yet, in spite of her faults, we could not help but admire her for her honesty.

Bette Davis had indelibly stamped her mark on the unforgettable character in the original, which was filmed at RKO in 1934. A second version, circa 1946, was produced by Warner Brothers and starred Eleanor Parker. Whenever a remake is attempted, unfortunately, it is inevitably compared to the original rather than being judged on its own merit.

Although Kim was severely blasted by most of the critics upon the film's release, her performance, seen today, is creditable in many ways. In the first version, Bette Davis was extravagantly praised for her acting, but that performance was not without fault. A mean, cheap, and completely selfish woman can be played on many levels. While Davis pulled out all the stops with her characterization, Novak was more subtle and wisely underplayed the part.

As Kim put it:

> I don't know whether audiences will hate or feel sorry for this girl. Somerset Maugham created Mildred from an actual person whom he knew in his youth. He has said, in spite of her faults, she never pretended to be anything other than what she was. That's the way I tried to portray her.

There were problems connected with this production from start to finish. One can only admire Kim's guts and determination in going on with and completing the film. It was one of the most difficult periods she was ever forced to endure. With all of the obstacles she faced, one has to agree that she turned her performance into a personal tour de force.

Unlike any role she had played before, the part of Mildred demanded every last ounce of her strength and histrionic ability. Kim perfected an accent that made even the genuine Cockneys on the set believe they were back within the sound of Bow Bells. It took painstaking study on her part, but Kim was anxious to transfer every detail of Mildred's character to the screen.

After mastering what she felt was a true Cockney accent, she found director Henry Hathaway wouldn't buy it. But then Hathaway had never wanted her in the first place, and it is doubtful that he would have been pleased with anything she did. He had originally wanted to team Marilyn Monroe and Montgomery Clift for the leads. When this wasn't possible, he decided a younger actress should play the role.

Hathaway openly stated:

I wanted a younger actress like Tuesday Weld because Mildred is such a stupid fool. Only a young girl could be that stupid and she should be a teenager.

Hathaway said of Novak, "Do I have to have her in my picture? I begged them to let me have who I wanted. How the hell they expect me to transform her into a teenaged Cockney waitress beats me." And there was one point where MGM had all but decided to replace Kim with Elizabeth Taylor to appease the complaining Hathaway, but Taylor's price was $1,500,-000. They decided to leave Kim in the role. This decision did not please Hathaway, but there was little he could do about it. Novak would remain in the film with or without his approval. This must have caused further ill feeling and added to his resentment of Kim.

Between Hathaway's hostility and having to contend with the intricacies of a difficult accent, Kim was perfectly miserable. Hathaway wasn't popular with the other actors or the crew, either. The director ran a stern ship and had long been considered hard on his performers. He had said, "Everyone has got to fight for his own breaks. Young people today don't like to fight anymore, they're too polite. They want offers on a platter. You don't get anywhere by being polite." Hathaway's rigid thinking was, "Actors who couldn't stand up to tough direction shouldn't be in the profession at all."

Finally, the bomb exploded. After completing the shooting of one of the early sequences with Kim, Hathaway said, "Cut. Stop the camera. I quit!" Walking over to Kim, who was still in a state of utter amazement, Hathaway put an arm around her shoulder and said, "I won't go on with this goddam picture, not for another minute. I want no part of it. Sorry, honey, but there it is."

It must be a devastating experience for any actor to know that the director doesn't want him in the production. The director is the father figure, the master, the guide you rely on to lead you through the dark distance. When you don't have his respect, what is left?

During the interim period, Bryan Forbes (who scripted) took over the directorial duties until Ken Hughes was signed for the job. Hughes steered the film through to its completion, but, by the time the final shot was lensed, *Bondage* was five weeks over the production schedule at an additional cost of a million dollars.

The next unpleasantry Kim had to endure was the rudeness of her leading man, Laurence Harvey. As she said, "For some reason, known only to him, he refused to talk to me except in the line of duty." This didn't make their scenes together (during three quarters of the film) any easier. The cause of the antagonism, Harvey explained later, was that he, as a legitimate actor, was humiliated at being cast opposite a woman who knew absolutely nothing about acting and used only "her body and immobile expression to force a dramatic point." An angry Kim's answer to this was, "If I'm cast in roles I can't handle, then it's the studio's fault, not mine."

The fact that she was top-billed over Harvey didn't help matters either, and Harvey was more interested in the movie he had just produced and directed in Spain, *The Ceremony,* than he was in *Bondage.* Whenever he wasn't needed on the set, he was off in a cutting room working on his own film. The late actor's favorite subject was himself, and there was a long list of leading ladies who said they would never work with him again. His feuds with female costars were becoming legendary, and he was acting like a spoiled little boy. Elaine Stritch, who starred in the stage play *Time of the Barracudas,* didn't speak to him offstage during the entire run of the play after he told her what he thought of her acting ability.

Harvey's consistent rudeness to Kim made her ill at ease during the entire filming of the production. Within the context of the plot, Harvey is made jealous by a love letter from a rival shown to him by Novak, and he strikes her across the face with all the vengeance that has been stored inside of him. The blow was hard enough to make Kim stumble, and, considering Harvey's feelings for his costar, he must have relished the moment. It was realism at its best.

Kim's first three encounters with Harvey in the film occur at the tea shoppe where she works as a waitress. For one entire week, she trotted back and forth in the tea room set, juggling pots of tea and plates of toast and cakes. About the experience Kim said:

By the time we had finished these scenes I felt as though I never wanted to see, much less eat in, a tea room again. Believe me, I'll never hurry another waitress as long as I live.

This was Kim's first location filming outside of the United States. *Of Human Bondage* was filmed on locations in Dublin and at the Ardmore Studios in Ireland. To add further tension, there were also British union problems festering at the time. Shooting had been delayed by a strike threat which jeopardized both the location sites and Ardmore Studios. Ardmore Studios had been built four years earlier with the optimistic intention of making Ireland an important film-production center. The *Bondage* group had moved in only after weeks of tiresome negotiations between the producers, Seven Arts, and the representatives of certain British and Irish unions. One of the main reasons for shooting in Ireland was that there are more genuine late-Victorian backgrounds than in London, because of the wartime bombing and the architectural inspirations of the post-war property developers.

About the experience of working abroad on her first film, Kim said:

I'd never worked abroad before although I'd been to Europe on trips. But that's something else again. Filming is much the same the world over, but there are certain nuances of differences between procedures in Hollywood and shooting overseas. You always learn something new.

Going to Ireland was an experiment. I tried to cut the umbilical cord with this picture made away from Hollywood. After the way things have gone, I won't be too anxious to repeat the experience. It may be necessary to make pictures in other countries, but I'll be careful, very careful, in the future.

The important thing to me is to believe in what I'm doing. It's the same as being a salesman. You find it so much harder to sell if you don't believe in your product. I want to be sure of the people I'm working with. That's not always easy in a new setup. Many good ideas are ruined because of personality clashes.

There's always someone to say that an actor is the last person to know what's good for him. Often that's true, but you must have a deep trust in the person who's saying it. Trust is essential for an actor. I value honesty in human relationships. I'm not a quitter. I don't walk out on a deal, no matter how much I might be tempted to do so.

To survive, you have to cultivate patience, toughness, resilience, yet somehow remain a human being. People should spend more time planning pictures before dragging actors halfway across the world to act for them. Then the people responsible for the artistic side should listen to what others have to say and consider other points of view instead of bulldozing their way through regardless.

During the filming, Kim lived in a suite at the stately old Connagh Hill Hotel which overlooks the green fields of the Emerald Isle to Killarney Bay. She said, "I'll never forget the beauty of this lovely country." Kim found Ireland an ideal milieu for her first away-from-home film venture. On her rare afternoons away from the set, she built up an Irish wardrobe of tweeds and sweaters that gladdened the hearts of the Irish Export Board.

In the midst of all her troubles on *Bondage*, Kim met a columnist for the *London Express*, Roderick Mann. His proved to be a sympathetic shoulder to cry on, and he soon helped Kim over her depression about the film. But Mann, like others before, later tried to press the issue of marriage, and this sent Kim on her own independent way.

*Bondage* was Kim's first costume film (although one could argue that *The Eddy Duchin Story* and *Jeanne Eagels* were, too, since they took place in different eras). *Bondage,* however, offered more. It was turn-of-the-century, and Kim was adorned with the trailing skirts, peek-a-boo high waists, Merry Widow hats, veils, and parasols of the period.

In the early part of the film, she wears cheap gaudy clothes. But after she gets her hands on the young medical student who gives her money, she is able to provide herself with more opulent attire. Designed and created by Beatrice Dawson, her wardrobe included elaborately fringed kimonos, beflowered petticoats, and dresses covered with lace and jet.

Along with everything else that had gone wrong during this production, the final blow came when the nude shots from *Of Human Bondage* were banned in the United States as "offensive to public morality." The photo that started all the commotion was actually

*Of Human Bondage*

one of great beauty. It showed Kim sprawled across a brass bed with a feather boa strategically placed over her bosom and derrierre. The look on her face was that of a wistful child. The scene called for a nude Novak to be lying on her stomach with her back exposed while the rest of her body is covered by a sheet. Midway through the scene, she arises (carefully holding the sheet in front of her) and reaches for a feather-boaed kimono that she clutches to her bosom for the remaining moments of the scene. Shocking? Hardly.

When Kim was asked if she minded doing the scene, she replied: "Not as long as it gives something to the picture and helps the story." The director convinced her that it would, and, in the line of duty, she did it. At the time of release, *Of Human Bondage* was denied Production Code approval because of its "controversial nude scene," and censors screamed obscenity.

Advertisements played up the scene. A seductive Novak draped in feathers bore the caption: "*Some Women* can't help being what they are . . . there would always be men in her life . . . all kinds of men . . . and always Philip to come back to . . . to degrade and despise."

About the episode, Kim said:

If I had known [the photos] would be banned when we were making that picture, I would have quit then and there. I think this film could have marked the end of my Hollywood career. I just couldn't bear any more of that nonsense. The scene in question and the stills involved were prudish in comparison to many of the films being made today.

\*          \*

*Of Human Bondage* is the gripping and controversial story of a beautiful but calculating girl who plays cat-and-mouse with a man's love and comes close to ruining his career. The heartbreaking relationship between the sensitive young medical student, Laurence Harvey, and the cheap, avaricious, Cockney waitress, Novak, holds the spectator in a relentless grip. The man is plagued by a club foot, but his only real weakness is being totally blinded by love for a woman who is fundamentally a whore and incapable of any lasting relationship. This is the bondage, the prison cell, of human incompatibility. Such bondage is doomed to disaster.

W. Somerset Maugham's story of unrequited love, set in Edwardian London, was given a visually flawless production. The colorful costumes of the period, the settings of a picturesque, gas-lighted era—including a giant fireworks display at the Crystal Palace and backdrops ranging from interiors of St. Luke's teaching hospital, street scenes, and drawing rooms to the squalor of the Paddington slums—added variety and interest.

Harvey first notices Novak in the tea room where she works. He sees her several times while he is in the company of his fellow students who stop in regularly—mainly to see Novak. In spite of her wisecracks and the coarseness that is part of the character, there is a softness under it that is touching and appealing. In the tea shoppe, during an encounter alone with her, he tries to get better acquainted.

Harvey:   Don't go for a minute—stay and talk.
Novak:   What about?
Harvey:   Anything! Just talk! . . . where's your boyfriend today?
Novak:   Which one?
Harvey:   The gentleman with the carnation.
Novak:   Oh, you mean Mr. Miller. He's away this week on business.
Harvey:   How does he manage to live without you?
Novak:   I have no idea, it's his worry.

(She orders and brings his tea.)

Harvey:   Is he in love with you?
Novak:   Who?
Harvey:   Mr. Miller.
Novak:   I don't know—you'd better ask him, but I don't know what it's got to do with you if he is.
Harvey:   Well, what I really wanted to ask you, since I mean, if you're not married or engaged or anything like that—you're not, are you?
Novak:   Go on.
Harvey:   Well, I wondered if you'd come and have dinner with me one night—maybe see a show—would you?
Novak:   Yes, alright. I don't mind.
Harvey:   You would, when?

And they make arrangements to meet on Thursday at Victoria Station. Harvey searches for her in the second-class waiting room but, in her desperate need to be a "lady," Novak is seated in the first-class section. In a hat with a veil, Novak studies her reflection in a mirror as she powders her nose, revealing a beauty never more stunning than at this moment.

*Of Human Bondage*

and begins to talk to Harvey only to be shushed by the lady seated behind her. Reverting to the guttersnipe that she is, Novak shushes the woman right back. She passes the time during the balance of the performance with the opera glasses focused on a male friend seated in a box seat.

Later that same evening, Novak gives further insight into her character in their ensuing conversation.

| Harvey: | You're looking especially beautiful tonite. |
|---|---|
| Novak: | That's because I'm being nice to you . . . I remember a poem I learned in school once. There was a little girl who had a little curl right in the middle of her forehead—and when she was nice, she was very, very nice. and when she . . . |
| Harvey & Novak: | Was bad she was horrid. |
| Novak: | You remember that too? Am I that little girl? |
| Harvey: | Sometimes. I've got a surprise for you. |
| Novak: | What? I love surprises. |
| Harvey: | No, no—later. |
| Novak: | Oh well, why don't you take me someplace where we can be alone? |
| Harvey: | Where? |
| Novak: | Well, you could always take me back to your place. |
| Harvey: | To my place? |
| Novak: | Don't you want me to? |
| Harvey: | Yes, of course. You are in a strange mood tonite, aren't you? |
| Novak: | And when I am nice—I am very, very nice. |

During their conversation, Novak's eyes light up when Harvey mentions a "legacy" on which he lives. One scene on this first date, in the restaurant where they are about to dine, shows that Novak is briefly annoyed while waiting for her glass to be filled. She childishly extends it toward the waiter—not realizing that Harvey must first taste the wine before she is served. As the evening comes to an end, Novak allows Harvey to kiss her and he wants to know if he matters to her at all. She is evasive and says, "Questions. I hate questions. You're always cross-examining me. I like you . . . of course, I like you." But she will not commit herself beyond this statement. She tosses the whole incident off with a curious laugh. She has used him and likes the feeling of power that she holds over him. About a future date for the next night, she playfully toys with him and says, "If you don't take me out, some other fellow will," and abruptly departs for her place as Harvey watches her go.

They attend the opera, and, as she amuses herself by fiddling with her opera glasses, Novak is completely disinterested in the whole thing. She eats a chocolate

Novak is impressed with the surroundings at his place, and now he is waiting on her as he inquires whether she would like tea or coffee. He surprises her with a ring and asks her to marry him. As she tries on the ring, she ponders, "Do you think we'd be happy?" Then she says, "Come here . . . say nice things to me. I like it when you say nice things to me. Makes it easier." Harvey admits that he is desperately in love with her and that she has changed his entire life.

Later, dressing after a bed scene with Harvey, she announces that she is going to be married but that he is not the lucky man.

| Harvey: | You're not exactly dressed for congratulations. (she continues to talk about the wedding.) Will you tell me why you gave me the privilege of kissing the bride? |
|---|---|
| Novak: | Well, I had to make it up to you somehow, didn't I? I wouldn't have let ya if it wasn't goodbye. I mean her precious is all a girl has . . . after all, you are one step ahead of [her intended] Emile. |
| Harvey: | Thank you for telling me in such a pleasant way. |

188

*Of Human Bondage,* with Laurence Harvey

*Of Human Bondage,* with Laurence Harvey

wanting to hang on to her pride but, nevertheless, still testing Harvey and her power over him, she is once again victorious. All Harvey's thoughts of McKenna are forgotten, and he takes Novak back with the promise that he will take care of her until she has the baby.

Novak:    I'll never forget you wanted to marry me. I'll do anything you say. Anything you like, now. I mean, if you still want me.
Harvey:  Would you? Why?
Novak:    Well, I owe it to you. Do you still care for me?
Harvey:  Yes, I care for you very much.
Novak:    Well then, after all, you can't blunder . . . now there's no risk, is there?

Harvey goes to see her in the hospital after she has had the baby. Once home, she gives up the baby (a girl) to a woman who will care for it and is impressed that the woman is "quite a lady." When Harvey disapproves of what she has done, Novak says she has to work and promises to go to see the baby regularly.

Novak:    I'm sorry, Philip. And you're so good to me. I'm awful to you. Am I that awful?
Harvey:  No. You're just bearable.
Novak:    It isn't as if I didn't know it, is it? I just can't help myself sometimes. What are we going to do this afternoon? Can we go out and celebrate?

After getting Harvey's promise to take her out because she loves "posh" places, she asks if his friend, Jack Hedley, can join them because "he makes me laugh." And laugh she does, in the company of the two men, although she has spent most of the evening dancing and laughing with Hedley.

A few days later, she is modeling a dress for Harvey that she has just purchased. When he accuses her of flirting with Hedley and tells her Hedley doesn't think too highly of her—that she's just "another cheap conquest" to him—she produces a letter she received from Hedley that morning. Even now, Novak cannot remain faithful to her benefactor, and she excuses her actions in this way: "I like you very much as a friend but you can't live on friendship now, can you?"

Enraged by the fact that she is having an affair with his best friend, he breaks with her, seemingly once and for all. Pointing out what he has done for her, he declares he is just sick and tired of being made the fool.

Harvey:  You can make up your stupid little mind—one way or the other. Either settle on my terms or else get the hell out of my life.

Although she suggests a meeting at the tea shoppe the next day, he declines. Novak gives him back the ring saying, "Wouldn't be in good taste, would it?" And then, with a bit of conscience, she adds, "You're not angry are you? Wouldn't have made you happy in the long run." And she is off again and running.

Because he has fallen in love with Novak, Harvey has neglected his studies and closed his eyes to her shallowness. As a result, he's been subjected to repeated rebuffs and humiliations. Now that she has told him that she is going to marry another man, he resumes his work and passes his medical examinations, encouraged by the gentle understanding of Siobhan McKenna, a widow who has given him the companionship he's needed during this difficult period.

The claims which Novak has fastened on him, however, are not easily broken, and manifest themselves on the day when Harvey returns to his lodgings to find her huddled on the staircase. She confesses that she is pregnant and has been deserted by the man who had promised to marry her. The tears are perfectly timed as she tells him that the man already had a wife. Novak touchingly says, "I wish I was dead." Still

*Of Human Bondage,* with Laurence Harvey

*Of Human Bondage*

Novak: [Lashing out with venom] I never liked you! From the beginnin' but you forced yourself on me. Why you don't know—you revolted me. I wouldn't let you near me, not if I was starvin'! [After Harvey has slapped Novak hard across the face] If you only knew how much I hated you!

Harvey: From now on, I don't care what you do, who you go with or who you sleep with, understand? Go to Griff and let him keep you in the manner to which you've become accustomed.

It is Hedley, later, who informs Harvey that Novak is now "on the streets." Harvey goes in search of her and looks into the faces of the prostitutes in the low-class area. Finally, he sees her and calls her name. (It is a compliment to Novak as an actress that she acted with her whole body in this scene. When discovered by Harvey—as the camera—on the street, she showed her condition even before she turned around. Had we not been prepared for a sick woman, we would still have seen one—seen the change in her and the fall from what she was—in the curve of her shoulders, the way she handles her body, and the way her dress has slipped to one side. It's also apparent in her rhythm, the way

she is functioning *totally* within the scene, which is subdued and devoid of hope.)

Novak: Always turnin' up like a bad penny, aren't ya?
Harvey: Where do you live?
Novak: Wanna go home with me, darling? C'mon then.

They make their way to her place where she continues to abuse him in her own familiar way.

Novak: What are you waiting for? Put your money down and let's get on with it.
Harvey: Stop it! Now, pack your bags, I'm taking you out of here.
Novak: Look, why don't you leave me alone. I don't want anyone feeling sorry for me.

Knowing that she'll never really understand him, Harvey does get her to go home with him once more. The baby (Because she couldn't afford its keep) has been in her room; he promises that it will be boarded out once again.

Some time later, sure of her ground, she toys with one of the feathers from her boa-trimmed kimono in front of a mirror as Harvey comes in.

Novak: I thought perhaps you might like to see me as I used to be . . . I love you. I want to make it up for all the rotten times I've given you.
Harvey: I'm sorry but it's too late.
Novak: Why?
Harvey: Perhaps, it's because I once loved you too much.
Novak: Please, please let me . . . let me make it . . . please.
Harvey: You disgust me!
Novak: I disgust you!
Harvey: Yes.
Novak: Well, that's a laugh! I disgust you! You're the one to talk, I suppose. I suppose you think you're God's gift to women or something. Well, you're nothin'—that's all you're fit for. All you can do is to think about it. Like some dirty little school boy. That's all up here with you. Y'know what I think about you?
Harvey: No, I don't want to know what you think about it. It doesn't matter. It's all too late now.
Novak: It's all too late, is it? You ought to take a look at yourself. I used to laugh at you. I still laugh at you. But you were too easy—you bored me. . . . I could just twist you any way I wanted to. I used to feel sick when you kissed me. Do you know that, I felt sick? I felt sick! Afterwards, after I let you, do you know what I did? I used to wipe my mouth. But I got my own back. We laughed at you, Miller and me. And Griffith laughed at you. We used to talk about you when I was in bed with them and they were making love to me. Y'know what we used to call you? What I used to say? I used to say, wouldn't the cripple

*Of Human Bondage*

*Of Human Bondage*, **with Laurence Harvey**

like to be here kissing me now? That's all you are! Just a cripple! A bloody cripple!

Harvey: Don't tell me, Mildred. It's no news to me. Tell yourself, if you want to, but don't tell me.

Novak: Don't you go! Don't you go, I haven't finished yet. Don't you dare go! I haven't finished. I haven't finished with you! I haven't finished . .

Their paths cross again some time later when Harvey is working in a clinic. He is washing his hands, his back to the next patient who has been seated by the nurse. When he turns, he sees the patient is Novak. She is hostile. "I don't want any favors. Just give me some medicine and I'll get out of here." Harvey warns her of the possible seriousness of her illness and insists some tests be made. He offers to make arrangements for the baby's care during her hospital stay, but Novak tells him the baby is dead.

When the results of the blood test are available, Harvey goes once more in search of Novak. She comes into her room with a customer, after plying her trade on the streets, and sees Harvey. He informs her of the risk she's taking and asks, "I don't want to frighten you but have you ever seen anybody die of syphilis?" He wants to help Novak but she isn't about to let him as she snarls, "Who wants help from you, you dirty

cripple?" He leaves a sobbing Novak alone.

A short time later, he is informed Novak was admitted to the hospital the previous night and is dying. Harvey goes to see her, and she uses him to get her way one last time. "I'm awful sick," she says. "Promise me something. You were always good. Promise me. I want a proper funeral . . . like a lady."

In the final scenes, the drama reaches a heartbreaking intensity, engendering pity and sympathy for the misguided girl despite the weakness of her character. Harvey tries to comfort Novak in her final moments and tells her he still loves her. After her last breath, the camera lingers on the dead Novak in one of the most poignant death scenes ever captured on film.

With the passing of Novak, Harvey tries to face up to life and build a new one in the patient arms of Nanette Newman, a girl he met previously, who has been waiting in the hope that he would eventually come to her. Harvey realizes that Novak went through him like the worst kind of disease—the kind that doesn't show. But in spite of everything, he fulfills his promise to her by giving her the proper funeral that was her last request. She is buried like a lady, the lady she always aspired to be.

*Of Human Bondage,* with Laurence Harvey

*Of Human Bondage,* with Laurence Harvey

understated, well-timed, and moving.

The role provided Novak the opportunity to vacillate between brassy vulgarity and stark sensuality. She emerged as a pathetic and bereft creature.

This is melodrama played to a fine pitch and there were a number of moving and compassionate moments. The story is, essentially, somewhat dated soap-opera, and the film makers seemed to be aware of that fact. However, Kim breathed life into its scenes. On the whole, she is convincing and most critics approved of her work in part, if not totally.

The *Los Angeles Herald Examiner* said:

In many scenes, Harvey appears to be going through the motions rather than giving a definitive performance. Miss Novak, though, has far more opportunities to display a broader range of acting talent, and she succeeds in giving the more compelling performance, especially in two or three scenes where she is played against Harvey's staid manner.

*Motion Picture Herald* reported:

As portrayed this time by Kim Novak, at her best, the unreasoning trollop of Maugham's tragic imagining leaves nothing undone or unsaid to justify the honorable, upright Philip Carey, created four-square by Maugham and played with a wealth of reserve and restraint by Laurence Harvey, in his devotion to her life and welfare until death. Whether her performance, or his, or both together, will bring tears to the eyes of today's women in sufficient number to spin the turnstyles satisfactorily is one of the moot-est questions facing exhibitors as Autumn moves in and election campaigning steps up competition for public attention. Who can tell what a handkerchief picture will do before he plays it?

*Variety* mentioned:

The role that "made" Bette Davis doesn't serve the same purpose for Miss Novak. Yet she gamely tackles a wide range of emotions and seems to be far more aware of the demands of her role than is her costar. Her gradual degradation from goodtime floozie to the dregs of the gutter is an exacting task and she manages to hold onlookers' interest in her fate.

James Powers in the *Hollywood Reporter* said:

Miss Novak actually does quite well with some scenes, although she will never erase the memory of the coarse brutality of Bette Davis' portrayal in the first film version.

And probably one of the finest appraisals of her work in this film came from *Newsweek* magazine, which capsuled Kim's performance with praise in this way:

*Of Human Bondage* was not a huge success, but it had moments that were somewhere between just right and unforgettable. Kim gave her all and did a creditable job by giving the character of Mildred a definable presence and a complexity that emerged as much from attitude as from the dialogue.

On the plus side, Kim had more presence and composure than in many of her other films. Her use of low register in voice was effective, and she was wise not to imitate any more of the Cockney accent than the rhythm and the lilt. She has character, cruelty, and a lack of regard for anyone else's feelings. She was totally self-centered and heartless, but also aware of her short-comings. And the awareness allowed her to play scenes on two levels. She was especially good in her multiple moments, playing two or more things at once, a bitch with a conscience. But more than this, Kim made Mildred a human being, not a stereotype.

A good example of her two-level playing occurs when Kim leaves Harvey to get married. Her feeling of awkwardness with him, as a result of her conscience, comes through as she tries to wriggle out of the situation. Her death scene is also delicately handled,

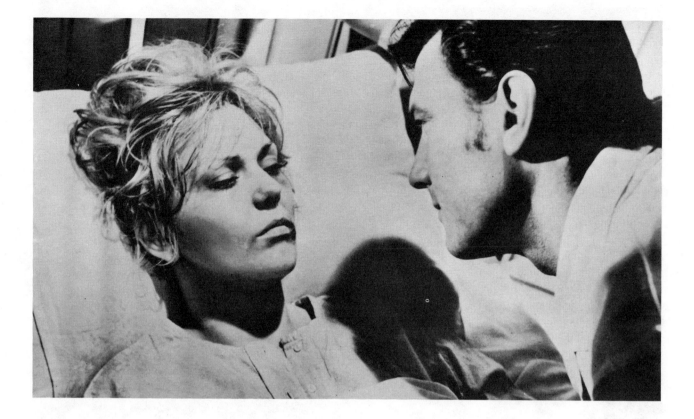

Anyone who cannot approve of Kim Novak's performance as Mildred in the new *Of Human Bondage* is petty and peevish. She is masterfully, even frighteningly, credible. Indeed, if there is any fault to find with the way she plays the round-heeled love of the lame but game medical student, that fault is her excess of verisimilitude. She clasps the squalor of Maugham's famed novel so tightly to her bosom that the film sometimes seems like "Person to Person." Admittedly her accent drifts around some, floating at random from Cockney to Liverpudlian to a Dublinish brogue; and at moments of stress, it is less Eastcheap than Southside (Chicago)—as when she glares at Philip (Laurence Harvey) and announces: "I doan wan' ennybuddy feelin' sorry fuh me." But at such a moment, she is more Mildred than anything Somerset Maugham ever dared imagine.

This summed it up perfectly.

# 12

—————— *12* ——————

Kim, during her climb to the top, had always cooperated completely with the studio publicity department and had gone all out in an effort to try to please everyone. As her stature grew and she became a world renowned celebrity, she realized that she had forfeited her most valuable possession—her privacy. Now that her contractual obligations were completed and, since she was no longer tied to a studio, Kim decided to change all of the things that had pressured and annoyed her in the past.

As a result, she became something of a riddle to the world of motion pictures. In keeping with her new way of life she rarely appeared in public and she seldom gave interviews. On the screen, she began to project a Garboesque remoteness and a mysterious quality that added to her charisma and became her trademark.

Just before *Of Human Bondage* went into general release, David L. Wolper (who had a successful documentary television series titled *Hollywood and the Stars*) made Kim the subject of one of his in-depth studies of motion picture personalities. Aptly titled "In Search of Kim Novak," it aired on 9 March 1964 on the ABC television network.

Joseph Cotten, who performed the task of narrator for the series, spoke of Kim in this way:

There are many Kim Novaks. One is the screen goddess described by press agents with breathless words like, lush, languorous, dreamy and bewitching. A second Kim Novak, pictured by the press as an international siren escorted by celebrated figures like Glenn Ford and Cary Grant, is followed by the gaze of an intrigued world. And there is still another Kim Novak, the girl who has carefully shielded her personal life from public glare, and this is only the beginning of the picture. Tonight, we go in search of Kim Novak, on *Hollywood and the Stars.*

They proceeded to show Kim the private person, some 300 miles from the film captial, on the wildly beautiful coastline near Monterey, California, where she lived in perpetual seclusion from the rest of the world. There, in her miniature stone castle above the sea, where she dwelt with Pyewacket and Warlock, was seen by millions of viewers. Kim's private life was a dramatic contrast to her public image, and, as she put it:

The very first time that I came here I knew that this is where I wanted to live. It's like another planet from that world called Hollywood, and, when I'm here, I'm almost another person. I've always felt a sense of the unreal about Kim Novak, the publicized glamour girl, the sex symbol—that she's part fiction created by Hollywood and the press.

I come here to be free of that. To be alone to do the things

With Warlock

Gull House

that I like best, especially to paint. Ever since I can remember I've loved to express myself in color and images.

Kim proceeded to show viewers samplings of her work as an artist.

I did this head of Christ as if he were sorrowing for an indifferent world. My friend, Walter Keane, the San Francisco artist, as I see him—the tragic clown. My father—as part of a petrified forest, unable to express his emotions and imprisoned within himself like the trees that have turned to stone.

Even though my mother is still alive, I've painted her here as a symbol of a mother's influence long remembered— even after death. I'm happiest painting because it's the one way I know in which I can say all the things that I feel—freely and completely—and in my own way. That's why I can spend weeks here at a time painting, sculpting—not seeing anyone—not even answering the phone. Usually it's someone who wants to speak to Hollywood's Kim Novak—but she doesn't live here. I do!

I've never really experienced a drive for fame and all that goes with it. Quite the opposite, I adore my solitude. I can be alone without being lonely.

Although she enjoyed her solitude, she was not the recluse that she appeared to be in print. And there were those times when she felt the need to be with people. During these moments, an occasional jazz concert or party in a towering redwood forest brought Kim together with her friends. They were members of the famous artists colony at Big Sur: musicians, painters, writers, and Bohemians. Kim described them in this way:

My friends here are not afraid to be themselves. They conform to nothing except their own beliefs. Most of them haven't seen a movie in years and they don't depend on newspapers or magazines. The fact that I'm a movie star has no real meaning to them. People accept you here for what you are—not who you are.

When I'm not with friends or painting, I might spend the day on guitar lessons or making up songs, or just watching the waves. I love nature. I love the sea. Because they're honest. They don't pretend to be anything but what they are, which isn't always true of people.

Regardless of how Kim felt personally, she was still an actress, and her interludes by the sea would constantly be interrupted by the demands of her profession. She managed to keep her professional and personal life in proper perspective and to enjoy both. She knew that, as long as she could manage to return to the sea, she would never again have the feeling of being closed in by what was expected of her professionally.

At home painting in the solitude of Big Sur

Though she sometimes questioned it all, she wisely looked at it in this way:

I sometimes wonder why it all happened to me. I had no experience. I had no training to be an actress. But fate brought me here and it kept me [in Hollywood]. And I am grateful. It's given me so many opportunities. I can travel and do things for myself and my family. And it's given me freedom. That's the most important thing in my life.

For Kim, part of the price of her "freedom" was being drawn back to work and the confines of Hollywood, back to the secluded house she still maintained in Bel Air. It was surrounded by the homes of many of Hollywood's leading stars, but Kim knew very few of them and socialized with almost none. About her home in town, Kim said:

Unless I come to town on business, I never stay here. I think of this place as a giant clothes closet. I keep all the frills that I don't normally wear. I like pretty clothes, but, by now, they've become more or less the tools of my trade.

Kim still retained the William Morris Agency as part of the show business machinery that surrounded her and looked out for her best interests. For a girl who preferred to be a loner, she continued to find her life unavoidedly entagled with lawyers, contracts and agents. For their influential services, the Morris office, headed by the powerful Abe Lastfogel, took the customary 10 per cent of Kim's substantial income.

Continuing to act as the buffer between Kim and this complex business world was Norma Kasell, still her manager and closest friend. In discussing their long-time friendship, Norma Kasell said:

I first met Kim when I was a promotion executive for a Chicago department store. Kim was thirteen at the time—extremely shy and awkward—but she had a special kind of appeal and, almost against her will, I pushed her into doing some modeling and appearing on my radio and television shows. That began to take her out of her shell. She soon started to win beauty titles like "Queen of Lake Michigan" and "Miss Deep Freeze" and then, while on a modeling tour in California, she was spotted by Columbia talent chief, Max Arnow, and given a contract for a hundred dollars a week.

Once more, in speaking of those early days, Kim said:

When they put you on that silent treadmill, it's like a nightmare. You're no longer a person. You're a property. A thing. The studio tells you what to say, how to dress, and whom to date. Sometimes I resisted but, often, I did as they asked because they were the experts and I was a beginner. Besides, I'd signed a contract and I really did want to try and do a good job. I wasn't learning much about acting, but I sure was learning a lot about performing.

I was twenty-one years old and people were soon telling me that I was the biggest box-office attraction in Hollywood. I found myself being swept along by this sudden and incredible career. And I wasn't even sure if being a star was what I really wanted.

During her years of growth in the industry, as a reaction to the price of fame, Kim found herself constantly searching for opportunities to be "herself." She loved observing people, something she had enjoyed since her teenage years, but it was becoming increasingly more difficult to do it. She did, however, manage to solve the problem.

I started wearing a wig in public right after *Picnic* as people began to recognize me. There was so much I wanted to learn. I needed to look and I needed to see. And you can't really look at people when they're staring at you. With a wig on, I can wander through the city or even go shopping without being seen. When I'm not recognized I can meet all kinds of interesting people who would withdraw if they thought I was her. That's why I loved New York. There, if only for a while, I could lose Kim Novak.

In her search for anonymity, Kim was seen less and less and almost never attended big premieres or par-

I'm very proud that my shy, quiet, little girl has become a movie star but I've asked her many times to give it up. To get married and have children. As an actress—she'll never have enough time or energy for a husband and a family. Now she may have a career, but I've always felt that happiness is more important than a career.

But Kim had her own views on this subject:

I can understand girls settling down and having a family—like my sister Arlene. I'd love to have a family, too, but I've found that when men want to marry you they become possessive and want to change you. They want to make you like themselves and then you have nothing left to give each other. I'll marry but only if and when it's right. When I'm wanted for what I am. One of the reasons I love to be with children so much is that they do accept you for what you are.

Not ready to settle down, Kim wisely knew that a life of this kind might be right for most girls in her age bracket but it was not right for her. There was still too much she wanted to see and accomplish before she could settle down and devote herself to just one person; and she was enjoying being "in love with life" too much to concentrate on being in love with just one individual. As she put it:

Wherever I go, even on short visits home, I find myself looking for the excitement of activity. Unlike many of the wistful girls that I play on the screen, I guess I'm restless and, when the pressures of my work build up, I just have to get out and do something like skiing or ice skating. I've never been much of a spectator. It's the doing that's fun for me.

In revisiting familiar sights in Chicago, and seeing her old neighborhood, she thought back to days that seemed far removed from the life she was now living. She remembered, while standing in front of her old school, "I won an art scholarship here while going to school and then the chance at Hollywood came along. Sometimes it's hard to imagine that that was almost ten years ago." Hollywood, of course, had changed everything, and she'd found a whole new world miles from Chicago.

While she sought freedom in her personal life, Kim also needed the release that she found through performing. She said:

I loved the freedom that acting could give. You can not only express yourself—you can become so many different characters. But this rarely happens. Hollywood usually prefers to use me as a sex symbol rather than to search for anything deeper. Perhaps that's the right way to make movies but, if it is, my feelings about being a Hollywood star will always be divided.

ties. Fans might catch a glimpse of her once every year or two but that was it. About these public appearances, Kim said:

Sometimes, as an actress, it's almost your duty to attend these rituals. And, though I smile and I go through the motions, I guess I'll never get used to them. In a way, you have to make believe. You have to play a role. The star. The glamour girl. That gives you an uneasy feeling. Even though you appreciate their attention, you wonder if people who come to watch would like you if they knew you as you really are.

Through it all, Kim emerged from her various facades during periodic visits to Chicago with her family, relatives, and friends. About these times, she reflected:

My memories of Chicago are warm and happy ones. When I was growing up, I was given a lot of freedom to find my own way. I especially enjoyed riding off on my bicycle into the woods to sketch and make up poems. In a sense, I've never really changed from that phase, and I realize that all the more whenever I return and am with my family.

The Novaks remained closely-knit. Kim's father had retired from his railroad job, and he and Mrs. Novak watched their daughter's remarkable career with mixed emotions. As her mother said:

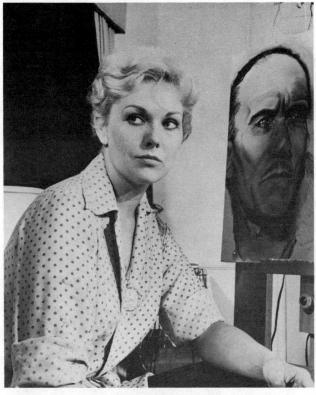

At work on a painting of her father

Still, I've always tried to bring everything that I could to my acting—especially with a role as challenging as "Mildred" in *Of Human Bondage*. She was unlike any character I've ever played before.

Much as she had enjoyed the experience of creating a character of dimension during the four-months filming *Bondage,* when the assignment was completed, she hurried eagerly back to her home in Big Sur, to her painting and her special way of life. Kim described her feelings in this way:

Sometimes I just don't realize how happy I can be until I come home to Big Sur. Acting can be challenging—an adventure—and there's always something new to look forward to on the next film. But within myself, there's a part of me that can never be satisfied with acting alone and that's why I return here where I can be really complete. For me, this is not so much a place. It's a way of life. A state of mind. Different worlds. And unless I give up Hollywood completely, some day, I'll always live in two worlds.

\*         \*

Kim was tempted to leave her ocean retreat for the opportunity of working with Billy Wilder on *Kiss Me,*

*Stupid.* Wilder had a long string of hits under his belt, including *Double Indemnity, Some Like It Hot, The Apartment,* and *Irma La Douce,* and Kim was excited and flattered that he picked her for the lead in this property. Wilder specialized in contemporary stories about contemporary people, the funnier the better. This time out, he and I.A.L. Diamond collaborated on a screenplay which took an amiable look at a series of events that befall an odd assortment of characters in the town of Climax, Nevada. The comedy was suggested by an Italian play, *L'Ora della Fantasia (The Dazzling Hour)* by Anna Bonacci. Kim had one of her most challenging comedy roles as "Polly the Pistol," an accommodating young gal in Climax. Dean Martin was set for the male lead.

The film went before the camers on 6 March 1964 and was completed on 7 July, a total of 85 shooting days. But twenty-four of these were repeats of scenes staged originally with Peter Sellers, who was forced to withdraw on 6 April because of a severe heart attack. He was replaced by Ray Walston. Most of the film was shot on a huge set built on two sound stages at the Samuel Goldwyn studio. Kim had four days in Twentynine Palms, some 250 miles east of the studio in the high desert, where exterior sequences involving the Belly Button Cafe were filmed.

In *Kiss Me, Stupid,* Kim wore one of the most modest wardrobes ever designed for a star. She had only two changes—a cocktail waitress uniform and a dress that, for story point, had to look too small for her. Both outfits were designed by Bill Thomas. Though the color lavender was a Novak trademark, Kim didn't wear anything even closely resembling it in the film. Her waitress uniform was red, white, and blue (red bandana top, blue skirt, and white rhinestone in her navel), and her dress was pink. There was one other piece of wardrobe for Kim, a black coat made out of a new synthetic substance known as Corfam that she wore while being transported back and forth to Ray Walston's home from the Belly Button Cafe. During wardrobe fittings for the picture, Kim's sense of humor showed when, on St. Patrick's day, she reported for a fitting wearing an emerald, rather than a rhinestone, stuck in her navel—and completely broke everyone up.

However, all was not fun and games for Kim on this set. There was an unexpected fall that caused her a great deal of pain and grief. Her secretary-companion, Barbara Mellon, had to rush her to a hospital in the middle of the night when Kim couldn't straighten up

The completed portrait of her father

*Kiss Me, Stupid,* with director Billy Wilder

or move her arms. She was weighted in heavy traction and had plenty of time to think during the sleepless nights of her confinement, of an earlier experience which was similar.

When she was eight years old, away at camp and learning to ride a bicycle, she had gone whizzing down hill on a boy's bike. As her speed increased, a solid brick wall loomed straight ahead. The crash couldn't be avoided, and she spent the next three months in a hospital, helpless, in full traction. Although she'd recovered, she was never to be free of a dangerously tricky back. As Kim explained:

> I have two vertebrae that have almost nothing between them. Just the thinnest layer of "padding" is what it really amounts to. The padding is worn down until there's barely any protection. Just the slightest thing, and it presses on the sciatic nerve.

The fall on the set of *Kiss Me, Stupid* didn't seem very serious at first. Kim merely tripped over someone's foot that happened to be in her path. There was even a split second for her to shield her face with her hand and prevent a blackened eye or broken nose, but she could not shield her body from the fall. Since she felt no pain, Kim told the worried cast and crew that

she was fine and went on with the scene.

Ten days later, her back started to bother her and, she recalled:

> It wasn't bad at first. I didn't know there had been nerve damage. I just thought my back must be a little out and I went to my masseuse. She gave it a couple of twists and pushes and it felt a little better. That night, however, it got worse. So the next morning I returned and she gave me the same treatment. Of course, this was the worst thing I could have done. All massage did was irritate my back more. The last couple of days before going to the hospital I was crippled over and in tears.

> I wouldn't go to the doctor because I'd started the picture. I kept thinking it would all work out. Finally, the masseuse told me she thought something was really wrong and that I should call a doctor.

Eventually, Kim was rushed to the hospital where the doctor advised her to stay in traction for two weeks, but she insisted on returning to work. Her doctor gave her a strict regime to follow, including pain pills and double injections of novocaine, which got her through the most strenuous scenes. Kim said:

> I took the pain pills. I had to. And for a while I was getting novocaine shots on either side of the sciatic nerve. Between scenes, I'd stand on a slantboard instead of sitting

205

down. I kept a moist heating pad in my dressing room. Taping my back was impossible because I was wearing a low-cut costume that goes way down in the back.

My doctor told me not to do anything physical. But it had to be. The director, Billy Wilder, is the most considerate man I've ever known, but when he'd ask if it would bother my back, I'd just say, "Oh no, it's fine." I didn't want to complain. If you're doing a movie, you can't pamper yourself that way. A lot of people have to work when they have troubles. Naturally, a doctor will give you a list of do's and don't's but, if you're working, a lot of other people are involved, and you have to go on with the business at hand.

When I got out of the hospital, the first scene I did involved climbing in and out of a tow truck, which is a very high thing. Then I had to jump and run up a flight of stairs. My character, Polly the Pistol, has her chest pointed up, and her hips pointed out. She's sway-backed in the middle. The doctor said I must hold myself completely straight, but during the whole movie I had to stand sway-backed, which put my back into a spasm. A couple of times my leg started to shake and I couldn't control it. But somehow I finally managed.

Kim was willing to jeopardize her health and safety for one reason. Because of the rough time she had endured filming *Of Human Bondage,* during which she had been crucified in print by her director and costar, she wasn't about to let anyone think she was playing the prima donna on this production. Consequently, she refused to baby herself in any way. Although her *Bondage* criticism had caused Kim to suffer inwardly, she would not refute the stories. As she put it:

What's to be gained from recriminations? And I just can't do that anyway. Let time and truth tell the story. All I want, all I ask, is respect as an individual. Just for people to give me a chance without getting a preconceived idea of what they think I am. I was so happy on this picture. It's the first time in my acting career that I've ever really found the joy of acting. I felt so good about it that nothing really bothered me. I just didn't let it.

Words of praise were lavished upon Kim by both her costar and director.

Dean Martin said:

I think she's wonderful. Kim is a real fine pro. I'd heard stories. I don't know where they came from. All I can say is they are nuts. She's one of the nicest persons I've ever worked with. I didn't know the seriousness of her condition at the time and she never said anything. There was one scene where I must have really hurt her but Kim didn't say a word. She's tops in my book.

And Billy Wilder said:

Working with Kim on this picture has been such a tremendous pleasure that I still can't believe it. Never a

*Kiss Me, Stupid*

tantrum or a problem, like I'd been led to expect. Instead, just magnificent, superb cooperation such as you get only once in a while from your bridge partner. Kim is a fine actress. She delivers her lines like they were music. And she is gorgeous to the camera. A real pro if I ever saw one, and I most certainly hope to work with her again.

The operation that doctors felt was necessary was never performed on Kim for reasons which were sound. She said:

I wouldn't consider it for a minute. You can't build the back up. You can't change it except possibly through an operation where they insert something between the vertebrae in order to give more space. But, as far as I'm concerned, there's nothing much they can do. I think it's awfully tricky and dangerous to fool with the back.

Although surgery had been a salvation for many others with similar problems, such as Elizabeth Taylor who underwent an operation of this type, Kim had her own approach to the matter:

*Kiss Me, Stupid,* **with Ray Walston**

*Kiss Me, Stupid,* with Ray Walston

To me, it's a matter of feeling that you can't let something like this stop you. You just can't allow it to. You just have to feel that you've got a job to do and you've got to go in and do it. If you go around playing it safe all your life you just can't get anything done. You do everything you can to conserve your strength for the important thing you have to do. And you have faith that you will be able to do it.

While it may have been simply a question of mind over matter, it worked for Kim, and she was physically able to do what was expected of her because of her strong belief that things would work themselves out. Her determination and guts proved once and for all that she was stronger and more dedicated to her professional duties than had been supposed. Though reputed to be "difficult" and "hard to handle," Kim turned out to be the exact opposite during the entire period of production. Billy Wilder was delighted with her enthusiasm and spirit and gave Kim one of her biggest laughs. At the conclusion of shooting, Wilder, in the great tradition of Ross Hunter movies, presented Kim with her film wardrobe—valued at about $8.98 in the open market—and said, "Anything Ross Hunter can do, I can do cheaper."

The most startling prop built for the film was an eighteen-foot cut-out of Kim which was set up in the desert to advertise the Belly Button Cafe. An idea of its size can be drawn from the fact that the glass in its navel measured three and a half inches across. It was rigged by special effects man Milton Rice so that at night the navel, which was lit up by electricity, would seem to revolve. In fact, the production designer did such a good job of transforming the Twentynine Palms Elk's Club into the Belly Button Cafe, that many of the local inhabitants thought it was real. More than a dozen girls stopped there to see if they could get jobs as waitresses.

During the course of the story, Kim and Ray Walston did a hilarious take-off that started innocently enough with Ray as a married man, but soon got out of hand when Kim kicked off her shoes, and passion began to beat its wild rhythm into their frustrated lives. Once Kim and Ray dropped their inhibitions they had a ball. During the scene where Kim and Ray did their impromptu dance, Gene Kelly dropped in to watch filming and Wilder promptly put Kelly to work blocking out the routine. Gene was told by the director, "Your contribution will be unbilled and unpaid, naturally."

\*          \*

*Kiss Me, Stupid* begins with Dean Martin concluding a singing engagement in Las Vegas. Heading for Hollywood in his Dual Ghia, he has been detoured through the little town of Climax, Nevada, where he stops for gas. The gas station attendant, Cliff Osmond, has a life-long interest not in pumping gas, but in writing lyrics for the music composed by his friend, Ray Walston, the town musician. As song writers, they have an unbroken record of failures and are beginning to believe that the song publishers in New York and Los Angeles don't even listen to their songs but simply steal the stamps off the return envelopes.

When Osmond recognizes Martin, he also recognizes the opportunity is at hand to have one of the nation's leading singers listen to, and possibly promote, their songs. Osmond, after being unsuccessful in getting Martin to listen to one, disconnects the fuel line in the Ghia. To further delay Martin, Osmond says he'll have to send to Los Angeles for the necessary new part.

Walston graciously volunteers to let Martin spend the night at his house while his auto is being repaired. After hearing Martin ask about what kind of action the town offers in the way of feminine companionship, Walston informs Martin that all the action is at a roadhouse on the edge of town, aptly named the Belly Button Cafe, where the cocktail waitresses are very friendly and there is "love for sale on the premises." Then, having a violently jealous nature, Walston suddenly realizes that Martin is no one to have in the same house with his attractive wife, Felicia Farr.

After purposely starting an argument with his wife, Walston is delighted when Farr rushes home to her mother for comfort. After getting Farr out of the house, Walston and Osmond plan to bring in one of the waitresses from the Belly Button Cafe to impersonate Walston's wife so Martin can get all the "action" he wants.

The accommodating waitress turns out to be Novak, who is known to most of the men in the town. In costume, complete with a rhinestone in her navel, Novak has a Jersey-Brooklynese accent and a cold to top it off. Osmond asks how she gets the rhinestone to stay in place and she knowingly answers, "I glue it in!" After first trying to beg off because of her cold, she finally gives in and agrees to go along with Osmond's proposition that she be hired for the night. But first she has to get a coat, after carefully warning him that she is "not covered by Blue Cross."

In her live-in trailer, which is parked behind the Belly Button, she stops to bid her parrot adieu for the

*Kiss Me, Stupid*

*Kiss Me, Stupid*, with Dean Martin

night. (The parrot's name in the picture is "Polly Unsaturated" and she loves to watch television. Really a male from the upper Amazon named "Pirate," it had been rented for the film. Though Pirate had a fluent vocabulary and was a good talker, his voice on the sound track was supplied by Mel Blanc.) Kim warns the parrot that too much television is bad for its eyes, grabs her coat, and is ready for her "assignment." When she realizes that she is to be transported in a truck, she's not happy.

Novak:  Are you kidding? I'm not going in any truck.
Osmond: Get your kiester in here!
Novak:  Y'know what you are? No gentleman.

And with that, they're on their way to Walston's.

Bringing Novak in to Walston, Osmond says, "Just wait till you see what I brought for dessert," and introduces Walston to his "wife for the night."

Walston: Shall we get organized?
Novak:  Look, I'm a good sport, you can ask anybody, but none of that crazy stuff, huh? Y'see, I got this bad cold . . .
Walston: D'ja ever hear of anybody with a good cold?

After telling her to "get out of those clothes," Walston comes in with one of his wife's dresses saying, "That's the only way it'll work." Novak has second thoughts about the whole thing and asks, "What are you, some kind of weirdee?" Not knowing what she has gotten herself into, Novak sneezes and loses her "navel" from its spot while shedding her uniform, then gets into a dress that's just a little too tight.

While cooking meat sauce for spaghetti, Walston finds out that Novak is a former manicurist from back east who got involved with a "hoola hoop salesman" who brought her to Climax and left her. As Novak tells it, "When I woke up in the morning, the guy was gone, the car was gone—that was it!" Without a car to get the trailer out of town, she has been stranded ever since and reveals her fate in this way: "Around here, I'm just somebody the bartender recommends."

Walston informs her of his plan and of the fact that she must impersonate his wife for Martin. Novak answers, "Don't worry, I know my job!" and carries it off beautifully. During the course of the evening, Martin asks Novak why Walston calls her by her nickname of "Lamb Chop," and Novak thinks fast and answers, "Maybe it's because I wear paper panties."

After dinner, Martin, Novak, and Walston move into the living room and Novak suggests that Walston play one of his songs. Everything is going fine until Farr suddenly appears on the home front. Walston quickly insults her and sends her away. Martin likes the song he has just heard and volunteers to keep Novak busy so Walston can make him twelve copies to take with him when he leaves. Martin fills Novak's shoe with champagne and enjoys the evening. Walston is supposed to leave them alone but has second thoughts about the whole thing when Martin says, "Something tells me, we're going to have a ball."

In the meantime, Farr has found her way to the Belly Button Cafe where she orders "another bloody Mary" after having more than her share. When she thinks she is going to be sick, the owner of the establishment, Barbara Pepper, puts her in Novak's trailer to "sleep it off."

Back at Walston's, he has further concern about leaving Novak alone with Martin. Novak tries to convince Walston he should go by saying "Look, Mr.— I got a job to do and you're in the way." Martin, as anticipated, makes a play for Novak but, as not anticipated, the insanely jealous Walston forgets who is supposed to be doing what to whom and throws Martin out of the house telling him, "If you want action—go to the Belly Button." And Novak doesn't understand any of his actions.

Novak:    Big idiot!
Walston:  I'll say he is.
Novak:    I mean you. Ya fixed yourself good. Ya had everything going for ya and ya went and loused it up. Why?
Walston:  I didn't want him to think you were a pushover.
Novak:    What difference does it make? One man more or less in my life. I'm Polly the Pistol, remember? I come highly recommended by the bartender.
Walston:  Well, I'm not the bartender and you're not Polly—not tonight! Tonight, we're Mr. and Mrs. Orville J. Spooner.

Walston is concerned that she has a cold and that it has been a long day. Novak and Walton spend the night together.

Martin has, in the meantime, meandered down to the roadhouse where the bartender touts him on to the most popular waitress in the joint, Polly the Pistol, fastest draw in the west, thinking that Novak is back in her trailer. Under the circumstances most auspicious

for romance, Martin meets Farr who is "sleeping it off" in the trailer. Farr is mistaken for the hooker and eventually Martin falls asleep. He drives off the next morning after leaving $500 for the "services".

Novak is brought back to the trailer by Walston after an evening together which has obviously been very special to both of them. Walston wants to pay her the money promised because she has been trying to save enough to get a car that will take her out of town, but she refuses his help.

Novak:    You wouldn't pay your wife, would you?
Walston:  But you need the money if you're saving up for that car.
Novak:    What car? I gave up on that . . . I'll never get out of this town.
Walston:  Don't say that.
Novak:    Oh, you don't have to worry. If we ever run into each other, I'll pretend I've never even met you.

They part tenderly with Novak saying, "You cured me of my cold."

Inside the trailer, after Walston has departed, Novak confronts Farr and the latter says, "You took my place last night, so I took yours," and Farr turns over the $500 to Novak. In a moment of quiet reflection they both think back to the events of the night before. Both obviously enjoyed the chance to trade places, and Novak says, "It was fun being a wife for the night." As an afterthought, Novak says, "And if you should find a loose navel floating around the house— it's mine." Farr confides that she is not going back to the house, and Novak gives her a solid bit of advice:

Maybe I shouldn't butt in but I think you're making a mistake. If I were you—and I was—I wouldn't leave Orville . . .
It's like a trailer without a car—ain't goin' nowhere—so when you find a good guy you should stick to him. I deal with married men all the time. Heels! Believe me, you got a wonderful husband.

Farr listens and returns home.

Several days later, Walston hears his songs sung by Martin on television and can't believe his good fortune. In front of the local television store, Walston is beseiged by admiring townspeople as Novak drives out of town in the car she has finally managed to obtain with the $500 from Farr. Farr caresses Walston fondly and whispers, "Kiss me, Stupid."

*          *

211

*Kiss Me, Stupid* was not the critical success it was expected to be, largely due to the fact that the Legion of Decency gave it a "C" or "condemned" classification. As a result of the Legion's action, the film was not released under the United Artists banner as originally planned. Instead it was distributed through Lopert, a wholly owned subsidiary of UA.

Harold Mirisch, president of the Mirisch Company, acknowledged that attempts to alter the film to change the Legion's classification had not been successful. "We made a lot of changes," he said, "but they [the Legion] insisted on more of them. It would have meant bringing Kim Novak back to reshoot and we couldn't do that." (Kim had already left the country and was in England working on another adult-themed film, *The Amorous Adventures of Moll Flanders,* by the time these events occurred.) Following objections from the Legion and other sources, Wilder reshot a sequence with Felicia Farr and Dean Martin in which the culmination is left to the audience's imagination. *Kiss Me, Stupid* finally received an MPAA certificate, and no further changes were requested for industry clearance.

Kim was well cast in the role of Polly the Pistol, and her comic timing was excellent. She was believable at all times, with a touch of pathos about her that made you "buy" her character. Her movements were timed perfectly and she made excellent use of her body. She used her voice well, and, between the Jersey-Brooklynese accent and the cold, she was right on target. Wilder, who is usually a peripatetic director, wore his customary cap and showed Kim exactly how he wanted things done. And she had a wonderful time doing them, despite the pain from her back while bringing them off.

Kim has been an actress with different reputations—the loner, the rebel. Stories had floated about that she was temperamental and displayed a moody behaviour on film sets. These became a choice topic for scandal magazines. However, everyone connected with *Kiss Me, Stupid* dispelled these rumors about Kim because, to them, she was the epitome of good etiquette and the ideal professional star. How these rumors started in the first place remains a mystery. Her cheerful disposition and friendly cooperation completely dispelled any "legend" that she was hard to handle.

While this film seemed to have created a new image, Kim maintained that she was still the same girl she had always been. If treated with respect and affection, she would respond in the same manner. If not, she'd stand up defiantly for what she maintains are "her rights." As she put it:

> I shall always question something that isn't good or that I don't believe in, because if it isn't good and I don't believe in it, then I just can't sell it to the audience.

\*　　　\*

Audiences, en masse, enjoyed the picture at the time of release, but perhaps its greatest success has come with young college students who are currently seeing it on campuses and loving it. Reviews for the film were mixed.

*Variety* said:

> Coming into the market on a wave of notoriety generated by one of the sharpest condemnations the Roman Catholic Legion of Decency has issued in many years might conversely benefit *Kiss Me, Stupid* in the beginning. However, once this curiosity factor is exhausted it is doubtful that this new Billy Wilder-I.A.L. Diamond sexploitation comedy will exhibit any exceptional boxoffice staying power. For, putting aside the LOD objections, Wilder is far from being in top form as a story-teller and commentator in this instance, and he has got at best only plodding help from two of his principals, Dean Martin and Kim Novak.

James Powers, in the *Hollywood Reporter,* noted:

> Miss Novak, who has been faulted in the past for insufficient energy and expressiveness, is also quite good. She is funny as the dumb b-girl, and she has a kind of innate pathos that Wilder extracts skillfully.

Brendan Gill, in the *New Yorker,* said:

> The stars of *Kiss Me, Stupid* are Kim Novak, Dean Martin, and Ray Walston. Miss Novak is young enough and pretty enough for her part, but Mr. Martin and Mr. Walston are no longer in the first flush of manhood, and the romping about they engage in here caused me more than once to wonder how close Dr. Paul Dudley White might be to the nearest telephone.

*Cue* Magazine pointed out:

> There are some very funny moments and ribald dialogue (some jokes were cut, too), but it is mostly coarse and heavy-handed, with Kim Novak slinking around as a sensitive prostitute embroiled in partner-changing.

The *Film Daily* stated:

> A sly, irreverent comedy that bounds gleefully over the social scene is offered by Billy Wilder in *Kiss Me, Stupid.*

This Mirisch Corp. presentation, a Phalanx Production, released through Lopert Pictures Corp., is graced with a splendid commercial cast headed by Dean Martin, Kim Novak and Ray Walston. The comedy and complications are adult. One gets the feeling that behind the facade of humor, producer-director Wilder is casting a cynical reflection on the manners and morals of modern society.

Harrison Carroll, in the *Los Angeles Herald-Examiner,* said:

For Kim Novak, the role of B-girl, Polly the Pistol, is virtually a character part. She plays the whole picture sniffling and sneezing with a cold. Yet, oddly enough, she is practically the only character who wins any sympathy.

And Raymond Durgnat, in *Films and Filming,* observed:

As the tart with a gentle heart, Kim Novak's performance is her familiar one, but as touching as ever. Here is a part Marilyn [Monroe] might have played, and the comparison underlines how, where the screen Marilyn was only a performer, a comedienne, Kim's slower, heavier style is essentially a tragedienne's. Whether or not she can act, in the orthodox sense of the word, I still don't know, and probably never will, but for my money her screen presence is, artistically, both powerful and authentic.

It is interesting to note that throughout her career Kim was never actually credited with knowing how to act while, time after time, she gave praiseworthy performances that were completely overlooked by everyone except her loyal public and devoted following. But then countless other performances by many great actresses were completely underrated until years later at film retrospectives where they were judged to be artistic classics.

One thing was now certain. Kim's popularity was international, this having been proven several years before at the Brussels World Fair. Four questions were offered visitors in an exhibit demonstrating an American voting machine. Visitors were asked to vote for the greatest European immigrant to the United States; the *"favorite all-time actress,"* the most famous state in the United States, and our greatest statesman. The answers were Albert Einstein, Kim Novak, New York State, and Abraham Lincoln—with the runner-up to Kim receiving less than half the accredited votes. This definitely had a lot to say for a girl who was totally underrated by many for her thespian capabilities. The public was still very much on her side.

Part III

_____

*Appreciation*

# 13

The two most infamous characters of bawdy eighteenth-century novels were *Tom Jones* and *Moll Flanders,* and it was a toss-up as to who was the bawdiest rake. Since *Tom Jones* had been brought to life and enjoyed phenomenal success in Tony Richardson's joyous movie version, it was only fair that Daniel Defoe's classic, *Moll Flanders,* about a lady of easy virtue, be given equal time. Hopefully, it would enjoy the same critical success and become as financially rewarding at the box office. Because it was to be afforded the same time, place, circumstance, costumes, language, and photographic effects, the chances were indeed most promising.

There was only one problem in bringing this property to the screen. The producer, Marcel Hellman, was having difficulty with the casting. Intent on finding the right actress to play the title character, he was looking for an actress with "a gay and earthy quality needed to do *Moll* justice," and his search was endless. During the shooting of *Kiss Me, Stupid,* Hellman visited the set and watched Kim being directed by Billy Wilder. After seeing her in action, the producer said, "I liked Kim and thought she would be ideal for our picture."

Kim, too, after speaking to Hellman, was interested in doing the property which would afford her the challenge of giving life to one of the lustiest ladies in English history. She began doing research on the character before leaving for England and the actual filming. Everybody, from the general reader to the most highbrow expert, agreed that Defoe's creation was a bewitching girl—if a little easy-going as to morals—and not very conscience-stricken when she had to "borrow" somebody else's money or valuables. After considerable study of the original novel and, obviously, of her role in the script of *The Amorous Adventures of Moll Flanders* (as it would be titled), Kim had her own interesting views about Moll's character:

> The way I see Moll, she was a very honest, strong-willed, and basically good person. But she kept landing in trouble because she led too much with her heart, following her impulses.

> I felt that Moll was bright but not in any educated or intellectual way. She had innate intelligence, like an animal. She could learn from some things—but not from others.

There was another point about the character that Kim wanted to put over—"the certain innocence she kept right to the end." As she put it:

Moll had a strong feeling of trust in people. She winds up with money, but she doesn't have all this from planning it out. However, don't get me wrong. When money comes across her path, she is pretty bright about getting her hands on it.

Kim may not have been a professor of English literature, but it didn't bar her from discussing one of fiction's most famous characters. In fact, she probably had more right to talk about *Moll Flanders* than the average professor because, in preparing and creating the role, she *was* Moll. As she pointed out:

> In playing Moll, I used my instincts rather than my intellect. Also, we can't forget that Moll Flanders was a product of the age she lived in—and a very bawdy, free-swinging, and colorful age it was. I kept that in mind as I did the part.

When Kim left the United States for London and the assignment in *The Amorous Adventures of Moll Flanders,* she did not have the faintest idea that this production would radically alter her lifestyle. Just as *The Notorious Landlady* influenced her decision to leave Hollywood for the more peaceful and quiet life of Big Sur, the production of *Moll Flanders* was instrumental in introducing her to leading man, Richard Johnson, who would take her for his bride upon the film's completion.

Kim arrived in London on 16 July 1964 by Lufthansa Airlines for the first conferences on the film, which was to start in September for Paramount release. In addition to Richard Johnson, a first-rate cast was assembled, including Angela Lansbury, Vittorio De-Sica, Leo McKern, George Sanders, and Lilli Palmer. Terence Young, fresh from his success with two James Bond 007 films *(Dr. No* and *From Russia with Love)* was set for directorial duties. This was Kim's second filming venture abroad, and, after all she had endured during the foreign location for *Of Human Bondage,* it took a lot of courage on her part to work once more on foreign soil in her first film in a British studio.

The wardrobe department worked overtime in caring for 1,500 eighteenth century costumes, twenty-eight of them belonging to Kim. She loved the costumes but disliked the confining pinch-waist corset she was forced to wear for authenticity and said, "An eighteenth-century number like this boned old thing is quite a sore trial for a twentieth-century girl." And she explained further:

*The Amorous Adventures of Moll Flanders,* on the set

I love the costumes, but this corset is something else. It's complete with hip pads for the desired hour-glass effect, which is great, but it takes me twenty minutes to get into my dress because of all these petticoats and even worse, all the laces on the corset. Just compare that with the thirty seconds it takes me to slip into a modern dress. Also, the corset gets uncomfortable after a while, and I always have to run off to the dressing room to loosen it.

Much of the action of the story took place around the manor house at Chilham Castle. Part of the time, Kim lived in the castle's keep, which, typical of this picture, was eleventh-century Norman and had luxurious, modern apartments hidden neatly out of sight. Another aspect of the "old and new" theme of the two-and-one-half weeks of location shooting in Kent was tiny Chilham village (pop. 1,232), mostly fifteenth century and named as one of the twelve prettiest villages in England in an opinion poll run by the British Travel and Holidays Association. For scenes shot in the village, the unit had to take down television aerials atop the ancient cottages and remove or cover with bushes and vines the signs, drainpipes, and other items not in existence at the time of the story.

Kim arose at 5:00 A.M. every day in order to get to Shepperton Studios in time for her 6:30 make-up call, and she didn't return to her rented Chelsea home before 8:00 P.M. This schedule not only curtailed her social life but also cut her off from the outside world as well. Eventually, when Kim commented that she didn't even have the opportunity to read a newspaper and catch up with world events, producer Hellman provided a Rolls Royce equipped with its own television set. The Rolls also came equipped with adjustable rear seats and window curtains, enabling Kim to catch up on her sleep during the ride to the studio in the morning. The TV set helped her to catch up on the news telecasts on the way home at night.

She also found England's news photographers as ruthless as the *paparazzi* of Italy in getting the shots they wanted. After the experience with the semi-nude photographs that caused so much commotion before *Of Human Bondage* was released, Kim was apprehensive about repeating this encounter during her nude swimming sequence for *Moll Flanders*. The producer had barred all outsiders from the set, but one enterprising Fleet Street lensman smuggled his cameras onto the grounds of the castle in a bag of golf clubs and quietly proceeded to snap the sensuous Kim—and, the next day, the results were flamboyantly splashed across a half page of the *Daily Express,* one of Britain's leading newspapers.

Director Terence Young had the cameras set up by the lakeside and ready to roll when another problem occurred. They were shooting the scene where Kim takes her nude swim before being disturbed by Richard Johnson. Enter the ducks bounding and noisily splashing in the water, making the lake a very pleasant rural scene indeed—so picturesque, in fact, that Kim, walking onto the set, was moved to remark that the prop department people had "really done their stuff." The big laugh that followed sent the ducks soaring back into the air and quacking excitedly as the director moaned. An undismayed Kim grabbed a few crusts from the morning tea-break and started throwing about some goodwill crumbs for the wayward ducks. Young called for his actors to take their places, and the ducks paddled on their way. Kim shed her dressing gown and slipped into the water ready for the cameras, but the ducks paddled back completely surrounding her.

By now, a groaning Young called a halt again and decided the ducks would have to go. More crusts and crumbs were collected, and Kim's stand-in was rowed to the other side of the lake with the ever hungry birds in close pursuit. The arcs went on once more, Kim's gown came off, and finally the cameras were rolling—but minus ducks.

Another scene for the picture did not go exactly as planned, and Kim had the black-and-blue marks to prove it. She found out that romance afloat is strictly for the birds—and seagulls at that! After two days in a bunk, elaborately decorated as the resting place of a wealthy eighteenth-century sea captain, for a romantic sequence with costar Richard Johnson, Kim found herself black-and-blue all over. One of the most torrid scenes in the film, it took two days to complete and, during the entire sequence, the "cabin" was realistically "tossing" as if the "ship" were at sea. At the end of each take, the two stars would make for the camera platform and "dry land" as quickly as their two feet would carry them, but nothing seemed to ease their seasick feeling or the bruises they incurred in the line of duty.

Producer Marcel Hellman, a soft spoken man not given to tossing compliments around, summed up Kim with three words that many another star would like applied to her. Hellman said Kim was "a real professional." He also added:

> Kim understands a very great deal about this business. Besides acting, she knows a lot about photography and costumes, for instance. I know very few other actresses or actors who take as much interest in the various phases of making a picture as she does.
>
> Further, she is a person who likes to see everything done perfectly. And, interestingly, being a painter, she has a fresh, different point of view about everything.
>
> Kim is wonderful as Moll and I think our picture will give [her] a new scope. I think she'll be able to do more comedies very easily. In fact, she has so much talent that really, she can do anything.

For the role of Moll Flanders, Kim changed the color of her usually blonde hair to a golden red for the duration of filming, and kept it that way throughout the personal appearances she made in connection with the movie's opening. The long-haired look that was needed was achieved via a generous fall that was attached to Kim's own shorter, cropped hair, giving the look that characterized Moll. Unlike the dye route she underwent for *Picnic* (when she returned to blonde as soon as the film was completed), this one didn't bother her at all.

In fact, Kim was not bothered by a lot of things; she was the happiest actress in the British Isles during this

With Chili, her newest pet

filming. She was ecstatic about the weather and the lovely English countryside, and she adopted a new pet, Chili, a Scottish highland terrier. The entire experience was far different from the unpleasant one she had had on *Bondage*. As she described it:

Making pictures here isn't much different from working in Hollywood. It's pretty much the same except we have tea "breaks," which I don't mind.

Besides shooting most of the film here at Chilham Castle, I'm also staying in the castle's Keep, or tower, while we're working here. It's the oldest place I ever stayed in. Parts of the Keep date back to Roman times, about 2,000 years ago.

This picture is a ball! My director, Terence Young, is a doll, and my part calls for a lusty Moll Flanders to have a lot of fun and romance. There's nothing very complicated or hard about the character. She's basically a fun-loving wench.

In bringing Moll to the screen, Kim had her fourth try with an accent after *The Notorious Landlady, Of Human Bondage* and *Kiss Me, Stupid,* and this time out she didn't press for effect. It was a straight accent with a sound similar to Greer Garson's speech, especially in her pronunciation of certain syllables.

When Kim left for London to film *The Amorous Adventures of Moll Flanders,* no one envisioned the possibility of a romance with her leading man, handsome British actor Richard Johnson. In fact, he wasn't the first actor considered for the role. Both Richard Harris and Warren Beatty had been mentioned previously, and Johnson was a last minute choice. Kim was never the kind of girl to become deeply infatuated with her leading men; making movies was strictly a serious business with her. The closest she had come to romance with coworkers would, more accurately, be labeled compatibility—what she had experienced with Frank Sinatra and Richard Quine.

Kim and Johnson were total strangers when she arrived in London. They met, before filming began, at Shepperton Studios. About this encounter, Kim said:

The moment I met Richard I felt the warmth of his presence. His charm and his manliness were at once apparent to me. I had never in my life met a man remotely like him.

And of his impression of Kim, Johnson said:

I felt I had known Kim forever. I had seen her in many films and was strongly attracted to her. She exuded a special charm and magnetism and, if I may be so bold as to say, a lusty sexuality.

Meeting her in person only magnified those attributes I had come to appreciate on the screen. Somehow, I told myself, this girl has *it*—she has everything I could ever want or need in a woman. And more!

Their romance was by no means instant, however, and Johnson put it this way:

It sort of started in a small way and then it got along. Kim kind of grew on me as the work on the picture progressed. About halfway into the film [around mid-October], we were in the caravan [studio trailer] playing cards. There were a few of us from the set and we were waiting to shoot one more scene before calling it a day. All of a sudden I turned to Kim and said, "Why not let me drive you home tonight—and take you out to dinner?" She thought that was a jolly good idea [and we went] to Daphne's Restaurant in London, a very charming place.

They dated numerous other times during the making of the film, but not as often as Johnson would have liked because he was doing double duty by making another film, *Operation Crossbow* with Sophia Loren, at the same time—thereby limiting his off-camera availability to a minimum. By the time *Moll Flanders* was completed (Johnson was still needed for the other film), Kim and Richard had made arrangements to meet in the United States. As Johnson said:

We had it all planned. I would come over and meet Kim's parents. Mind you, we hadn't yet talked about getting married. But we didn't have to. I sort of had a feeling that would come along naturally, all in good time.

I believe people should wait as long as they have to before they jump into matrimony. It's supposed to be a permanent thing and shouldn't be rushed.

Kim never did rush into things and had long been considered Hollywood's most eligible bachelor girl. When she departed for England, there was no serious "romance" in her life and, although there had always been someone linked with her romantically in print, these confirmations rarely, if ever, came from Kim. Perhaps the greatest insight to Kim's thoughts about marriage came from her sister, Arlene Malmborg, who put it this way:

Kim has very deep feelings about marriage and that is why she hasn't leaped into it. There would be fewer divorces if people considered all things or factors more carefully.

Most pleased about the whole affair was Paramount Pictures, who used Kim and Richard's romance (and, by then, marriage) as a selling point when the film was released.

\*      \*

*The Amorous Adventures of Moll Flanders* begins in an orphanage in the year 1720. A pretty little girl is asked what she wants to be when she grows up and she answers, "a gentlewoman." And who's to say she won't be, with those eyes? The village mayor is amused and touched by the child's answer, and he hands her a shilling which becomes her lucky piece.

Delayed credits are flashed on the screen, and, as the story continues, the child has grown up to be Novak at the age of seventeen. The mayor took her into his home as a servant in the household and, through her voice-over, we are told:

> My years in this house were exceedingly happy for, though only a servant, I was treated as one of the family and, like its other members, I've been encouraged to follow my studies, to keep myself spotlessly tidy . . . to . . . in other words, my education was in no way neglected . . . I was treated as one of the family and I enjoyed all the advantages of a wide education.

In addition to music and lessons in deportment and manners, she soon picked up the ways of ladies and gentlemen, and her charm has attracted the whole family to her, including the eldest son, Daniel Massey. When Massey promises to give her "more gold than you've ever seen," Novak is not impressed and says she has her own wages. But when he promises her marriage, she yields to him. His promise is false, and, minus her virtue, Novak is abandoned by Massey.

One day, while bathing in the nearby lake, Novak is disturbed by two highwaymen, Richard Johnson and Leo McKern. They develop more than a passing interest when they see her clothing on shore, and she is rescued by the mayor's younger son, Derrin Nesbitt. However, the sight of Novak emerging nude from the lake is more than Nesbitt can bear, and he quickly marries her. The match is doomed from the start. Nesbitt is a drunk, and, one night, his carriage over-

*The Amorous Adventures of Moll Flanders*

turns, leaving Novak a widow. Again she is heard in voice-over:

> Never, ladies, never, marry a fool. Any husband rather than a fool. And this one came to a fool's end! The family, of course, made sure I got nothing by his will—and so next morning, early, I left the house to make my way in the world. And now I was faced by the worst of devils—poverty.
>
> A girl can be kept by a man, or she can keep herself, but make no mistake—even when independent, she is still looking for a keeper. And I confess, I was not suitably affected by the loss of my husband. Though a widow, I felt I should soon be a widow consoled.

The penniless Novak, starting life anew, is hired as personal maid to a lady and her paramour count: Angela Lansbury and Vittorio DeSica. The penniless Lansbury and DeSica are constantly pursued by creditors but manage to keep up a good front. And DeSica can't keep his eyes off the "new maid."

Lansbury sends Novak to London with baggage before she and the count join her there. Novak meets the only other passenger, George Sanders, aboard the

*The Amorous Adventures of Moll Flanders*, with Richard Johnson

stagecoach, and he assumes her to be a fine lady. During the journey, the coach is waylaid by highwaymen Johnson and McKern. Johnson believes Novak to be a wealthy noblewoman, and he cannot erase her beauty, or her imagined fortune, from his mind.

In London, Novak takes up residence in Lansbury's house, where the first to call is Sanders. He mistakes Novak for a guest in the house and is overjoyed to find her alone. He tries to make the most of this opportunity but to no avail. Lansbury and DeSica arrive and the latter waits patiently for an opportunity to seduce Novak.

Meanwhile, Johnson and McKern are making their plans for easy riches. Johnson is going to masquerade as a gentleman and attempt to marry the lady he believes Novak to be. With the aid of Lilli Palmer, Johnson dons the clothes of a sea captain and calls on Novak. They are immediately impressed with each other.

Novak: And where will you steer me, Captain?
Johnson: Have faith, mum. I'll steer you through hell for the heaven you promise with those eyes.

A courtship blossoms and they fall in love. But they are both under false impressions. He still thinks she is a fine and titled lady, and he has led Novak to believe he has "estates in Virginia plus a fleet of three ships." After their first "date," Novak suggests a more intimate evening aboard one of his ships so they can dine in his cabin. Since he needs a ship to prove his authenticity, he goes to Palmer for aid. She says, "This is an expensive courtship," but provides the ship.

Each is impressed with the other's "way of life" and both are willing to change their individual life styles.

Novak: How I'd love to sail the salt seas and see strange peoples' lands. How exciting it must be!
Johnson: I'm learning that life ashore has excitements, too.
Novak: You wouldn't grow weary of the daily round and your own fireside?
Johnson: Not if there was someone to share it with.

A riotous scene follows in which McKern gives the impression that a whole crew is aboard, and, because he can't do anything right, for a time, it appears that the ship might even sink.

With Richard Johnson

Palmer keeps prodding Johnson with "winter's coming and a rich widow can be comforting," since she is eager to get back the return on her investment in Johnson's plan to marry "well." That night, thoroughly ashamed, Novak and Johnson confess to each other their true identities, and then angrily call each other names. After cooling down, they confess their attraction for each other, with Johnson declaring he cannot marry her until he is rich. Novak touchingly says she doesn't have much left "but it's all yours," and offers her lucky shilling.

After they spend the night together, Johnson leaves the sleeping Novak a note saying goodbye and asking forgiveness, but he has a last-minute change of heart and comes back for their farewell, saying, "One day, perhaps, we'll make our fortunes."

Returning to the home of Lansbury and DeSica, Novak finds her employment coming to an abrupt end after DeSica lunges for her in a madcap romp where she fights to save her honor. The hilarious scene ends

*The Amorous Adventures of Moll Flanders,* with Vittorio DeSica

up with feathers from bed pillows everywhere as Lansbury confronts the two in a very compromising situation. A revengeful Lansbury has her erring paramour arrested and sent to debtor's prison, and she banishes Novak from her house.

Jobless and desperate, Novak calls on banker Sanders who is overjoyed to see her. He marries her, but Novak soon learns that "wealth and position and comfort by day will not make up for insincerity at night." On her wedding night, Novak sees Johnson on the street below, from her bedroom window, and does not return to Sanders's bed to consummate their marriage. She sets out after her true love but is unable to catch up with him.

After searching relentlessly and in vain, Novak turns to Palmer for help. The latter teaches her the tricks of thievery as a way of life and a chance to "make her fortune" and save for the day when she will meet her lover again. This gives Novak an opportunity to wear a variety of disguises and different colored wigs because Palmer warns, "No gentleman must look at you twice." Novak becomes adept at catching her victims offguard and stealing everything from purses to jewelry. Unknown to her, Johnson is doing the same thing.

Palmer wants "brocade and lace" and teaches Novak how to go about "boosting" them. Then comes the fateful day when the lovers' paths cross once again. Novak is stealing lace in one shop while Johnson and McKern are robbing the store next to it. Everything goes wrong, and Palmer says, "There's the ruination of the finest pair of thieves in town." Novak, Johnson, and McKern are all arrested, flung into Newgate prison, and sentenced to the gallows.

Again, Novak is heard in voice-over:

> Those who have enjoyed the wicked part of my story would rather, perhaps, I left the good part out. But can they be thought to relish my sins and my crimes and find my repentance tedious? Would they rather this story were a complete tragedy and hurry over the instructive details of my confession and come to what I believed was the last day of my life? Under the awful threat of the gallows, I'd come to sincere repentance. It would certainly have lasted, I think, until the Friday but, on Thursday, the very day before I was due to be hanged . . .

*The Amorous Adventures of Moll Flanders*

At that fateful time before the forthcoming executions, the Board of Governors is paying a visit to inspect the conditions of the prison, and Novak's husband, Sanders, is among the group. Lansbury is also at the prison at that very moment begging for DeSica's life. When Sanders gets a look at Novak in the condemned hole, it proves such a shock that he collapses and dies on the spot.

Novak, being his lawful spouse, inherits Sanders's fortune with the help of Lansbury, who informs her that she can buy her release for the amount of five hundred pounds—and then cons her into "springing" a like amount for the release of DeSica after hearing her do the same for Johnson, McKern, and Palmer. All sentences are reduced to transportation to the Colonies.

Novak and Johnson are married aboard ship, and Novak insists on rewarding the captain who performed the ceremony with her lucky shilling saying, "I shan't need this any more."

\*　　　\*

*Moll Flanders,* with Richard Johnson

At the beginning of the film, Paramount wisely added a pleasantly tongue-in-cheek foreword to *The Amorous Adventures of Moll Flanders* saying "Any resemblance between this film and any other film is purely coincidental" in answer to any claims that it might be a copycat version of *Tom Jones.* This attitude happily carried throughout the film. *Moll Flanders* wasn't an imitation of that *Tom Jones,* but just another good-natured romp through the eighteenth century, and, while it had neither the style nor skill of its predecessor, it was persuasive and full of fun, spirit, and bounce.

Kim was at her best in the role of the lusty lass who learned quickly the ways of a sophisticated world. Her pretty face and the low-cut fashions of the period made it quite obvious that she was endowed with the physical equipment to conquer that world. She was a perfect choice for the role and had a good time during the making of this delightful romp into the past.

There were a number of physical scenes that gave her her first opportunity to become an "action" actress in every sense of the word. The heretofore "melan-choly blonde" (as she had been described so often) was allowed to let loose with no holds barred.

Many enjoyable moments were memorable—a cafe brawl, a chase involving horses and a carriage, a lavish ball, and several romantic interludes of an intimate, but not offensive, nature. One of the funniest scenes took place aboard the ship to which Johnson, posing as the owner of a whole fleet of vessels, lured the trusting Kim. His romantic advances were hopelessly botched by the efforts of the well-meaning Leo McKern, trying to give the impression that a whole crew was aboard.

Audiences and critics alike were able to enjoy the film.

Eleanor Perry, in *Life* magazine, said:

The exceedingly pretty Kim Novak plays Moll and it's probably the most energetic, most relaxed and best performance she's ever given. Her leading man is a dashing and handsome English actor named Richard Johnson whom she recently married and it's rather fun and nice to see them together on the screen.

The Technicolor looks great and there is some clever cutting, derivative of early Orson Welles and late Jean-Luc Godard and a few directorial touches which will make you laugh. Example: Kim and George Sanders are preparing for the nuptial bed. Kim undresses in the heavy-limbed despair of slow motion. Sanders in the jerky puppet eagerness of fast-motion. You may hate yourself but you'll laugh.

So it's a copycat version of *Tom Jones,* and if you didn't see the original you might even like it.

James Powers, in the *Hollywood Reporter,* noted:

This kind of movie, *Moll Flanders* or *Tom Jones,* requires the lightest of hands and the swiftest pacing. An amorous female is not quite so funny as an amorous male, but it might be made to be. *Moll* does not succeed, mostly because Miss Novak clearly is working against the notion of bed-hopping as a career, as it is presented here. Miss Novak's heroine seems to be hoping for better things, not content with things as they are. It takes some of the innocent lechery out of the story to have the heroine a reluctant participant.

*Variety* said:

There may be certain dispute over Miss Novak's impersonation of Moll, who revelled in scandalous behavior (to her, completely natural) and bounced from one bed to another in her attempted stride upward, but there's an earthiness about the actress which she utilizes to good advantage. She has no inhibitions, and is willing to enter into slapstick affray with fists and feet and whatever comes to hand to entice any man for gain, and she doesn't mind turning clown, if the occasion warrants it. She wears her flouncy costumes well, in all stages of dress and undress, and whatever may be lacking in her acting is more than recompensed by a gusty presence.

And the topper came from *Newsweek* magazine's evaluation:

Kim Novak is adorable as Moll, reading her lines with all the vulgarity that Defoe's heroine would have found quite natural and comfortable. And she looks splendid . . . there is a focal point of which director Terence Young has taken great advantage: on the right side of her mouth there is a sort of laugh line that appears whenever Miss Novak smiles, or pouts, and it makes her face as sweet and sexy as Hogarth's "Shrimp Girl."

Richard Johnson, her co-star, is also appealing, in a kind of Sean Connery way. (Miss Novak found him attractive, and is now Mrs. Johnson, which is something to think about during the film.)

The many supporting players—Angela Lansbury, Vittorio DeSica, Leo McKern, George Sanders, Lilli Palmer, Cecil Parker, Richard Wattis, and Hugh Griffith—are all splendid. But DeSica, as the impoverished (and fake) nobleman, and Sanders, as the old rakehell, are particularly fine. The extraordinary thing is that Miss Novak plays with them, holding her own perfectly well, and more than holding her own.

*     *

After the film's completion, Kim admitted that her scenes with Richard Johnson were quite different from any she had ever done before with a leading man. As she put it:

They're really what I would call "love love" scenes and I enjoyed them immensely. I found that I loved everything about Richard—his English ways, his way of speaking, his way of thinking and his mannerisms. I invited him to come to Chicago for Christmas and to meet my family. Then we would go on to my place in Carmel.

Neither Kim nor Richard wanted to rush into anything as permanent as marriage. He had been married before and didn't want to make another mistake. To reporters who cornered him in New York, on his way to meet Kim in Chicago, he was pressed for an answer as to whether or not he would marry Kim and he said:

This is so much more than just a friendship. We really haven't gotten down to discussing marriage as such—but I don't believe two people in our position really need to. I think we both understand each other and know what we want.

Kim met Richard at Chicago's O'Hare Airport, and they drove off to her parents' home in West Chicago.

However, by this time, the story of Richard's arrival had leaked out, and persistent calls from newspapermen all over the country overwhelmed the Novak home. Kim would not say there was going to be a marriage, but, conversely, neither would she say there was not. She did say:

It is a desire on our part to be together. It isn't that I'm afraid of marriage. I've never been afraid. I'm simply being careful because there is so much more to lose in a bad marriage than there is to gain in a good one. But Richard is a man I'm not afraid to marry. He is different from almost any man I've known. Life with him could not be dull or boring.

Kim also had other things to think about. She was a devout Catholic (although not a regular churchgoer, she believed in being the best kind of person she could be) and had been brought up to be cautious about marriage because it must be a one-time, lifetime contract. When taking Richard to her home in Big Sur, Kim dreaded the attention that was bound to be theirs at the airport. So she eluded the press by wearing a black wig and dark glasses as she flew out of Chicago, and Richard followed some time later, also hiding behind dark glasses. Eventually they caught up with each other, and Kim welcomed him to her world of nature's handiwork.

The girl who had run away from marriage on countless other occasions had finally been captured romantically and seemed very happy about it. The couple slipped away to Aspen, Colorado, and were married on 15 March 1965 with the civil ceremony beginning exactly at 3:13 P.M. on a snow-covered meadow near this ski resort town. The picturesque clearing, called Beaver Dam, a half-mile west of the resort ranch where they were staying, provided the perfect setting "close to nature and close to God." The Pitkin County Court judge left his courthouse office through a rear door to meet the wedding party (which included witnesses Norma and Hollee Kasell) and go to the secluded spot. While crowds of newsmen had clustered around the front of the courthouse, and were still waiting for the newlyweds to appear, the actual ceremony was taking place elsewhere.

Kim was a nervous bride during the outdoor ceremony, and almost blew some of her lines, but this was not uncommon for a happy bride. Kim wore a dress of white organdy with silk brocade, a matching coat and white silk shoes, while Richard stood beside her in a navy blue business suit. She carried yellow daffodils

Wedding to Richard Johnson

and her normally blonde hair was still red from *Moll Flanders*.

There was an odd forecast of things to come on that March afternoon. A platform had been built behind the ski lodge, so that the bridal party would have absolute privacy, and Kim fell off that platform and almost broke her back. She was helped to her feet by Richard, and the ceremony proceeded, but somewhat nervously.

Afterwards, the couple had a few words for the world. Richard said:

Kim is everything I could ever want or need in a woman and more. Each minute is exciting and a new adventure with her. We are looking forward to the beautiful years ahead.

Kim was equally breathless and said:

I'm sure I was right not to settle for less than I believe in. I feel that Richard is the right man for me. Love without understanding and friendship would never have been enough. Now I have all of this and more.

Was it really Kim Novak speaking? Kim, who had gone on record with the opinion that a "a good love affair is better than a bad marriage," who had insisted marriage wasn't "a natural way of life," because "nothing in nature is that way—joined or bound together"? There was still something of her need for freedom in the design of her wedding ring, which consisted of "silver and gold threads that wind around each other. Like two individuals who don't change and

become one but entwine their lives." Kim further explained:

Richard will love me for the way I am. He understands that I want to have certain freedoms—to paint when I feel like painting, or to write when I feel like writing, or to follow some other avenues of self-expression when the spirit moves me.

I always felt if there's an inner security only because of one's love—that's a dependent kind of thing. I think it has to come from believing in the other's inner strength plus the ability to share your lives.

And to clear matters once and for all in order to explain to the world that she wasn't "copping out" on her personal beliefs, Kim added:

No, I haven't changed my ideas about marriage. It *isn't* natural, but of course it's part of our society. It's hard really to explain what I mean ... I think there's a danger in marriage of having to *owe* something instead of *giving,* freely. People are marrying too young today. They are being pushed into it by society, and the person you marry becomes a substitute for the parent or teacher.

Single life is beautiful. Everyone should live alone for a while, ideally in a place like Big Sur, but anywhere really. Things have changed so much since the days when everyone stayed in his home town and settled there. Now you can easily travel and get a chance to find out *who you are* and *what you are* and *why you are.*

After their wedding ceremony, Kim and Richard returned to the ranch where they were staying and spent two weeks honeymooning and skiing before taking a leisurely drive and returning to California to settle in Kim's cliff-top home.

There wasn't nearly enough time for them to enjoy just being together because, shortly after their honeymoon, they had to travel to promote *The Amorous Adventures of Moll Flanders.* They gave endless interviews, with reporters more interested in their personal lives than in anything connected with the film. Those who were not familiar with Johnson's work on the screen flocked to theaters to see the man who had finally captured the elusive and "free spirited" Kim Novak. Kim openly admitted, during those early days of marriage, that the hardest thing for her to learn was the art of sharing. As she put it:

Sharing is beautiful but Richard is having to teach me a bit on that. You know it's natural to me to be by myself. And it's hard to share one's thoughts ... one's feelings ... and all of that. But it's a beautiful thing.

In order to really make this marriage work, both Kim and Richard knew that they would each have to "give

With Richard Johnson

Kim made Richard very aware of animals, nature and the good earth—things he hadn't thought much about since he was a young boy. And their different strengths and temperaments seemed to be blending perfectly. As Kim said, "I have highs and lows, and Richard is rather even in temperament—which makes for a good balance for us."

\*          \*

Before the anniversary of the first year of their marriage, there was a lot of balancing to attend to. Work had kept them apart some of the time and living conditions had also changed both of them considerably. Kim planned to sell the home in Bel Air that she had maintained for so long a time, and Richard was selling his bachelor house in Belgravia in order to buy a larger home.

Tragedy had also struck Kim. She had signed to do a picture in England called *Day of the Arrow,* with David Niven, for Filmways and MGM. Things had not gone well on this production from the start. Michael Anderson withdrew from the film, due to ill health, and J. Lee Thompson was signed to take over the directorial duties of a picture that had now been retitled *13.* This time, the number thirteen proved to be unlucky for Kim.

In November of 1965, and with only two weeks of shooting to be completed, Kim injured her back in a riding accident. While doing an important scene on location in France, she was thrown from a horse. Her back injury forced the suspension of shooting on the movie, which now had been retitled *Eye of the Devil,* and the $3-million production was shot around Kim as the company awaited her return.

Finally, all scenes not requiring Kim's presence had been completed, and the company was awaiting further word regarding the condition of its injured star. Kim remained in a London clinic with Richard at her bedside. After a brief stay, she emerged and did one more day's shooting, but this so exhausted her that she was forced to return. It was then that her husband announced the probability of her being unable to complete the picture.

With only two weeks remaining on the shooting schedule, there were discussions as to whether to replace Kim and reshoot scenes in which she appeared, or await her return. Kim's role spanned nearly three-quarters of the footage, and, when it was learned that

in" to each other because of their individual life styles. Kim would have to get used to spending time in England, and Richard would have the same experience in the United States. Kim eagerly looked forward to all of it as she described her husband's home in England:

It's a very liveable place and it's done in exactly the taste you would want. It's cozy and warm and the coloring is lovely. Actually it's terrific. It's very near a stable and I love to ride. London offers just about anything you could want in a city. And then of course if you want to go into the country, it's handy too.

But she had no plans to live permanently in England, as she clearly stated:

We plan to spend time [in London] and live here [in Big Sur]. Richard loves it here and I must say the place opened up to him. I've always sort of taken that as a factor. Because you know, it's a funny thing—there are certain people you can bring up here and I swear the sun won't come out for them. And it rains or something. But the sky opened up and everything was very beautiful. It seemed as though it welcomed him as much as he welcomed it.

The uncompleted version of *Eye of the Devil*

she would not be able to resume work for eight weeks, she was replaced by Deborah Kerr, who flew in from Switzerland to take over the role.

Kim remained in the London nursing home for six weeks until she was finally permitted to leave for the United States and spend the holidays with her family. Doctors thought that her back condition might be more improved by the following summer. She was depressed, having lost a role that had provided a great change of pace for her, and knowing that the pain she was suffering would remain with her for some time to come.

Richard's film assignments were to keep him abroad indefinitely (although he did manage to join her for the holidays) forcing them to spend their first wedding anniversary separated by a wide expanse of ocean.

In retrospect, it is doubtful that *Eye of the Devil* would have done much for Kim's career. It was an eerie story of a cult devoted to devil worship and evil deeds, with a husband determined to be sacrificed while his wife does everything within her power to understand and try to prevent his destruction. The picture was finally released as a programmer in late 1967, after being held in the studio vaults for over a year.

Following her painful weeks in the clinic, Kim was

forced to wear a steel brace on her back, and many thought that she might never be able to work again. Ill health, tension and the constant separation did not help her marriage.

\*  \*

Thirteen months after the wedding, Kim was ready to file for divorce. However, there was one complication. Just before the announcement of their impending split, Kim and Richard were seen by millions of television viewers throughout the country when they were presenters on the annual Academy Awards show. As they came to the front of the stage together, she in a shimmering and curve-hugging sheath and he in a tuxedo, they appeared to be one of the happiest couples in filmland, as the sound of applause greeted them from an exuberant, jam-packed audience.

Because she was and always has been such an honest person, this was probably one of the most difficult moments Kim ever had to force herself through, because she felt like a fraud. As she put it:

There we were at the Academy Awards show, with everyone looking at us, and only the day before we had talked about getting a divorce and had already made preparations for our separation.

We were a phony couple that night. Even though I could barely fight back the tears, knowing I would be going through the ordeal of a divorce, I put on an act. I put my arm through Richard's and looked up at him lovingly, and he looked at me with the same expression.

I had to go through with it—and it was rough. We had promised months before to attend, and, if I tried to back out at the last minute, then everyone would have known for sure that something was terribly wrong. But most of all, I went through with it for the sake of the industry. Millions of people would have been disappointed, and that is supposed to be a happy night.

They had scheduled Oskar Werner and me to present two cinematography awards and then at the last minute Oskar couldn't make it. One of the directors put his arm around me and said, "I've got a great idea. Why don't you and Richard make the presentation?"

I had to do it. I was so nervous I didn't know what I was doing. On stage we fumbled with the envelopes together and then handed over the Oscars [to Ernest Laszlo for *Ship of Fools* and Inger Stevens accepting in place of Freddie Young, who was not present, for *Doctor Zhivago*].

Backstage, everyone was wonderful, and there were handshakes, kisses and embraces. Then afterwards, at the awards ball at the Beverly Hilton, we dined together, with champagne and soft lights. I was kind of glum, but I tried to chase the blues away by dancing —with someone else. It was the toughest role of my life.

231

*Eye of the Devil*

*At the Academy Awards with Richard Johnson*

Maybe I waited too long. I was over thirty. We both had careers and were used to our own ways of life. We couldn't change them to suit each other. I'm used to solitude, and our work kept us apart so much that we didn't have enough private life left over for just the two of us. Marriage had to be a fifty-fifty proposition. I guess with us all we had was about twenty-five-twenty-five, if you know what I mean. I'm a very independent person, and no one can ever make me do anything I don't want to do. I need a lot of attention and a patient man. Marriage is a full-time job at best, so with us trying to make it on a part-time basis, with just the little time we had left over for each other, our marriage never really got off the ground. We were like strangers. So if you are honest with yourself, no one can live a married life that way. It would all be the same kind of fraud as those final days. Maybe it takes more courage to admit a mistake and try to start over again.

Still very hurt by the emotional letdown of the whole experience, Kim knew that time would be the greatest healer of all and that it would change a myriad of things.

In the eyes of the world, Kim had reverted to total hibernation—with Pyewacket, Warlock, Chili, and a black mynah bird named Choika—in her isolated villa. But Kim didn't hibernate. She packed up the animals and disappeared into the redwood forest not far from Gull House where she could commune with nature and where no one could demand anything of her. "You can't imagine how wonderful it is to wake up under those magnificent trees," Kim later expounded complacently. And the giant redwoods helped her to throw off her depression and become her own person once again.

On 26 May 1966 Kim, using her married name, Marilyn Pauline Johnson, won a divorce without any contest of action from Richard. They remained friendly and still had the greatest respect for each other as individuals. Kim's request to assume her maiden name was granted and she refused to talk to newsmen who gathered outside the courtroom. And in spite of the fact that she was forced to charge mental cruelty, she testified that Richard was "always nice" to her.

After kissing her elderly lawyer on the forehead, Kim hurried back to her fortress-like castle in Big Sur to try to reorganize her life. Although she must have felt sadness and disillusionment, Kim also realized that she was once again the "free spirit" she intended to remain. Alone by the sea, Kim reflected on her situation:

# 14

The accident which occurred when she fell from the horse during the filming of *Eye of the Devil* kept Kim off the screen a lot longer than she had expected. It almost appeared for a time that she was permanently jinxed as far as returning to the screen was concerned. As soon as the back pain eased up and allowed her to feel somewhat normal again, fate dealt her another cruel blow.

On 26 August 1966, Kim miraculously escaped serious injury when her station wagon lost a wheel, left the highway, and overturned twice. She was travelling on the rugged California coast south of San Francisco near the town of Santa Maria, en route to her home in Carmel, when the accident occurred, near the Santa Maria Bridge on U.S. 101, the famed highway about 140 miles northwest of Los Angeles.

Kim was taken to Sisters Hospital in Santa Maria and released the next day, at which time she was transported by ambulance to St. John's Hospital in Santa Monica. Although she had spent a restless night, Kim was grateful to have survived the experience with little more than a lacerated hand and middle finger requiring fifteen stitches.

As she described the ordeal at the time:

I'm lucky to be alive. I didn't realize anything was wrong with the car. I thought the wind was whipping it. Suddenly a wheel came off. I realized that I couldn't do anything. My two cats were on my lap and the two dogs beside me. I swept them off the seat onto the floor and then fell on top of them. I figured I couldn't save myself, but I was going to save the animals. This is what saved me. Lucky that I wasn't wearing seat belts.

All of the animals escaped injury. The station wagon flipped end over end in a double somersault as it plunged down the 8-foot embankment and finally came to rest 125 feet from where it had left the highway. New tires had recently been put on the car, and a preliminary investigation indicated the lug nuts on the wheel were loose, possibly caused by a mechanic's carelessness.

What the public did not know was that this wasn't Kim's first accident in recent months, but her fourth. Each accident had followed the same pattern, with Kim driving alone when, without warning, mechanical failure had sent her car spinning out of control. The first time Kim had experienced car trouble, it had turned out to be just a minor mishap, although serious enough to prevent her from continuing her trip in the vehicle. The second time, her station wagon had spun out of control on a rain-slicked West Los Angeles street and collided with two other cars. Fortunately, neither

**With director Robert Aldrich and the cast of** *The Legend of Lylah Clare* **at a rehearsal meeting**

Kim nor the occupants of the other cars had been seriously injured. With number three came the anguish of having her car blow up in the middle of the dangerously crowded Hollywood Freeway. Kim had been driving a little foreign sports car, a Karmann-Ghia, at the time; and, like the other accidents, this one had come without warning. When she experienced number four, Kim was more than a little stunned at what appeared to be a jinx in her life.

However, there was good news on her fourth miraculous escape. X-rays indicated that she had not re-injured her back, which had been hurt the previous year in a horseback-riding accident. Wire photos, appearing in newspapers throughout the country, showed a smiling but wan Kim with a bandaged finger.

The accidents, as well as a mud slide that finally caused her to give up her Bel Air residence, were never mentioned by Kim. "Why dwell on them?" she said. "They're in the past. I want to get on with the living. It's today that counts." But she did take the bad experiences as an omen that she wasn't meant to live or work in Hollywood for a while, and she retreated to Big Sur where she remained isolated in her fortress-like castle with its windows looking out towards the sea. High atop the rocks, she had the feeling of being in her own private domain, completely out of reach with the world. One had to drive through a winding dirt road off the highway to reach the house, and a sign clearly read "Private Road—Do Not Enter." Beyond the dirt road was a trench-like moat barring access even further, and there was no bell or window at the door to the house— just a peephole.

The almost fatal accident had changed Kim's entire way of thinking. "Alright, I've had it," was her thought. The sulphur baths in Big Sur helped her to recover physically, but surviving physically "was only part of it." As she put it:

I had to look for a deeper meaning from life before I could return to a studio. I've had more than my share of good luck. I started in films very young. I didn't have time to get to know myself. Then the accident happened.

At first the feeling was, "I really shouldn't be here." A fear took over. It passed me by this time. But next time . . . what was the purpose? Why was I spared?

For me, there was a special meaning to the accident which forced me to stop for a while. The time off was good. It gave me time to discover myself and I liked what I found.

I remember thinking, "Don't take life for granted." Suddenly something jars you. It's a shame to go through life and not appreciate all the good things in it. The accident

was really good luck for me. Making one movie after another isn't the whole bit for me anymore. I've learned to express myself also through my paintings and sculpture.

For the first time in her life, the insecure and shy Kim Novak had matured and "got her act together." She was finding herself in the process and liked what was underneath the whole facade. She at last had the time to probe beneath the surface. Living was becoming more meaningful with each passing day, and part of this was the result of her way of life. As she said:

I've sat in on some of those sessions with the hippie crowd that goes in for that absurd ritual of finding one's real self through the naked acting out of the emotion one feels at the moment. But this wasn't for me because I found it to be primitive, ugly, and debasing.

She was to find her answers in another way. She explained:

I am close to nature [at Big Sur]. I swim, laze in the sun, walk and enjoy the companionship of the animals I have gathered around me. I have dogs, a horse, and I've even acquired a goat, an African pygmy given to me on my birthday. I am alone a lot of the time, but not really alone, for I have my painting. I am trying different and sometimes interesting effects, utilizing driftwood which I find on the beach. I write and compose a bit and read a lot. When I want to be with others, I have the people of Carmel and the Big Sur. We have dances, and I love to dance. I'm not of Hollywood to any of these friends. I'm just one of them and we have lots of fun.

\*             \*

Kim, who said she loved life too much to use it all up making one movie after another, finally decided to return to the screen, after a two-year absense, in *The Legend of Lylah Clare*. In explaining her reasons for going back to work, she said:

I felt that this script offered me every sort of opportunity in the dramatic range, so I simply couldn't refuse it, even though it was something of a wrench luring me back to work.

Legends attach themselves to us whether we like it or not, and screen acting certainly contributes to development of a dual personality. I liked the idea of playing two characters. As the aspiring young actress who becomes a star in the course of bringing *Lylah Clare* back to screen life, the whole mystique of Hollywood is investigated. Besides, the script was offered to me at a time when I felt like doing a movie again. The timing was right.

Certainly there were things in the script that I could identify with, while certain other things gave me considerable hesitation. But Peter Finch and Robert Aldrich weighed in the balance.

I like to read over a script and find as many ways to identify with my character as I can. Then I discuss interpretation with the director to find out what he wants. In the case of *Lylah Clare*—I'm with it with all the old intensity that I've always applied to acting.

And I hope we achieved that sort of high camp facade we tried for, rather than a down-beat "biographical drama" about the tragic loss of a mythical star to the film world.

Movie-making is new and exciting today. The new freedom is compatible with the way I feel, a kind of way that is stimulating and exciting. Films like *The Graduate* are as good as living. It's free to do whatever—it's a painting as opposed to a photograph.

\*　　　\*

During the shooting of *The Legend of Lylah Clare,* Kim spent her off-camera hours studying and preparing the difficult intricacies of her character. Other cast members did not see much of her at that time.

Coral Browne said:

Kim Novak and I only had one big scene together and I only did six days on the movie. In that time I didn't come close to Miss Novak because of the time element. However, whenever we met on the set, she was most charming and I found her to be completely professional.

Milton Selzer recalled:

*Lylah Clare* seems so long ago to me and I can't recall specifics, but I do remember that the making of that picture was a very pleasant experience for me. I found Kim Novak to be an easygoing personality and a very nice person. She was friendly. She was good. I enjoyed the opportunity of working with her very much.

And Ellen Corby observed:

Although we had previously worked together on *Vertigo*—we did not come in contact with one another at that time. I did not get to know Miss Novak when I worked on *Lylah Clare* either.

The *Lylah Clare* script was rather inconsistent. I had little to do on it and made myself scarce—spending most of the time writing on my own material. I remembered one of Miss Novak's earlier films, *The Man with the Golden Arm,* and thought she was terrific in it but never had the chance to tell her so.

During the time on *Lylah Clare,* I remember Miss Novak as a hard-working and very beautiful actress who was extremely professional. She knew the business and what was expected of her and was always prepared to do whatever she could to keep things rolling evenly. I'm not sure she understood the whole story—I know I didn't.

There was a lavish wardrobe for Kim's role in *The Legend of Lylah Clare,* and designer Renie saw to it that the star's body-beautiful worked for her in every way, showing off the stunning wardrobe in startling and totally effective ways. Kim wore absolutely nothing under two of the most exciting of the thirty creations designed for her.

One of the revealing costumes was an at-home robe, made of Aba of Viachini wool crepe, printed in soft olive and turquoise in a Persian pattern. It was cut in a great square with only side seams and, as Kim moved in the Aba, she gathered it around her or let it flow freely, thus revealing every outline of her body.

The most exciting was a lush white evening gown that she wore when first introduced to the press and the world after being transformed into the star who would portray *Lylah Clare* in the early part of the film. Renie turned for inspiration to the ancient Greek ideal of beauty, as portrayed in works of art, for this dress that would flow over Kim's seductively graceful figure and well-proportioned torso.

The dress was made of the softest, almost transparent, white Alix jersey, and, while it covered Kim, it didn't conceal her charms. "Kim's fluid body, falling instinctively into the Greek 'S' curve of beauty, was the base on which the dress was draped and on nothing else," Renie explained. "Regardless of how she moves—running, dancing, making a grand entrance down a staircase—the dress flows and moves with her through the use of folds and drapes."

\*　　　\*

The plot of *The Legend of Lylah Clare* concerns an unknown starlet, Novak, who had worked her way through college on a circus trapeze and now hopes to become an actress. Agent Milton Selzer feels she is the perfect choice to portray a legendary film queen on the screen. In spite of the fact that her hair is darker and she wears glasses, Novak bears a startling resemblance to the star, Lylah Clare, whom Selzer had originally discovered.

Staying at a cheap hotel, Novak studies all the fan magazines and other material pertinent to the late star, as delayed credits are flashed on screen. Tossing and turning on her bed, Novak finally gets up, grabs her coat, and walks down Hollywood Boulevard in the early morning hours to the haunting strains of Devol's theme music. She pauses to look at the famous

*The Legend of Lylah Clare*

names—Fatty Arbuckle, Jean Harlow, Clark Gable, Marilyn Monroe, and Rudolph Valentino—embedded in the cement sidewalk. In front of Grauman's Chinese Theatre, Novak steps into the footprints of the actress whose life she has been studying.

Later that evening, Novak arrives at the home of director Peter Finch. The meeting has been arranged by Selzer because Finch is about to film the life story of the look-alike star, who was discovered in a brothel. The director is an egomaniac who is trying to make a come-back and catch his second box-office breath with this picture. He also happens to be the widower of the star, who died on their wedding day under mysterious circumstances. Finch's cruelty is displayed as he makes Novak, who is two hours late, wait outside in another room as he, Selzer, and Rossella Falk continue to sit, over after-dinner drinks, at the dining room table.

Novak is mesmerized by a painting of the dead star that hangs on a wall midway up a long, steep staircase. When the others enter the room, Novak asks, "Is that where it happened, up there?" The first version of the star's death is told by Falk, who was her friend and dialogue coach. Flashbacks show the star stabbing her attacker, and, because of her fear of heights, falling to her death from the non-bannistered staircase. Finch asks Novak to walk down the stairs so he can see how she moves. She controls her body well as she descends. The director, however, is cruel in his observation that they have discovered a "spastic Catherine the Great." After a few more insults, Finch touches her and there is an abrubt change within Novak. Her voice, much the same as the legendary star, complete with gutteral German accent, says, "Keep your filthy hands off me!" There is silence as Finch, Falk, and Selzer stare in utter disbelief at what they have heard. Novak pleads, "I'm not her! I'm not!"

Some time later, when they are viewing a film version of *Anna Christie,* Finch turns the sound down and realizes that Novak knows all of the dialogue since she is mouthing the words in the same accented style. Novak dismisses it by saying she "studied O'Neill in high school".

Novak's brown hair is bleached blonde, her name is changed (in spite of the fact that she tells Finch, "I'm happy with the name I have"—a statement reminiscent of Kim's own experience with Harry Cohn at the start of her career), and she is coached in preparation for her introduction to the press corps.

At the party, as she is about to make her entrance, Novak trades a glass of champagne for a long-stemmed red rose which she holds as she slowly descends the staircase in a revealing, clinging white gown. Looking every inch the movie queen she is about to portray, Novak charms most of the press people with

240

*The Legend of Lylah Clare,* **with Gabriele Tinti and Peter Finch**

her answers to their queries—until she is brought to meet Coral Browne, the powerful grande dame of the news corps. Browne is vicious, and they clash immediately. Novak, who has been jabbed on all sides by the cane the crippled Browne uses, says, "She just dirtied my dress." Novak asks for a cigarette, after previously saying she doesn't smoke, and her mood changes. When Browne asks Novak if she is having an affair with Finch, Novak again becomes the legendary star, complete with accent and temperament. After taking all the abuse she can manage, Novak verbally attacks Browne as "the wicked witch of the west" and a "dried-up, crippled freak." Browne leaves in a fury of denouncements after Novak has ordered her out of the house. Finch has not argued the point since he believes "a director should never undercut his star's big scene."

Before long, it is revealed that the deceased star liked men, women, and drugs, but not necessarily in that order. Everyone is beginning to confuse Novak with the original, and soon she believes the confusion herself. Finch completely dominates her, delighted with the results. Although he has known failure in the past,

he now has the will to try for greatness again. A total egotist, more in love with himself than he can ever be with another human being, he is reincarnating his former star. And Novak, under his spell, finds herself needing him as much as he does her.

His control over her is shown in a scene in the garden where Novak is clad in a bra and hip-huggers as she walks in a leisurely manner, accompanied by him. (Several years later, this same bra would go to the highest bidder in the famed MGM auction.) She is introduced to Finch's gardner, Gabriele Tinti, and there is an immediate attraction between the two.

Later, Finch and Novak arrive at the Hollywood Brown Derby. She is wearing a red cape as they make their entrance. Removing the cape, Novak is seen in a revealing red dress. The duo is joined by Ernest Borgnine, head of the studio, and Selzer. (This is a difficult scene for an actress. She must listen as the men do the negotiating and most of the talking. What Kim does with her eyes during these moments proves what a fine actress she really is, and she registers strongly. Her eyes look from person to person, and, perceptively, she sees through Borgnine.) When Borgnine suggests that she make the picture with another director, Novak remains loyal to Finch and reverts to the voice and manner of the legendary star. Completely baffled by the change in her, Borgnine agrees to Finch continuing as the director and acquiesces to all his demands.

Finch, who is about "to relive the most important part of his life", forgets who Novak is and calls her by the dead star's name. Novak flees from the table when she realizes that he will step over anyone in order to achieve his end: the making of the film.

Later, arriving home, Finch encounters Falk who does not approve of his treatment of Novak and says, "Sometimes, even a dog needs to hear its name called." Novak's bags are packed and Michael Murphy,

*The Legend of Lylah Clare,* **with Peter Finch**

Borgnine's son, who is infatuated with her, has been waiting in his car to drive her away from the house. At that moment, Novak sees Finch slap Falk across the face. The director tells Novak that he has sent Murphy away and he has also locked her out of her room.

Novak:    If you're going to keep me here and lock me out of my room, I'll just have to find somewhere else to sleep, won't I? Should be quite an experience. I've never slept in a mausoleum before.
Finch:    You're not to go in there, do you hear?
Novak:    Why? Is she still in here? Is that what you're doing, keeping her in a little container? Instant Lylah?
Finch:    Elsa, please, as a favor, I ask you not to.
Novak:    Please! Well, that's a new word in your vocabulary. Please.

Novak has gone directly to where she has seen Finch hide the key to the legendary star's bedroom and she uses it to open the door. Falk warns Finch, "If you hurt this girl . . . this time, I will really punish you . . . I'll kill you if I have to." Finch joins Novak as she enters the forbidden room which is still in a state of complete disarray, with everything just as it was after the fight on that fateful wedding day.

Finch gives his version of the star's untimely death. As he tells it, the star came home with her lover who came after Finch with a knife. They fought, and the lover fell to death, only to be revealed as a woman. The star looked down, forgetting her fear of heights, and fell to her death too. Finch asks, "Did she love me or hate me . . . what's the difference now?" Novak answers, "I don't hate you," and feels extremely compassionate toward him. She unfastens the back of her dress and slips out of it, as Finch kisses her and lowers her toward the bed. Later, in bed together, it would appear that they are totally in love, and Novak now puts her complete faith and trust in Finch.

During the filming of a difficult scene for the movie, they are on location at the beach, and Finch is deliberately cruel and sadistic toward Novak. He loses patience when she cannot do what is expected of her.

Finch:    It's a perfectly simple action. I don't see why you can't follow orders.
Novak:    It's not simple. I don't know what I'm supposed to be thinking. What am I feeling? Why? What am I supposed to feel?
Finch:    Feel? You stupid cow! All you've got to do is do as I say and then your feeling will be up on the screen. All I need is your face. I don't want your good will or your understanding.

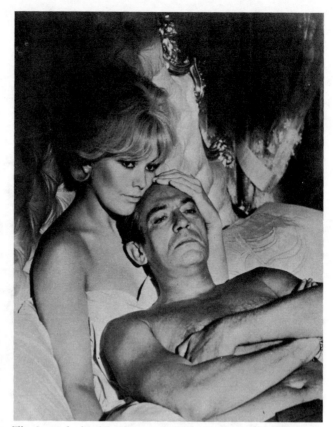

*The Legend of Lylah Clare,* with Peter Finch

243

*The Legend of Lylah Clare,* **with Peter Finch**

*The Legend of Lylah Clare*

*The Legend of Lylah Clare*

Selzer warns Finch not to push Novak too far and Falk says, "It is possible she doesn't understand," but the director is not willing to yield or respond to any warning.

That evening, Falk enters Novak's room as she is brushing her hair in front of a mirror. Falk helps an exhausted Novak to bed and gives her a sleeping pill as she massages her. Falk kisses the sleeping Novak on the cheek saying, "I'll always love you," and repeats the kiss. She, like Finch, is making Novak a substitute for the legendary star they both loved.

The next day, the company is shooting the staircase death scene and trying to complete the final footage for the picture. It does not go well. After three takes, Finch calls a halt and announces that the picture is completed. Later, Novak, Finch, Falk, Selzer, and his wife, Jean Carroll, watch the rushes. On the screen, Novak descends from another staircase (in her best Dietrich fashion) and sits at the bar. When the lights go on, Finch knows Novak couldn't play the scene he wanted because it was false, and he comes up with an idea for a new ending. He decides the ending will have to be on

the trapeze and Novak will have to "die in harness." When he is questioned regarding the fact that this was not the way the real star died, the director says, "We make the legends—the legend becomes truth."

Together again in bed, Finch and Novak confess their love for each other but they end up in an argument. Although Novak clings to the fact that "you loved me," Finch tells her, "You're an illusion . . . without me, you don't exist." Again, the legendary star emerges through Novak, and her temper flares.

Some time later, in the company of Tinti, Novak is completely possessed by the original star. While sipping champagne with him, she makes a phone call to Finch. "I decided to come back to work . . . you better get down here—*fast!*" she announces. Once the director arrives at her dressing room, Novak, still possessed, is in a vile mood and tells Finch to "Keep your filthy hands off me." Finch can no longer control the temperamental star as she says:

Alright, little man . . . now get your ass out there and tell them Lylah's coming. As soon as she gets her harness on! (And Novak follows this with hysterical laughter.)

*The Legend of Lylah Clare*

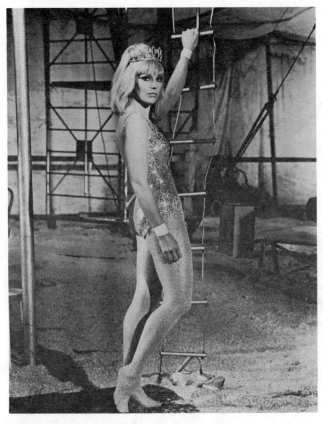

*The Legend of Lylah Clare*

audience. Finch also realizes that, in making this picture, he has sacrificed Novak's life. Although success has been achieved, it turns out to be an empty victory.

Outside the theatre, Finch is completely numbed by what he has done, and, when interviewed, can only mumble, "you make a terrible mistake and your only consolation is that you thought that you had learned something and then you gather up the courage to try again . . . till you suddenly realize that all you have learned is how to make the same mistake again, perhaps differently."

They are interrupted by a commercial. Serving as a mirror for the audience, Falk watches it on her television set at home. She loads two bullets in a gun (as she had warned Finch she would do: "If you hurt this girl . . . I'll kill you . . . ") that she holds in one hand as she sits with a drink in the other hand, waiting for the director to show up. The second bullet is obviously meant for herself.

Extensive coverage is given to the dog-food commercial and there is instant horror when too many dogs descend and bark threateningly. In the final freeze frame, the savage beast is revealed within the tamest pet and serves to symbolize the destructive selfishness within all human beings.

\*     \*

When she emerges from her dressing room attired in spangled tights and a red velvet cloak, she refuses the aid of a double. Falk is concerned and warns her not to "look down." Novak is then raised up to the trapeze swing. Her first attempt is perfect, and she completes the difficult flying feat. Finch demands another take "just for protection," and she does it again.

After the second take has been completed, Finch tries to get her to look below, saying, "your audience is down here," while Novak is trying to ignore him. Novak, via flashback, relives the death one more time, and, finally, she looks down and falls. Landing in the net, she is hurled from it and bounced to the ground, where she breaks her neck. Finch keeps the cameras rolling on the dying Novak and gets her to say the last line in the script, "I love you, Louis." The camera is still rolling as her eyes close and then Finch has the lens focus on the trapeze swing, still in movement.

This scene is repeated as Finch and the others view it at the film's premiere at Grauman's Chinese Theatre, and the movie is a huge success with the opening night

The famous Grauman's Chinese Theatre in the heart of Hollywood, and the setting for some of that city's most celebrated movie premieres, again became the scene for a glamorous and star-studded movie opening. All the usual "first night" festivities marked the occasion—lights, cameras, street crowds, TV and radio interviews with the famous screen personalities in the theatre forecourt.

The event was staged during the filming of *The Legend of Lylah Clare* and depicted the unfurling of a Kim Novak film in the story. And, just like the movie, when the actual premiere of the film version of *The Legend of Lylah Clare* was held and the picture was unveiled, the event was staged at Grauman's Chinese Theatre. This time it was for *real* rather than for *reel*. Kim arrived in town from her hideaway in Big Sur for the event. It was almost like the Hollywood of yesteryear. The bleachers around the famed old theatre were packed, and fans of all ages lined Hollywood Boulevard for two blocks at the gala premiere.

They were there to see Kim, the sex goddess, who

With fans and photographers at the premiere

had been away from the Hollywood scene for a long time. They carried signs—"We Love Kim," "Glad to Have You Back," "Sock It to 'Em, Kim"—and chanted, "We want Kim" over and over again. When she finally arrived, a roar went up from the crowd, some of whom had been waiting hours just to catch a glimpse of her. Like a true star, Kim didn't disappoint them.

She was dressed in a bare-midriff Indian-style ensemble of white kid, complete with beads and fringe hanging from the long sleeves, over a tanned torso. She wore a blonde Cleopatra wig, and, in her navel, was a

large diamond—"eight carats," she told a radio interviewer. With her was handsome, bearded Joel Thomas, who owned a restaurant in Carmel, and Kim and Thomas made a splendid couple.

As for the diamond in Kim's navel (shades of *Kiss Me, Stupid*), she admitted, confidentially, that it wasn't real at all. It was paste. After the movie, celebrities and the press sipped champagne in the forecourt of Grauman's. Then many of them headed for the Factory (which was an "in" spot at the time) and Kim arrived just as the establishment was closing. When she told the maitre d' she had never been there, he took her on a royal tour.

Still later that evening, patrons at Canter's delicatessen also got more than their lox and bagels when the glamorous sight of Kim dazzled them out of their seats. She walked in to order a stack of hot pastrami sandwiches on rye, with dill pickles, for a quiet celebration back at the Beverly Wilshire hotel. The late party was held in Peter Finch's suite and included Finch's wife, Eletha, and Kim's friend Joel Thomas. Also in the group were Michael Murphy (featured in the film) and Alida Aldrich, the daughter of producer-director Robert Aldrich, who had also worked on it.

*       *

As with most of the films that Hollywood has ever made about itself, the major thrust of *The Legend of Lylah Clare* is that success is tough, and Hollywood destroys.

Kim did a fine job in the film and never looked more beautiful. The first choice for this role was Jeanne Moreau, who would have been sadly miscast. Kim was far better suited to the part than the very talented, but older, French star. It would have been a difficult assignment for any actress. During a large portion of the film, when Kim assumed the role of Lylah, the voice of Hildegard Knef was dubbed to give the proper German accent required, along with the constant maniacal laughter, and this didn't make matters easy. It was strange to hear these sounds coming from Kim's mouth. The part, playing of two characters within the same personality, was reminiscent of her previous work in *Vertigo*.

Audiences found it confusing plotwise, but, nevertheless, it would later become a cult film. Kim gave a fine performance and held her own throughout the proceedings. Studying her work at great length, she revealed much that had not previously been noted in her characterizations, and she used her eyes to great advantage in scenes where she was given little or no dialogue. She had perfected her technique and was continuing to improve her craft. You believed what was reflected in her eyes.

*The Legend of Lylah Clare* is a fascinating film to watch and holds the viewer spellbound. You can never quite figure out exactly what was meant to be deliberate or understated. Kim was given a herculean task when asked to shade her character with so many hues, and to add smatterings of Garbo and Dietrich as well. It

is an interesting performance that becomes more hypnotic with each viewing.

Critics and reviews were equally mixed. Some put this film on their year's worst list while others were fascinated partisans.

Hollywood's *Citizen News* said:

The Legend of Lylah Clare returns Kim Novak to the screen after too long an absence, in a demanding role that is perhaps her best to date. For she is on the screen most of the film's two-hours-plus running time, dramatically pivoting between the naive young actress, Elsa, and the sophisticated, husky-voiced sex goddess, Lylah Clare.

Novak, Finch and Falk tie for honors in the acting department; with Miss Novak, as mentioned before, giving her best performance to date.

Charles Champlin, in the *Los Angeles Times,* noted:

As for Miss Novak, to say that the task of making sense out of Lylah (1) and Lylah (2) is beyond her gifts is misleading: the task would have overwhelmed Sarah Bernhardt in her prime.

As it is, she is put through some Big Scenes (maniacal laughter, that kind of thing) which are fiercely embarrassing to watch.

Richard Schickel, in *Life* magazine, pointed out:

Consider, for example, the principal characters. As Elsa Brinkmann, Miss Novak is required only to do a standard sullen ninny . . . but in flashbacks, where she's old Lylah, and in the film-within-the-film, where she portrays Lylah, she must do Garbo with a soupcon of Tallulah and Bette thrown in—and play it straight.

*Motion Picture Herald* said:

Altogether, its somewhat excessive running time aside, *The Legend of Lylah Clare* weaves an irresistible spell, the spinning of which is helped considerably by a stunning performance from Miss Novak. Always attractive to watch, she reveals here a mastery of technical skill not evident before.

John Mahoney, in the *Hollywood Reporter,* observed:

Both transference and transmigration seem to be implied in Miss Novak's assumption of Lylah's personality, her early reactions in that character repeatedly noted as being beyond her basic metriculation in the period. When she assumes that character, she is given a thick German accent, which aggravates the confusion by being generally unintelligible and frequently badly synched, very likely dubbed by an outsider. Physically, Miss Novak nears perfection, particularly as the star presence, in the process exposing more well-toned flesh than she has previously granted her roles.

*The Legend of Lylah Clare*

*Variety* said:

Film is at its best when it spotlights the dilemma of the girl reincarnating the dead star, especially when Elsa grotesquely switches to Lylah's vulgar German-accented tones and phrases, or when she imagines the scenes of her predecessor's violent demise.

Though only intermittently given a challenging scene or two, Miss Novak brings off her dual role as Elsa-Lylah well, and makes a physically splendid reappearance as well, not incidentally in some of the more revealing and striking gowns (by Renie) of her career. She brings off a near-nude scene with sexy aplomb.

And *Newsweek* magazine said:

In terms of its intentions, the film fights cliches with cliches. Does the legendary Lylah derive too directly from Garbo, Harlow, Dietrich, Monroe or other of the industry's prized legends? Of course she does, and so Aldrich and his writers admit it by endowing her with the most preposterously specific attributes they can find: Harlow's hair, Dietrich's voice, Monroe's pout and Garbo's career—a snippet of simulated old film shows Kim Novak, as Lylah, playing the Garbo role in *Anna Christie*. Does the has-been director's mansion smell of Swanson's house in *Sunset Boulevard?* Absolutely, and so a hyper-horrible Hedda-Louella character asks: "Aren't you borrowing a little heavily from *Sunset Boulevard?*"

Miss Novak, as Elsa and Lylah both, tries her best—a very good best, quite often—to do the impossible, which is to make us laugh at Elsa's imitations of Lylah at the same time she is scaring us with the possibility that Elsa is Lylah. The spectacle is odd, to say the least, when the meek, mousey unknown suddenly throws her head back and hurls forth a lusty laugh or, with the voice of an invisible ventriloquist, speaks Lylah's lines in Lylah's

Germanic baritone. Even then, however, the effect is more unwittingly foolish than intentionally witty, since nothing ever comes of it. Not a single soul in the film seems to notice, let alone react to, the sound of this alter ego zipping in from some Rosicrucian corner of outer space.

\*       \*

Upon completion of *Lylah Clare*, Kim returned to her Big Sur retreat and all one had to do was visualize a beautiful young woman alone—but never lonely. She lived in the house that hugged the seaside rocks near Carmel. She rode her horse, lazed in the sun, and enjoyed the companionship of her beloved animals. In addition to her Arabian horse, she had dogs, cats, and an African pygmy goat. She had her painting, her sculpture, and the folk songs she was writing. And, if she ever did feel the need for people, they were always available.

This was Kim Novak, the intense individualist whom Hollywood's old guard suspected of being a bit batty because she didn't live in Beverly Hills or Bel Air or even a Hollywood canyon. She didn't even make movies any more, except occasionally, when she chose to. But Kim had her own views, as she said:

> I always wonder what's the matter with them, why do they keep pushing and pushing, even after they have all the money they'll ever need? Isn't it enough to enjoy life, to live it as completely as possible?
>
> I've never had much ambition. God knows I'm grateful for what my work has brought me. Without it, I might not have any of the things I really love, like my house and my animals, like being able to do things for my family. I wouldn't change it for anything. But I wouldn't push any harder for any more.
>
> Being successful in the movies can spoil some people; they can get pretty impossible. I think it's because they become entirely consumed by just that, you know? It's their whole life; they have no other outlet.

But many questioned whether the house-by-the-sea and all that went with it was really true happiness for Kim. In reply, Kim put it in this way:

> Oh, God, yes! It's been the answer to so many things. After all, how many of us ever find the right place, the right people? I mean it's my place; I belong there.
>
> I'm anything but lonely. I'm independent; I don't require people in order to have fun. Yet I enjoy people, I enjoy sharing things with them. But I don't need them.

Kim was content to entertain casually at her home when the feeling moved her, but not to do anything lavish, as one would expect from a glamorous movie star. And who's to say she wasn't having more fun than her sister stars who lived in the heart of Hollywood and were never out of the glare of the limelight? As she put it:

> I don't entertain formally. I'll make a big pot of chili and have a bunch of friends over and we'll talk and play music. Things like that. A lot of the people around here are artists and musicians . . . all whom I would call free spirits. They have the courage to lead their own lives in their own kind of way, and they're not afraid to express themselves. We have a mutual respect and comradery.

As for romance, the man she was currently spending time with was still Joel Thomas. They had much in common. Each had their own horse and they enjoyed riding together. He loved the sea as much as Kim did, and they enjoyed many of the same other interests. However, she had no plans for marriage at this time. And, as for working in the future, Kim said, "I have no scheduled future. If a part is offered me and I find it irresistible, I'll go with it."

251

# 15

Soon after the premiere of *The Legend of Lylah Clare,* Warner Brothers-Seven Arts persuaded Kim to remain in Hollywood long enough to make another film, *The Great Bank Robbery,* which began shooting in late August 1968. Melina Mercouri had originally been cast for the female lead in this comedy-oater but bowed out at the last minute. Kim, as the replacement, was an odd choice to be cast opposite Zero Mostel.

She also had some unusual reasons for taking the assignment, her first western. As she stated:

> I should have done this years ago. I love it and I love riding horses which I do a lot. I also love the outdoors, and this picture has me in it all day long.
>
> *The Great Bank Robbery* is a funny way-out kind of mod western. It's *Bonnie and Clyde* in a different period. This time, it is set in 1880. There's physical action and a minimum of dialogue, both of which reflect my way of life—a kind of close-to-earth living. The film's plot is so funny it gives zest to each day's work.

The "physical action" that Kim referred to was similar to what she had done in *The Amorous Adventures of Moll Flanders.* She had a good time with it and was extremely proficient.

Fun was the order of the day during the making of *The Great Bank Robbery.* The mood on the set was light, and Kim thoroughly enjoyed the experience. She also applied her "do-it-yourself" philosophy in regard to her make-up, although she did leave the finishing touches to the artists employed. She expressed her feelings in this way:

> It's so easy, on a movie set, to get into the habit of having everything done for you. The most competent people are in our business, which is all the more reason why I feel I must do as much as possible for myself. It is one way to retain an essence of balance.

Her makeup for this film was quite different from the usual. It was the start of the "new look" that Kim would have in all of her future screen appearances. She used a very pale shade of lipstick, and, except for eye-shadow, eye-liner, and mascara (which made her eyes appear dark and dramatic), she had a more natural look.

In keeping with her "do-it-yourself" style, Kim assumed the complete care and grooming of her horse, Big Sur, which she rode for two hours after each day's work. Riding the animal to the studio every morning from the motel where she stayed while filming, she was a curious sight for passersby near Burbank. The studio gateman, too, was surprised to see a star arriving on horseback the first morning that Kim reported for work.

The horse was used in an important scene where Kim rode through the town, a la Lady Godiva, to distract the men guarding the bank. Kim's curves were shown to advantage through a long blonde wig, strategically placed daisies, and very little else. Director Hy Averback shot the scene for several days, and all who could possibly find a reason for being on this set tried their damndest to show up. Averback had Kim riding through the town at top speed, then bringing the horse to a halt and making it rear. Fortunately, Kim is an experienced horsewoman so she had no difficulty with the task—but riding bareback and bare did complicate things. Needless to say, she breathed a sigh of relief when the sequence was completed.

Kim also found it fun to wear period costumes once again. Although her clothes weren't nearly as lavish as those she had worn in *Moll Flanders,* she carried them with the classic style they required. In her opening scenes on the train, she wore a black dress of the period and a large brimmed hat with a bird perched on top. During the scenes in which she and the other members of Mostel's group are supposed to have walked twenty miles, Kim enjoyed "dirtying" her face along with the costume to help create the illusion.

Ruth Warrick was cast in the film as the second female lead. Warrick was a shapely woman, but, for her part of the widow, her bosom had been padded out to enormous size. At the time, Warrick stated, "I'm supposed to be pious, but as the picture goes on and guys make passes at me, it gets to be a bosom contest between Kim and me." "Yes," agreed Kim, "and to look at her like that gives me inhibitions."

There were hardly any reasons for Kim to feel "inhibitions" as far as competition from Warrick was concerned. There was more of Kim revealed in this film than ever before. Although she had previously shed her clothing (in *Jeanne Eagels, Pal Joey, The Notorious Landlady, Of Human Bondage, The Amorous Adventures of Moll Flanders,* and *The Legend of Lylah Clare*), this time she shed more and more frequently. In addition to the "Lady Godiva" sequence, Kim was seen throughout the film in various stages of undress. There was also a "bubble bath" and a "psychedelic trip on peyote" which prompted her (in the script) to do a "strip" to seduce Clint Walker and make him aware of her ample charms.

A major prop for the film was the world's largest passenger-carrying hot-air balloon that was used in the final sequences when Mostel, Kim, and the others try to make their escape. The balloon was ten stories high and 130 feet around. Its egg-shaped interior contained close to 250,000 cubic feet of hot air which was manufactured by four liquid-propane gas burners. Two teams of seamstresses built the balloon at a cost of $45,000. Six passengers could ride—but not necessarily with comfort—in the gondola basket, and it had to be properly licensed by the Federal Aviation Administration.

The balloon sequences were filmed at Sonora and Placerita Canyon. The site of the latter was the location of the Walt Disney Golden Oak Ranch and marked the area where the famed California Gold Rush took place in the 1840s. All of this added a further touch of realism to the proceedings.

\*　　　\*

The madcap plot of *The Great Bank Robbery* spoofs the outlaw image of the 1890s and begins with an ancient train steaming across the western plains. Aboard the train is a band of crooks posing as itinerant evangelists: Zero Mostel, the leader; John Fiedler, a dynamite man; Peter Whitney, an expert engineer; and Novak, a former "cooch" dancer and "illusionist" who is also Mostel's paramour. Although posing as a religious group, the four thieves are really en route to the small Western town of Friendly to rob the local bank.

As the train moves along, Mostel and his group give out with a hearty version of "Bringing in the Sheaves" with Novak throwing in several zesty "Hallelujahs" for good measure. Bandits, led by Claude Akins, interrupt the songfest, rob the train, and murder the crew. Once the bandits have departed and the smoke has cleared, Mostel leads his group to Friendly on foot. The idea of evangelism isn't appealing to Novak, who continues to beat her tambourine and sing as the disheveled group makes its way along the dusty railroad tracks. Novak considers their masquerade "a lot of trouble just to rob another bank."

Novak: Would the Reverend Pious please tell me why we have to do this?
Mostel: Would Sister Lyda please tell me how else we could rob this bank?

And Novak gives him her best *Lylah Clare* laugh. She'll

*The Great Bank Robbery*

*The Great Bank Robbery,* **with Zero Mostel**

*The Great Bank Robbery,* **with Clint Walker**

*The Great Bank Robbery*, with Clint Walker

go along with the charade to please her man.

Once in the town, Mostel continues his role as reverend of a nondemoninational sect spreading "the gospel of love through the church of the cosmic heart." Mostel is welcomed as a replacement for the present pastor who is leaving for missionary work in Samoa. After the dusty walk into town, Novak is hurried away from the townspeople by Ruth Warrick, who begins to wonder about the whole group when Novak says, "These clothes . . . I gotta get my clothes off," and proceeds to open the buttons of her bodice. Warrick takes Novak to her place where the latter relaxes in a tub full of bubbles.

Mostel, with his benign disguise and wiles, also enchants widow Warrick and the other ladies of Friendly. His first sermon is praised and Novak contributes to the service by being the organist. Safely installed as pastor, Mostel and his band then start digging a tunnel from the church to the bank, an establishment which is none too honest either.

"The good Lord will provide" when it comes time to cover the noise of blasting the tunnel—and, to do this, Mostel belts out the song "A Rainbow Rider" in which everyone merrily joins. It ends up in a free-for-all with Novak hanging from a chandelier and finally crashing seat first through a drum.

During the coming Fourth of July celebration, Mostel plans to strip the bank. His little band of bogus churchmen is joined by Sam Jaffe, who, in the guise of a portrait-painter of bank president John Anderson, will create a giant backdrop picture of the inside of the bank. During the actual robbery, it will be hung in front of the robbers so that people outside the building will see only an empty room. It will be Novak's job to divert the bank guards when the robbery takes place.

Unknown to Mostel and his group, two fumbling Mexican bandits, Akim Tamiroff and Larry Storch, are simultaneously planning to set off their own fireworks by ramming a juggernaut into the bank. To complicate matters further, still another tunnel to the bank is underway, this one from a phony laundry opened by Clint Walker, a Texas Ranger, out to seize ledgers that will expose the bank's crooked operations.

Novak is dissatisfied with one aspect of Mostel's program. She's getting "restless" because he hasn't made love to her since the planning started. At a town dance, Novak meets Walker, and his quiet manliness excites her. Before Walker knows it, Novak has kissed him, and he is apologizing to her for *his* forwardness.

Novak:   Did you like it?
Walker:  Just cuz I talk slow don't mean I'm peculiar.

Voices from Walker's men digging on the other side of the tunnel are being heard as both tunnels are nearing completion. And now everyone is beginning to suspect everyone else. Akins suspects Walker of being something other than a laundryman, and Mostel also begins to be suspicious of Walker's activities. As a result, Mostel orders Novak to go out with Walker, pump him for information, and keep him away from the tunnel for three hours. Novak's feelings for Walker fight with her loyalty to Mostel, so she is at first reluctant to accept the instructions. But finally she agrees.

Novak:   What if he attacks me?
Mostel:  That's the risk *he'll* have to take.

Novak sidetracks Walker, whose aides (six Chinese Secret Servicemen) continue digging. During the picnic lunch by a brook, Novak feeds Walker some "candy" that she had obtained from an Indian. The "candy" has been spiked with peyote, a drug like marijuana but made out of cactus, and it sends both into a psychedelic haze in which Novak does a striptease and seduces Walker. He, however, is not quite sure who has done what to whom, and thinks—maybe—that he has seduced her.

While Mostel instructs the Chinese laundrymen in the teachings of Christ, his partners dynamite the rival tunnel which they have discovered. After returning from his "trip" with Novak, Walker begins to suspect that Mostel may also be tunneling into the bank. Walker also suspects that Novak may be part of the robbery plot and he asks her to leave Mostel. In response, Novak kisses Walker while, at the same time knocking him out with a blackjack because she knows there is work to be done and "the great bank robbery" is about to begin. She does have second thoughts, although only for a moment, and Novak confesses to the unconscious Walker:

I'm sure gonna miss ya but I can't leave Harry [Mostel], see, cuz he needs me. Not the way you do but, well, I've been with him all these years, see, and he kind of loves me in his way. I figure I owe it!

And, although she does have strong feelings for Walker, she is duty bound.

*The Great Bank Robbery*

At 5:00 A.M., Mostel and his group crawl through their completed tunnel into the darkened bank. To prevent their activity from being seen, they hang the backdrop in front of the vault; Jaffe has painted it to look exactly like the actual vault. Novak provides her promised distraction for the guards on the upper floor by appearing in the night as the ghost of Lady Godiva, a naked apparition on a phosphorescent horse. She not only distracts the guards—she stuns them!

At the same moment that the cannon is fired to mark the dawn of the Fourth of July, the vault is dynamited open. However, just as Mostel thinks his plan is successful, the Chinese Secret Servicemen, who have dug into Mostel's tunnel by mistake, stumble into the bank. After a free-for-all, the Chinese are chased through the bank, captured, and jailed by Mostel before they can spread the alarm. Walker, meanwhile, is still tied and gagged. Mostel and company take their loot and their musical instruments and head for the nearby balloon-launching site, where "the preacher" is scheduled to deliver "a sermon in the air" before their getaway. As a goodbye gift, Novak leaves the ledger for Walker after kissing him farewell.

Before the balloon can take off, John Larch, the sheriff, discovers the robbery and the imprisoned Chinese. From the note on the door, reading "It is better to give than to receive," he knows that Mostel is the guilty party. The chase is on! The sheriff releases Tamiroff, who has been in jail, and the Mexican bandit reaches the street just in time to see his gang, under Storch's leadership, assault the now empty bank with a juggernaut.

Mostel and his group are barely airborne when the word reaches the Fourth of July celebrants that the preacher and his companions are actually bank robbers. Bullets tear into the air sack and the balloon is crippled, unable to gain sufficient altitude for a clean escape. The musical instruments and all available ballast are jettisoned to gain height; however, the balloon remains low in the air and at the mercy of the prevailing winds. They ascend but are still dangerously close to the train below, which is filled with their pursuers.

Punctured by bullets, the balloon descends, and the passengers find themselves back at the bank. There Akins demands that Mostel hand over the loot. Walker, after killing Akins in a shootout, also demands the gold and reveals his true identity as a Texas Ranger. The idea of losing the gold is repugnant to Mostel. He doesn't want to surrender it and he doesn't want to follow the suggestion of Norman Alden, the pilot, that he dump it so the balloon can ascend. But Novak solves the dilemma for all. She jumps out of the balloon and embraces Walker, letting Mostel sail up and away to newer and more elaborate criminal escapades minus her curvy avoirdupois which is now being held in Walker's sinewy arms.

*        *

Although there were some genuinely funny moments in *The Great Bank Robbery*, it failed to make audiences roll in the aisles. A little bit of everything was tossed into the film with the hope of pleasing viewers, but the mixture only "clogged the drain" and didn't serve its purpose.

*The Great Bank Robbery*

Kim did what little was possible with a minimum of dialogue, but this was not a worthy follow-up to *The Legend of Lylah Clare,* and it did nothing for her career. Visually, she was stunning. Action-wise, she was fine. But the script just didn't afford her anywhere to go as an actress. While it may have been fun to make, its value to her ended there. Reviewers generally agreed that "Present-day cliches are tossed into late-90s western comedy for yocks, and maverick-style humor attempts fall short."

*Variety* said:

Larceny isn't limited to William Peter Blatty's [who would make his mark with *The Exorcist*] screenplay. Akins, Tamiroff, Storch and Miss Warrick steal scenes at every turn. Mostel has a few moments of brightness, but loses out for the most part. Miss Novak works energetically but unsuccessfully, and Walker, in the role of the restrained hero, is restrained.
Songs, "The Rainbow Rider" and "Heaven Helps Him Who Helps Himself," by Sammy Cahn and James Van Heusen, are okay. Pic is too long, goes in too many directions, and reaches for gags. As in the case of the balloon, it limps more often than it flies.

*Motion Picture Herald* noted:

Kim Novak, whose lines consist mostly of "yep" and "nope," is usually seen either in the bathtub or tearing off her clothes. In the Lady Godiva scene, she takes them all off. She is not at her best in this burlesque role.

And John Mahoney, in the *Hollywood Reporter,* said:

Kim Novak co-stars as Mostel's extra-evangelical mistress, neglected as Mostel sets out to steal the money Akins has stolen from the train and had corrupt mayor John Anderson deposit in a "robbery-proof" bank. She gives a satisfactory performance, though comedy is not her thing, and is at her best bodily corrupting Walker, who responds with the reassurance, "Just because I talk slow doesn't mean I'm peculiar."

\*            \*

After completing her first western, Kim headed back to Big Sur to be by herself. As she put it:

I've been trying to find the real me for a long time. The image that Hollywood had of me wasn't me and I knew it. Then when I moved up north to be by myself, I learned what I was really like.

Now I really appreciate things. I always have, but now I feel each moment is important and this is the way I want to live. There's a little cove right underneath my house overlooking the ocean. I watch the whales migrate, and one day one of them came into my cove and had a baby. I watched as they rejoined the herd going south. It's wonderful being so close to nature.

During my brief marriage to Richard, I tried, I really tried. I tried to live in London and all, but just couldn't. I was unhappy and couldn't make anyone else happy. I'm happy now and I feel this helps the people I'm around.

I don't want a lot of possessions. They can finally hem you in. I want to be able to pick up a bag and go anywhere when I feel like it. But if you have a big house, cars, gardeners, cooks and all that, by the time you get through making all the arrangements to go, the exhilaration has gone.

Kim had nothing planned to follow *The Great Bank Robbery.* If a script came that interested her, she would make a decision about returning to work at that time and not before. As she said:

*This Land Is Mine*

Commitments! When I read about actors having commitments for the next three or four or five years, I just shudder. They're prisoners. They can't take a vacation, they're committed. I love my work when I work. I love my home and my life. It's wonderful and I am finding myself.

\*　　　\*

All was not to be peaceful for Kim on her mountaintop retreat, however, when she found herself in court in Salinas, California, in April 1969. Neighbors were complaining about the fact that she boarded so many animals on her property, and the Monterey County Board of Supervisors brought suit against her demanding that she be restrained from keeping some of them.

Although the neighbors said the animals disturbed them, Kim won her case. Yet victory was not altogether pleasant. Kim was deeply hurt by this action and felt it was entirely unwarranted. Some time before, she had purchased additional property near Gull House as an investment, and she now considered building a new home in that more isolated area. As she put it:

> It may sound ridiculous, but I've bought another place only fifteen minutes from my home. It's right in the Redwoods and a completely different atmosphere. I could never live in a big city and be with lots of people all the time, so I'm looking forward to living there in the not-too-distant future.

Neighbors rarely, if ever, saw their famous neighbor except on occasions when she went into the nearest town to purchase provisions for herself and the animals. Local residents now referred to her as The Hermit of the area—but these were not the friends she had made when she first came to settle there; those people remained loyal to their "free spirit." In an effort to maintain her privacy, Kim further annoyed the troublesome few because anyone coming near her property was kept at a distance by her goat, affectionately named Creature, and a Dalmation christened Paloosa. All Kim had ever wanted was a peaceful existence. And now she was thoroughly convinced that one day soon she would be forced to move further into the redwood area in order to find it. Thus she put Gull House on the market and went ahead with plans for building. But her move would not be an immediate one.

She did consent to do a promotional tour in behalf of *The Great Bank Robbery* when it was released but, after that, the world would see and hear very little of her for a while.

\*　　　\*

Her next appearance was on a documentary television special. Since Elizabeth Taylor had shown TV viewers England, and Sophia Loren had done the same for Rome (not to mention Melina Mercouri's tour of Greece and Inger Stevens's of Sweden), what would be better than to have Kim in the naturalistic setting of Big Sur? "This Land Is Mine" aired on the ABC television network on 6 April 1970.

Since the rugged majesty of California's Big Sur held "the kind of beauty that can really make you cry—but tears like no other tears," as Kim described the area, she was agreeable to appearing as the viewers' guide when producer Lester Cooper pitched her the idea. Having lived in the area for a number of years, she was a logical choice.

This documentary, dealing with America's vanishing natural beauty, showed Kim in the area surrounding Gull House, accompanied by her goat and one of her dogs, Chili. Photographed on the rocks, Kim looked down at the ocean below and later was seen fording the Big Sur River astride her horse. Casually attired in black pants and a purple top with a gold chained medallion and gold link belt, Kim, with her hair falling loosely, seemed completely at ease amid the familiar surroundings she loved so dearly.

Kim also did the vocalizing for "Tides," a ballad she had written with Al Shackman. Her voice was pleasant, and Kim's guitar strumming to her own composition was in keeping with her mood of the moment. She seemed totally relaxed and very much at ease. This also gave the viewer a good insight as to why Kim loved the area so much. One could readily agree that this was "a very special place."

\*　　　\*

Finally, in the fall of 1972, Aaron Spelling and Leonard Goldberg (who headed Spelling-Goldberg Productions) tempted Kim to make her television acting debut in an ABC-TV "Movie of the Week." Having long been a television holdout, Kim agreed to do *Home for the Holidays* because she felt it would afford her an emotional workout in a taut and tense drama. She knew it wasn't a great script but figured it would at least prove that she was still alive. She had recently read a question-and-answer column to which someone had written asking if she were.

Shortly before *Home for the Holidays* was to go into production, however, Kim had to bow out. Her mother had suffered a stroke in Florida, and Kim rushed to her bedside. Kim was replaced by Eleanor Parker in the telefilm which aired to no more than lukewarm acceptance by the critics.

\*　　\*

In December of the same year, Kim found herself back in England for a return to filming at Shepperton Studios where she had previously done *Moll Flanders*. It was ironic that, once again, as had happened at the start of her career, she was a replacement for Rita Hayworth. Production had started on *Tales That Witness Madness* with Hayworth in the starring role of this all-British-cast horror-drama. After a few days of shooting, Hayworth did not appear on the set. She couldn't be located (although it was later reported that illness had forced her exit), so the producer summoned Kim to take over the role. Within a matter of days, she was on her way to England to star in her first film, ending a three-year absence from the screen.

Kim was intrigued by the maze of devious twists and turns in the screenplay and the fact that *Tales That Witness Madness* embodied four self-contained films in one, with linking sequences set in an eerie clinic. In addition to the aspects of the role that appealed to her when she was told about it was the fact that the shooting schedule was very brief and she would not have to be away from home and her animals for any great length of time. Her part was completed in a week and she received $100,000 for her services.

The irony of the situation was the fact that history was repeating itself. After being touted as Harry Cohn's replacement for Rita Hayworth's throne at Columbia Studios, Kim once again found herself taking over for the same actress. There are those who have speculated as to which of the two ladies was the more fortunate as far as this particular property was concerned. Nevertheless, Kim plunged into the assignment, determined to give it all she could.

Actress Mary Tamm (who played the role of her daughter) remembered the experience in this way:

My acquaintance with Kim Novak was brief. One week to be exact—and during that time I think we only worked together on two or three scenes. At the time, my impressions were probably slightly colored through my nervousness—not only about Miss Novak's reputation but also because this was my very first screen role.

However, I can say that I was very impressed with her as an actress—she was extremely professional, and with none of the unapproachability one usually associates with big stars. She was very charming and friendly towards me and executed her role in the picture more than efficiently, as she stepped into the part at very short notice and completed it within a week. Obviously, she must have worked very hard on the role in her own time. I personally think that she has great charisma on the screen.

From a professional point of view—she is an unselfish actress, as one example from our work together illustrates. We filmed in extremely cold weather, and I had a scene with her where I was dressed only in a bikini, and as you can imagine—it was freezing! I remember her being very concerned about my not catching cold, and trying to get through the scene as speedily and efficiently as possible for my benefit. I found this attitude admirable and refreshing. I thoroughly enjoyed working with her very much.

\*　　\*

*Tales That Witness Madness* begins with a connective device linking four separate stories of the supernatural and is recounted by one of the doctors treating four of the patients in a mental hospital. The head of a research clinic, Donald Pleasence, discusses the inmates with old friend Jack Hawkins, and together they view the patients through glass-walled rooms. The patients are Russell Lewis, Peter McEnery, Michael Jayston, and the lone female, Novak. Each has his own fantasy. Pleasence recounts four violent cases that supposedly prove a mysterious theory, and we are enlightened as to how each of them arrived at the hospital.

In the first grisly episode a boy has an imaginary tiger that he seems to see but his quarrelsome parents do not. We know almost immediately what can be expected, and the naughty little boy has figured out a sly way to end Mommy and Daddy's late-night brawls for good.

The second story is a truly frightening tale about a young antique-shop owner who is possessed by a photograph of his dead uncle. In a houseful of furniture he has inherited from his aunt he finds a bicycle that can pedal its rider backwards in time to another century and another life.

In the third tale, a man carts into his house a tree with a rather human shape. The tree cries when it is neglected. We see the man's wife objecting to the falling leaves on her living room rug and the tree becoming jealous of the wife. In time, the man takes a fancy to the tree's shapeliness, and, after he disposes of

*This Land Is Mine*

*Tales That Witness Madness*

his wife, he and the tree remain together.

The final segment is aptly titled *Luau*. It concerns a wealthy literary agent, Novak, who arranges a luau for one of her clients. Unknown to her, the client, played by Michael Petrovitch, is a practitioner of voodoo, and he casts a shadow on her life using a South Seas tribal myth.

According to ancient superstition, Petrovitch's mother's soul will only be saved from eternal torment if her celibate son carries out a human sacrifice at the next full moon. The victim must be a virgin girl, and, at a ceremonial feast after the killing, Petrovitch must burn some hair from the girl's head as a token to her mother and must eat of the young maiden's flesh.

Petrovitch and a companion, Leon Lissek, arrive as houseguests in Novak's luxurious home in England. Novak solicits her daughter, Mary Tamm, to help entertain Petrovitch. A complaining Tamm changes her mind when she sees the dark young stranger.

There is a very good scene between Novak and Tamm in which Novak says, "I forget, we don't talk about how old we are." Tamm counters with a bitchy, "Either of us." While Novak is in sexual pursuit of her handsome writer-client, he is more interested in her daughter. Novak continues to proceed with the elaborate plans for a full Hawaiian feast in her client's honor.

Petrovitch is entranced and disturbed by Tamm's innocent sensuality and more than ever aware of his solemn and grim duty. After establishing the fact that Tamm is a virgin, he knows that he can assure that the spirit of his dead mother will rest in peace. Petrovitch and Lissek make the preparations for their ritual killing.

While busy with her own preparations for the party, Novak is unaware of the ritual that is being performed around her. Later that evening, there is a full moon. The festivities are in progress. The music is playing. While Novak is getting into the swing of things by repeating Petrovitch's ritualistic mumbo-jumbo of "Mamaluke . . . Mamaluke," we are aware of what the medium-rare roast beef she is about to eat really is.

Is it any wonder that the four inmates are tormented and suffering from obsessions and hallucinations? After telling the tales, Pleasence presents his theory to Hawkins. The unconvinced Hawkins has Pleasence carried off by burly attendants, only to be, himself, attacked by the invisible tiger at the fadeout.

\*     \*

*Tales That Witness Madness*, with Mary Tamm

*Tales That Witness Madness* was Kim's first, and hopefully her last, experience in the horror genre. In accepting the role, as previously stated, she was intrigued by the "twists and turns" in the screenplay. In the final release print, most of the "twists and turns" did not intrigue the audience. The fact that she was supposed to be eating her own daughter's flesh was just more than some members of the audiences could accept.

Ever since her hypnotic performance in Hitchcock's *Vertigo*, Kim had been searching for a suspense film that might equal its success. In the role of the beautiful "Auriol Pageant," a woman who suffers strange mental agony over the fate of her innocent young daughter, Kim failed in her search.

The part would have been better played by an older actress. This character called for a more fluttery type who could be believed throughout. Expecting any actress to be "giddy and man hungry at the same time" (as one reviewer put it) is a tall order—and when she looks like Kim, it's even harder to believe. Although she tried valiantly to convey what was expected—because the dialogue was minimal—Kim wasn't able to take it any further. She had accepted the role hurriedly; it was simply a case of miscasting.

Nothing was spared to make *Tales That Witness Madness* a class production. Ace art director Roy Walker (who worked on such examples of beauty as *Ryan's Daughter*) created a set that matched the nightmare

267

*Tales That Witness Madness,* **with Lesley Nunnerley**

effect of the tales. The clinic was all in white—floors, walls, ceilings—and the four patients were observed in ultramodern and impersonal surroundings. Against this white background, in the opening sequence, is Novak, black-clad from neck to toe. The visual effect is startling.

About the production, director Freddie Francis said:

You really can't complain about being type-cast as a dispenser of macabre movie magic. We have had the help of some of the best actors and technicians in the business. Spine-chillers have attracted much of the cream of the profession. Who am I to be snobbish? My bank manager is a very happy man and if he's happy so am I. Cinema is make-believe and so much of this type of film is purest fantasy. You've got to let audiences get ahead of you, but first make sure they're on the wrong track.

If audiences were on "the wrong track," critics were definitely on "the right track" in reviewing this entry

in the horror sweepstakes. And one couldn't argue with their observations.

*Product Digest* said:

Best of the mediocre lot (if there is such a thing) is the final one, which stars Kim Novak as a rich literary agent . . . The return of Ms. Novak to the screen after an absence of four years might have been a selling point for the picture had she not appeared just the other day to much better advantage on television in an entertaining feature made expressly for that medium *The Third Girl from the Left).*

*Variety* stated:

*Tales That Witness Madness* is a deliberately comedic quartet of horror short stories, interconnected by scenes at a clinic . . . Freddie Francis as usual directs with flair, economy and effect. Kim Novak seems to be the only non-British cast member. Norman Priggen produced smartly for World Film Services. Episodic films are generally jinxed at the b.o., but perhaps among the popcorn-and-horror-buff trade, where the film has its potential, an exception will be proved. The Paramount release is a fun programmer, but the domestic R rating (there's some nonerotic nudity) may limit its b.o. spectrum ... Finally, Novak is featured [in the last segment] titled *Luau*, [and] this segment ends with a Polynesian banquet where the guests get more to eat than they bargained for. Novak's acting is awful, never in command of the role in which she must be giddy but man-hungry at the same time. But the plot gimmick sort of carries the ball to conclusion.

Alan R. Howard, in the *Hollywood Reporter*, noted:

Three out of four is a respectable ratio, and since the first and weakest episode in *Tales That Witness Madness* is the shortest, this movie produced by Norman Priggen and directed with care by Freddie Francis is an entertaining amusement.

Kim Novak stars in *Luau*, a terrifying tale of voodoo in which a nervous, superficial literary agent (Novak) stumbles upon madness during the sexual pursuit of her handsome writer-client, played by Michael Petrovitch. Novak gives perhaps her first character performance, and her other-worldly presence mixes well with the outrageously fluttery agent.

Kim had put an end to her self-imposed vacation to star in *Tales That Witness Madness*. She never spoke of how or why she happened to replace Hayworth in the film and turned it off with, "That's between the producers of the film and Miss Hayworth."

While Kim had remained off the screen too long a time to have returned in such an ill-fated property, she had learned many years before that one couldn't possibly be a winner at all times. Sometimes it was just impossible to rise above bad scripting. But, very shortly, she would be able to surpass this performance with one of substance and far greater realism.

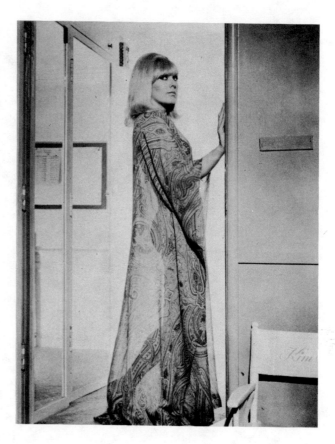

# 16

Since her previous attempt to do a movie for television, which had been halted due to her mother's illness, Kim continued to read the scripts submitted to her, rejecting all of them. She preferred to wait until the right property was proffered and continued to hold strongly to the idea that she had to believe in what she was doing in order to deliver her best.

It was Edward Rissien, executive vice-president of Playboy Productions, who finally succeeded in enticing Kim away from her favorite role of solitary artist and animal lover. "It took a lot of reassurance to get her," he said, "but what really did it was Dory Previn's script."

The property was *The Third Girl from the Left*, and it became Kim's first full-length television movie. "I liked the script," she said at the time, and added, "There aren't many stories written for women these days and this really delves into one."

It was a new departure for composer-lyricist Previn who wrote the screenplay. Her biting dialogue and insight stemmed, she admitted, from hindsight. She'd been a chorus girl, and her story posed an interesting question. "What happens to old chorus girls? Are they disposable? Do you throw them away like Kleenex?" To answer the question, Previn focused on "the last of the species"—an over-the-hill chorus girl who finds herself at the end of her reign with nowhere to go.

Tony Curtis and Michael Brandon were set for the two male leads, and Hungarian-born Peter Medak directed. It was Medak's first film assignment in the United States.

\*       \*

*The Third Girl from the Left* begins with a realistic view of chorus life backstage in a New York cabaret. As the credits are flashed on the screen, there is a series of in-depth close-ups of Novak applying makeup before a dressing room mirror as she attempts to lop off fifteen years for the ordeal she is about to face. The haunting look on her face sets the exact tone to exemplify the vulnerability and toughness embedded in her character.

Mascara-ed, sequined, and rhinestoned, Novak next stands ready to face her audience at Manhattan's Carioca Club where she has danced for fourteen years. Suddenly, at the age of thirty-six, her world of dance and daydreams is rudely shaken. Her boss shunts her from the front line of the chorus to the back, where she becomes a symbol of all women who have been used as

*The The Third Girl from the Left*

*The Third Girl from the Left*

sex objects and then tossed aside. As he bluntly puts it, "When the face goes, baby, you've had it." The personal hurt, embarrassment, and fear register in Novak's eyes while she continues in silence.

In her offstage life, Novak still cherishes hopes that her thirteen-year affair with an egotistical stand-up comedian, played by Tony Curtis, will end in marriage. He gives her mink coats, yet she has always worked and paid her own way. Her years of loyalty have not been easy, and she has had to put up with his self-indulgences and other women.

Curtis leaves for a Las Vegas engagement just when Novak needs him most, after being relegated to the back line of the chorus. The whole experience has left her devastated, and, with Curtis away, she is, therefore, vulnerable to the advances of a delivery boy dropout, Michael Brandon, who is twenty-three—the exact age she was when she fell for Curtis.

Novak's self-delusions are further challenged when she is pursued by the younger man. He gives her youth, freedom, and, she succumbs to his allure, and even resolves to go off with him on his return to college. Their scenes together are quite touching.

With Brandon, Novak has a very different relationship from the one she has known with Curtis. But, in spite of the happy times, it is apparent that Brandon, like Curtis, thinks of her more as an object than a person. Lines such as Novak's "Garbage is so depressing," and Brandon's "Garbage is great," show how far apart they are in their outlooks. At moments like this, the film has a kind of lost, ethereal quality that gently emphasizes its theme.

In one scene, Novak is taken to a swap meet by Brandon where someone wants to swap her for something. This is one more reference to "object" as opposed to "person"—and one more way of showing that

*The Third Girl from the Left*

she's a remainder from a time gone by.

After discovering Novak and Brandon in a compromising situation, Curtis berates her for her lack of morals. The realization that she has gone to bed with the younger man is more than he can face. Novak lashes out at him with all her pent-up emotion. She tells him he has never cared enough about her to take an interest in anything that mattered to her. He hasn't even bothered to look at the paintings she has done, including her most cherished work which hangs in her bedroom. It is the one thing that he has had ample opportunity to observe, but he hasn't made the effort.

In the end, with her bags packed, Novak realizes she has nowhere to go. The club has gone topless, and she's out of a job without even being asked whether or not she would be willing to continue. Through with Brandon because of the age difference, and wanting desperately to start a new life, she realizes that it's too late for her. She cannot cope. Thus she decides to return to Curtis—and more of his abuse.

The film ends with a freeze frame on her face. The anguish, helplessness, and disgust at having to settle for something less than she wants are all mirrored in her expression.

\*          \*

*The Third Girl from the Left* aired on ABC television on 16 October 1973, just prior to the release of *Tales That Witness Madness.* It was a perfect selection for an initial venture into television, and Kim was right to accept the role. After completing it, she said:

I was getting a reputation for being unwilling to work, which wasn't true. I have always said that when I read a script that could give me something better than what I have going at home, I would work. The part I played in this film was a chorus girl who was struggling to find herself and come to grips with relationships and life. I like parts with what I call counterpoint in them, playing against something to achieve something.

I had heard that the pace of television would be very difficult for somebody not accustomed to it but I didn't have any trouble with it.

It was great. I worked one stretch from five in the afternoon to seven in the morning. I have never minded working long hours or doing many takes as long as I feel people are working together to improve something.

I was nervous at first having never done television. But I'd rather work intensely for a short time than with less intensity over a longer period. It's hard to sit in the dressing room between takes. In television you can stay geared up always. You can keep at the right emotional level.

Kim entered television movies at a point where they most resembled the big studio movies in which she had starred for Columbia, Paramount, MGM and Warner Brothers. Movies made for television have a more leisurely time span for their production. They are not subjected to quite the same rush as the series episodes that require an actor to study next week's script while shooting this week's.

Kim celebrated her fortieth birthday during the making of *The Third Girl from the Left,* and, although she had usually been a "loner" during most of her previous films, this time she did not rush off to her dressing room between takes. She talked with other members of the cast and crew and became an integral part of the production group during her free time.

Michael Conrad, who appeared in the film, stated:

She attacked the dancing gamely and fitted in quite well with the professional dancers with the result that she was very believable as an older "gypsy".

*The Third Girl from the Left*, **with Tony Curtis**

I have always felt that acting is a spontaneous, fresh expression of one's true experiences and, while I considered Miss Novak to be quite mannered, I greatly admired her professionalism and her femininty. She is lovely and very deserving of her movie star status.

To prepare herself for this role, which required dancing, Kim worked untiringly with choreographer Miriam Nelson (who had previously aided her on *The Great Bank Robbery)* to perfect the dance sequences and master the high kicks, but this should come as no surprise to anyone who knew of Kim's determination. If she believed in doing something, she believed in doing it to the best of her ability. There were no short cuts in her personal and/or professional aims, and she never sought short-term methods when more time was necessary.

Dory Previn remembered their working relationship in this way:

I thought she was an excellent choice for the role of "Gloria Joyce" and working on the film with Kim Novak was very gratifying. She is a mysterious combination of a bewildered woman and a wise child.

Kim was the perfect choice to reflect the glamour and innocence that Previn wanted to permeate, and, therefore, illuminate her script.

Director Peter Medak was none to happy over the fact that he was allowed only three weeks to complete this film. He also recalled:

The one thing I will always remember about dear Kim is that every time we rolled the cameras—just a second before I said "action"—she would manage to produce a mirror and a hair brush and, with great care, she would start correcting herself. This mirror used to pop up from under carpets, inside freezers, scripts, pockets—virtually from everywhere. She is a typical example of how Hollywood could fabricate a human being.

What Medak did not take into consideration was the fact that Kim was the product of another era—an era where glamour was part of the profession—and that she had to have last minute reassurance before facing the camera. It had been deeply instilled in her that she must look her best when being photographed. While life at Big Sur could be lived in levis and denim shirts and minus makeup, time spent in front of the camera must project "the image" to the public. No matter what she might be doing internally, she must remember the external as well.

Medak used a number of distracting setups and angles and didn't always know when to bring out the film's sweet-tough quality and when to work against it. However, he did seem to have transmitted confidence to his cast. And where he failed to sustain Kim in those moments when he gave her the courage to dare to look foolish, she managed to survive on her own through sheer honesty and her prowess at projecting vulnerability.

It was a memorable role and certainly one that Kim can take great pride in having done. In summing up *The Third Girl from the Left,* Sue Cameron, in the *Hollywood Reporter,* said:

> It is an incredible part for an actress and it's easy to see why she wanted to go back to work. Kim Novak, long an underrated actress, gets a chance to prove here what an excellent actress she is. There is no other actress who could have played this part as well.

＊　　　＊

Not since *The Amorous Adventures of Moll Flanders* (and Richard Johnson) had Kim been drawn toward anyone she worked with as much as she had

*The Third Girl from the Left,* **with Michael Brandon**

*The Third Girl from the Left*

been to her *Third Girl* costar Michael Brandon. They hit it off right from the start and enjoyed talking together between takes. During the making of the film, they also spent much of their off-camera time together, and there were no glamour trappings when they did. Both were attired in jeans; Kim's hair hung loose and free, and she looked hardly a day older than she had a decade before. In fact, in some ways, she seemed younger.

Despite the difference in their ages, they remained bound together as two individualists who shared common interests. When the film was completed, their friendship continued, and Brandon headed for Big Sur. From Kim, he learned a way of life he had never known before and became aware of many things he had given no thought to previously. As he put it:

[Kim] is the first older woman I've been involved with. It's working because Kim's a realist, a giving woman, who's given up playing little games with people she cares about.

Animals also became important to Brandon during his time spent with Kim. Later, after his return to Los Angeles, he said:

Kim and I haven't spoken in months. We're in different worlds now. I'm back to civilization. The thing with Kim was that I was on her trip. I was the student—she was the teacher. I was learning about horses, animals, isolation and truth. You have to try to take that away with you. You come into a world that's a lie—and you have to find your own truth and maintain it.

Brandon credited Kim with making major "alterations" in his life by showing him the peace and tranquility an existence close to nature offers. He will always be grateful for her influence in getting him to open up as a person. Brandon stated, "My mother said I never cried as a child but I learned to cry, thanks to Kim." When the parting came, Kim and Michael had both gained enormously from their friendship and could look back on a meaningful and beautiful relationship.

\*      \*

During the making of *Third Girl*, Kim said:

I feel as if I've returned to civilization but it's not the sort of life I'd like to resume. Isolation is a way of life with me. Not that I don't like companionship or a few friends, but I prefer the company of my pets, and I know they love me dearly.

Kim now packed up and moved into the mountains, away from the sea where her new home nestled on twenty acres of forest land and lush vegetation. As she put it:

I drew up the plans for the new house myself. The doors leading outside are eight feet by four feet, large enough to allow the horses and llama to wander in and out whenever they choose. Of course, I have another living room upstairs where I can entertain people who don't particularly like to have the animals around.

Her plans had included sliding door panels that allowed the animals to roam around at will but could be closed when Kim desired privacy.

One of her favorite animals was a raccoon named Ume. About her little masked friend, Kim said:

He sleeps at the top of my bed every night. Sometimes he wakes me up in the morning by rubbing his paws gently over my face. Ume goes riding with me on my favorite horse, Nur Jahan—that means light of the universe. He also likes to ride the llama by holding on to his ears with both paws. All the animals love one another.

If Kim appeared eccentric—and to many she probably did—she wasn't deliberately trying to give that impression. She was simply deeply committed to nature, the ecological movement, and her relationship with the animals. In describing her feelings for them, she put it in this way:

I don't try to discipline them or make them do what I want. We are on an equal footing. It's true. We look into one another's eyes and understand unspoken thoughts. It's a wonderful feeling.

There's nothing so great as to get up early in the morning and ride Nur Jahan down the stream to the ocean and into the surf. He's so gentle—I ride him bareback and without regular reins or bit.

I don't coo or baby my animals, so they're not taking the place of children. The best thing about my pets is they don't know I'm Kim Novak—I'm just their friend.

\*      \*

In addition to her current cinematic efforts, Kim was also being seen in a film that was shown in museums and schools—something of a novelty for an actress

*The Third Girl from the Left*

who continued to reject scripts by the carload. In this instance, however, the project was one she felt compelled to do, and she proceeded to allow herself and her art work to be photographed for it. Her brief appearance, therefore, became a part of *The Celebrity Art Portfolio.*

Sponsored by The Franklin Mint, a commemorative coin company, *The Celebrity Art Portfolio* was directed by Richard D'Anjolell and filmed by Modern Talking Picture Service. The film dealt with screen personalities who painted as a hobby. The artistic endeavors of familiar movie faces was quite impressive and proved that any one of them might very easily make a living as an artist if necessary. Others whose work was represented in the eleven-minute short subject, in addition to Kim, were Candice Bergen, Richard Chamberlain, Henry Fonda, Dinah Shore, and Red Skelton.

\* \*

Kim began work on her second made-for-television film in November 1974 on location in and near the waters of Oxnard, California. The script was exciting, and one could readily see why she accepted it. Originally titled *The Devil's Sea,* it aired on 14 January 1975 on ABC as *Satan's Triangle,* and dealt with that mysterious and lethal area of the Atlantic Ocean known as the Bermuda Triangle.

Within this triangle, consisting of Bermuda, Miami, and Puerto Rico, some 1,000 persons and more than 100 ships and planes have disappeared. It is the contention of the Coast Guard and various oceanographers that the triangle is doubly hazardous because it is one of the two areas in the world where compass needles point to true north rather than magnetic north, and because freak weather conditions can easily occur without warning within the treacherous Gulf Stream. Since their explanation has never sufficed, and the mystery has remained unsolved, *Satan's Triangle* offered a possible theory for what might have happened to one of the boats and its passengers.

The film was slanted to appeal to the public's fascination with supernatural phenomena, and, while it is hardly a masterpiece, it does have some frightening moments and suspenseful special effects. Visually, it is a stunner, and, since the action takes place entirely at sea, there is a constant stream of rugged action. An excellent job of directing was done by Sutton Roley, who laced his well-told tale with sudden chills.

Roley remembers the experience in this way:

Kim Novak was probably as professional a lady as I've ever worked with. I just loved her. I'd heard all kinds of other stories about her working habits (one wonders how those rumors start) but she was absolutely marvelous in every way.

One day when we were filming about twelve miles out at sea, it called for a chopper to come down about twenty feet with a rescue basket. When the basket dropped, she was to get into the water and swim in toward the boat with Doug McClure. It was one of the first shots we did for the film.

When she came in that morning, and I saw her standing on deck, she seemed to be a little up-tight. I sensed something was wrong and said, "What's the matter, honey?" She said, "Oh nothing, Sutton, everything's fine—everything's fine." When we were ready to do the scene, she got on the railing and jumped into the water. She paddled her way out there and the chopper came down over her as was required by the script. The scene was completed.

Later, after she was back on deck, I saw her looking at me and smiling. I said, "What was wrong, Kim?" She laughted and said, "Well, you know Sutton, I didn't want to say anything but—I can't swim. The special effects man told me this undersuit that I'd be wearing would keep me buoyant and so I just took the chance and went in!" I said, "You're really something," and I meant it.

Another difficult time occurred for her when the devil (in the form of the priest) had to fall from the mast (which was about a fifty-footer) and we had rigged it up there with a pully and a rope. I walked over to Kim after I'd had [Alejandro Rey] up there and she said, "I know . . . you want me to go up." I said, "Would you?" She said, "Okay, Sutton, just do it fast!" I said, "Okay." We tied her ankles and pulled her all the way up in the air—held her there—and then let her down. After the take, I walked over and she said, "I know, you want to do it once more." I said, "Please." She said, "Fine." She was absolutely marvelous throughout the whole ordeal.

Kim was on the set all the time. You know most actresses go and sit in their dressing rooms, but she was always there between takes. She'd say, "Come on, let's go with this—let's get it done." There were no problems about anything including her makeup. She'd look in the mirror, fix her lipstick a little and say, "How is this, Sutton?" I'd say, "Well, maybe just a little bit . . ." She'd take and rub it off and say, "How's that?" I'd say, "Fine—let's go!" She was just perfect throughout the whole production. I've worked with a lot of the other kind of actress, too, so I know what a gem she is.

It was a highly technical film to do in the amount of time we had. We filmed at the Oxnard Marina and then went out about twelve miles for the water stuff. It was all shot in bright sunshine and there was no rehearsal whatsoever due to its very speeded up kind of schedule.

Kim was a pro, in every sense of the word, at all times. I think she has been underestimated as far as her talent and her capabilities. She is so deserving and I wouldn't say

With four of her "comrades" at home in Big Sur

anything about her that I didn't mean. I really would like nothing better than to have the opportunity to work with her again at some time in the future.

Alejandro Rey recalls:

Kim gave me a very interesting tip. I always read and reread a script a number of times. I'm always very prepared and usually come on the set with suggestions and whatever I can bring to the part I am playing. I gave our director, Mr. Roley, a suggestion and he accepted it. I gave another and it was accepted. Then I gave still another which he did not accept. Kim came to me and said, "You know, Alejandro, I've learned during my career that suggestions have to be measured very carefully. You lose points if you bring too many. You have to select those that

you feel are absolutely necessary. Then you will get the approval from the director and you keep the secondary ones to and for yourself." I thought this was very interesting and I did learn throughout the shooting on this film. It became a personal thing between Kim and I. We would talk about things in connection with the script. We would discuss at great length, and very carefully weigh, whether that particular suggestion had enough merit to bring it forth to the director or not. And we found in most of the cases that they did not. So we waited until there was something that was absolutely vital. Then it was worth bothering the director. I never worked with a finer director than Sutton Roley, who was equally at ease with both the acting and the technical parts of filming.

Kim didn't like the idea of rehearsing—at least in her scenes with me. She was always prepared for whatever

scene we were doing but she told me, and I quote, "I'd rather let you surprise me so that I can take from it . . . you and the scene." I happen to be an actor who likes to rehearse many times but there are a great many actors who are better on the first take. That's the way she felt in relation to working together. She wanted me to do whatever I was going to do in the take and not to rehearse it at all with her.

I don't mean for this to sound like a cliche but Kim was highly professional and very, very prepared at all times . . . I would have to say she was an absolute professional.

Michael Conrad, who had previously worked with Kim on *The Third Girl from the Left,* added:

Kim moved in beautifully during a tense moment between the director, Sutton Roley, and Doug McClure. Like a true star, she soothed the egos in a very direct and modest way and got the film moving again.

\*   \*

*Satan's Triangle* begins when two Coast Guard rescue pilots, Doug McClure and Michael Conrad, answering a distress call from a craft, rush to the zone of trouble. They spot the badly damaged luxury yacht from their helicopter, and see no signs of life aboard. They continue to circle over the ship and finally see two bodies on deck.

McClure is lowered down from the chopper. When he boards the vessel, it appears that all of the passengers have reached violent ends. What he finds is shocking, and the visuals reinforce this.

A body hangs by a foot, grotesquely, from a mast. Another is propped up stiffly on deck. McClure goes below and finds another male corpse which appears to be floating at full length in midair. He then discovers Novak, huddled in terror, in an aft compartment. She is alive but in a state of half-dazed fear. McClure assures her he will get her out safely.

In the chopper, Conrad is aware that the fuel pressure is dropping rapidly. McClure advises Conrad, via walkie-talkie, to get ready to lift a survivor. As they are being raised up to the helicopter, a mishap occurs, and the rescue basket carrying Novak and McClure gives way. They are splashed into the sea. Conrad has no choice but to allow them to swim back to the safety of the boat as he heads out for fuel and another loading device.

*Satan's Triangle,* with Doug McClure

Back on board, Novak warns McClure, "We're going to die on this boat, you know . . . just like the others." He assures her he is not ready to die yet, and, in reference to the yacht, he explains: "She's solid and she's sound. She'll ride it out. And so will we."

After they have changed into dry clothing, Novak relates the weird story of the events on board. We watch a flashback showing her account of what happened to her rich, obnoxious boy friend, Jim Davis; his mercenary skipper, Ed Lauter; another member of the crew, Titos Vandis; and a priest, Alejandro Rey.

Shortly after they had rescued the priest, an apparent survivor of a plane crash, the ship's engines would not start, the radio went out, and they were stranded. In telling her tale about the priest, Novak says of Rey, "From the moment he came aboard, a strange lightning started and the weather changed." In describing him, she adds, "He was handsome—too handsome—it would have been easy to forget he was a priest."

*Satan's Triangle,* with Doug McClure

During the flashback, there is a very good scene between Novak and Rey in which he tries to save the sinner and we learn more about her.

Rey:     Hold on to your faith. He will not forsake you.
Novak:  He gave up on me a long time ago, Father.
Rey:     You're wrong, Eva, we're all His children.
Novak:  What do you think that I was doing with Hal? I'm a prostitute, Father. That's all I've ever been.
Rey:     So was Mary Magdalen and the lord loved her. And He loves you.
Novak:  And do you love me, too, Father? Show me. Show me that you love me.
Rey:     I love you, Eva, as God loves you. [Rey takes a gold cross and places it around her neck.]

Novak continues her story until she has remembered all of the events that led to the deaths of the men. McClure, in putting the pieces together, comes up with a seemingly logical explanation for the unusual sequence of events. Lauter was caught in the hatch. Vandis was swept overboard. Davis was impaled on the bill of the swordfish that he caught. And Rey had fallen to his death and been caught up in the mast. McClure hopes he has dispelled Novak's fears once and for all.

Novak says to McClure, "Y'know something? I don't think I believe in the devil anymore." McClure proceeds to make love to her. Novak's gold cross, given to

*Satan's Triangle,* with Alejandro Rey

again, the wicked smile with the teeth showing, and the look of the devil in the eyes.

*       *

*Satan's Triangle* holds your attention every second because you are never quite certain what is going to happen next. Sue Cameron, in the *Hollywood Reporter,* said: "Novak is excellent in her very special part. It is perfect casting."

*       *

Kim was continuing to stick to her code of working when she found a script that appealed to her, and, with *Satan's Triangle,* Danny Thomas Productions had come up with one she thought held "an interesting idea," something she "liked."

her by Rey, disappears before our eyes once she has removed it from around her neck. McClure and Novak spend the night together awaiting the return of Conrad.

The next morning, the helicopter comes back to rescue McClure and Novak. Safely aboard, they now have eyes only for each other until the rescue team, on board the ship, announces its findings via walkie-talkie. It has discovered the body of a woman . . . long blonde hair . . . 5'8", about 125 pounds.

Inside the chopper, a frightening transformation occurs as the news is announced. We see Novak smiling a curious smile. We see teeth and the devil's look in her eyes, and we hear the sound of strange laughter.

Novak has been transformed into Rey, causing McClure to fall to his death, and making Conrad and the chopper crash. Rey appears to die too but, instead, he enters the dead body of McClure who surfaces and comes to life, awaiting rescue by an unsuspecting Swedish ship. Reflected on McClure's face, we see, once

283

## 17

Ten years had passed since Kim had been married to Richard Johnson, and, although both had moved on to other lives, they had remained the best of friends. The British actor had flown from his London homebase to see Kim on several occasions. They were photographed together in 1975 during one of his visits to her Northern California retreat, and they appeared to really enjoy being together. Each still felt deep concern for the other. At the time, Johnson shed some light on Kim's very private existence. As he put it:

Kim withdrew from the world for two reasons. First, she is a shy and basically insecure person who was built up into a sex symbol. Not that that's so unusual—it has happened to many so-called lucky girls who hit the big time in Hollywood. It has ruined many of them. Look at Marilyn Monroe. I think Kim identified strongly with Marilyn's problems. Marilyn's ultimate despair and suicide scared her.

The pressures of being a star laid heavily on Kim. I remember the time, when we still were married, that we went to a theater in New York. During the intermission, some guy kept staring at her with a rather ugly, lustful look. I finally had to threaten to hit the fellow before he would quit.

The second reason for Kim's withdrawal was a bitterness against critics' reaction to most of her film roles. Kim was never able to shake the image of a bubble-headed play-

mate-of-the-month type although any open-minded person who sees her films knows she is better than that. She always had to pay the price for that silly buildup she got at the beginning of her career. It isn't easy to hang on to your self-esteem when people are constantly making fun of your best efforts, especially when their words are prejudiced and not true. One day, she just said, "I can't take this kind of life anymore." Thank God she had the courage to get out of Hollywood before it finished her.

Kim hasn't turned into a nutty middle-aged woman who goes around her house talking only to her pets. In her environment, she's quite normal, I assure you. She keeps busy and is not a cranky female hermit. She just doesn't want to commit herself to any other person. Kim doesn't see people often, but she does have a boyfriend from time to time. There are a few men she can trust but you have to meet Kim on her own terms. She's the strongest-minded woman I've ever known.

About the reasons for the failure of their marriage, in spite of the fact that he had such a deep understanding of his ex-wife, Johnson added:

Some people aren't made for marriage. Kim is one of these. I guess I am, too. We were very much in love. In those days, Hollywood people hadn't taken up the fad of keeping house without marriage. There was a lot of nasty talk and headlines about our "sinful" carrying-on. All kinds of pressure was laid on us. We gave in to it and got married.

With husband, Robert Malloy

It was a terrible mistake. How could it work when Kim's life was in California and mine was in England? By admitting our mistake quickly, we managed to stay friends—good friends—in the truest sense.

The world lost a great movie star when Kim went into semi-retirement. She has a remarkable screen presence. No one who ever saw any of her movies ever forgets her. Producers know this. Why else are they constantly after her to change her mind and come back to Hollywood? She is one of the last of the big stars and she's had the courage to say good-bye to all that and lead her own life. On the whole, I'd say Kim has made the right choice. She is happy in her world.

One of the finest compliments any two people who once loved each other or were married can express is to hold each other in such high esteem. It also said a lot for Kim and Richard, both unique individuals.

*     *

In the decade since her divorce from Johnson, Kim had never found anyone that she, ultimately, wanted to marry. There was always something that stood in the way in those instances where she might have· been temporarily swayed. However, eventually, she did decide to give marriage another try. Although Johnson had stated that "some people aren't made for marriage" and that Kim was one of these persons, she did not think so.

On 12 March 1976, Kim married Robert Malloy in a simple outdoor ceremony. This time, the wedding was performed below the patio of Kim's mountaintop home beneath a pine tree with a view of the Carmel Valley hills. It was attended by only about a dozen friends and relatives, in keeping with Kim and Bob's wishes.

Kim's older sister, Arlene Malmborg, was her bridesmaid. Her matron of honor was her good friend (since they were both eleven-year-olds in Chicago) and former secretary, Barbara (Mellon) Wermuth. The best man was the bridegroom's brother, Bill Malloy.

The ceremony was performed by Judge Robert W. Hain of nearby Hollister, California. Kim wore a knee-length brown print dress with a cowl-neck and carried a small bouquet. Judge Hain said, "Kim was very, very nervous. But she finally got through the vows with some tears being shed." Afterwards, the bride and groom kissed and broke into smiles as the nervous tension eased. The happy couple, who had insisted on privacy for the ceremony, held a reception afterward.

Some forty friends wished them well and watched them as they toasted each other with a glass of champagne and cut a two-tiered wedding cake. Happiness was apparent, as a radiant and glowing Kim said:

> This marriage is forever and ever. I never dreamed I could be so happy. I've never cared as deeply for anyone as I do for Bob. I'm a very lucky girl. Our every interest coincides. Finding someone who is so perfect for me is a once-in-a-lifetime event.

Unlike Richard Johnson, who had lived in another country and found it difficult to adjust to Kim's lifestyle, Robert Malloy was a localite who loved the area that she lived in as much as Kim did. He was also in another profession so there would not be the problem of conflicting career assignments that would take one away just as the other returned home. This was the perfect mating of two very similar and private people.

It was the second marriage for both of them. Kim had first met Bob, a veterinarian, in September 1974, when he came to her home to treat a sick horse. About their new life together, Malloy said:

> We're very much in love and we wanted to be man and wife. It wasn't a step either of us took lightly. We've been planning it for several months and we didn't rush into this like a couple of kids. We like to ride horses, ski, go trout fishing in the mountains. We enjoy togetherness and we like the outdoors. Kim likes her privacy and shuns the stereotypical Hollywood lifestyle which I'm not into.

The couple spent their honeymoon on a camping trip. Later, Kim said:

> I have never imagined that I could be so happy and I've never felt a sentiment so profound. An event of this importance doesn't come to a person more than once in a lifetime.
>
> Bob is the perfect person. My name has been linked with many men and I have loved some of them. My voluntary isolation provoked many rumors—most of which were false. The truth was simple. I was alone. Now I have someone I truly care about sharing my life with.
> About future film assignments, I have many animals at the house who are all in need of me and I don't care to be away for too long a period of time. This would be unfair to my husband. He comes first.
>
> I live an existence of love and laughter. Bob is a born humorist. It is a veritable zoo at our house—a happy zoo. The respect of our desires and needs reciprocates and is in total accord. This is, without doubt, a question of maturity. I suppose one needs to be prepared and I was truly ready for Bob. I appreciate this love so completely.

At last, after years of waiting, Kim had found the ideal person she had searched for and hoped, one day, to meet. Now her dream had become a reality in the way she had hoped it would be.

*　　*

Kim had been very honest in saying that she didn't want to be away from home for any extended period of time. But, shortly after her marriage, she was offered a part that required her to be away for the briefest time of any assignment she had ever considered. Kim agreed to return to the big screen in a cameo starring role opposite Charles Bronson in *The White Buffalo*. This would be the first separation for the Malloys since their marriage, but Kim's part required only three days to film (for which she was paid $50,000) on location at a site near Canon City, Colorado; she had been given Bob's blessing to continue with her career if and whenever she wanted.

The role of "Poker Jenny" in *The White Buffalo* appealed to Kim for a number of reasons. It was patterned after the real-life Poker Alice Iverson, who was said to be one of the constant loves of the legendary Wild Bill Hickock. She moved through the same gaming establishments and stage-stop hostelries that were Wild Bill's field of action.

In describing the character that Kim played, Richard Sale, who adapted the screenplay from his own novel, wrote: "She was tall and pretty, she wore her pale-brown hair piled atop her head Boston-style, her slanting green eyes were candid, yet full of mischief, her mouth was broad and sensuous yet wry and honest." Kim filled all the necessary requirements despite the fact that her hair was blonde.

About her role in the film, which she laughingly called "a raunchy part," Kim said:

> I have been trying to preserve a certain life style that makes it difficult to find time to work in films. I like the motion picture industry but it's too time-consuming to devote my entire life to it. However, there is always an exception.
>
> *The White Buffalo* is a case in point. It's a marvelous part. The chance to work with people I admire and respect so much gave me little option but to play the role. Now that it's all over, I can say it was very worthwhile. I loved doing it very much and I think there is something interesting on the screen that audiences will enjoy. I wouldn't have missed it for anything.

The assignment reunited her with director J. Lee Thompson who had worked with Kim on the ill-fated *Eye of the Devil* a decade before. In its written form, one can see all that Kim envisioned in this script and, especially, that it offered a chance to broaden her scope as an actress. The role of "Poker Jenny" was far removed from anything she had done previously. This was a step in a new direction and one that afforded invaluable new dimensions. Kim couldn't possibly have known that producer Dino De Laurentiis' track record would suddenly go awry.

The project, at its inception, had everything going for it. De Laurentiis purchased the screen rights from Richard Sale and had him transform the work into a screenplay. He wanted it for Charles Bronson. Bronson and De Laurentiis had been associated previously on four box-office hits, with the total worldwide gross exceeding $150 million. De Laurentiis signed a strong and capable group of actors including Will Sampson, Jack Warden, Clint Walker, Stuart Whitman, Cara Williams, John Carradine, Ed Lauter, and Douglas V. Fowley for costarring and supporting roles. In addition, he interested Kim in returning to feature films for the first time since *Tales That Witness Madness*.

Problems arose because the buffalo depicted in the title was a member of that rare species of American bison known as the Woods Buffalo that is now extinct. A mechanical facsimile was created, but, when the Italian producer and his production team viewed the footage and realized that the mechanical creation looked like a puppet, they knew they were in trouble.

They hired Carlo Rambaldi to build them a better beast and started from scratch. Rambaldi, who had been described by De Laurentiis as "an Italian genius whose hands connect with his head," had previously created the title beast in the producer's remake of the 1933 classic *King Kong*. Like Kong, the buffalo was constructed as though with bone, muscle and flesh.

This nine-foot-high, fifteen-foot-long mechanical buffalo that repeatedly loomed out of the murky environment, thundered over the snow, and snorted a vaporous breath from his nostrils was to be perfect. He was cranked over plastic shavings, between a nailed-up forest of firs, by the aid of wires and pulleys. The fringe of his hair, which bobbed with every motion, was teased into shape by a man with electric curling tongs. And he was propelled toward the movie cameras by a mechanism guaranteed to make him convincing.

289

*The White Buffalo*, with Charles Bronson

His construction was equally intricate. The beast weighed 4,000 pounds and had sixty-four separate animation points. The inner, jointed, steel mechanism of his body was covered with light plastic, separated by layers of sliding material to make it flow. Yak fur, sewn over elasticized backing, stretched as his muscles flexed. When the buffalo galloped, a crane-like mechanism entered its back so that spineflex and foot movement were synchronized. He was pulled forward on a cable wire hidden beneath the snow.

In addition, there was a separate head for close-ups. It could wrinkle its nose, twitch its ears, open its mouth to bray, exhale steamy breath from its nostrils, and roll its eyes. As an actor, the White Buffalo turned out to be quite a mugger.

De Laurentiis had said, "I take my work to the people. I work for the audience. For no one else." Unfortunately, audiences and critics saw the beast of the title looking like a left-over carnival prize. With all of the concentrated effort that went into its creation, it is sad to note that it was not convincing. It still appeared to be just what it was—a mechanical creation.

Nobody ever starts out to make a bad film, but, in addition to the beast, there were other problems that contributed to this film's failure, including the camera work which was, at times, frightful. (The murky quality that was seen on the big screen was, however, mysteriously cleared up when the film was viewed on cable television.) The actors were all fine and their only mistake was in being part of a property that didn't hold up. As to her contribution, Kim rated four-star excellent, and what she did on screen proved she was more appealing than ever in this very different role.

*       *

The story of *The White Buffalo* recounts the search by two independent men to hunt and kill a fierce albino bison. Wild Bill Hickock, the frontier adventurer and gunman, and Crazy Horse, war chief of the Sioux Indians, are the main characters. These roles are played by Charles Bronson and Will Sampson respectively.

Bronson is haunted by a nightmare in which he is attacked by the animal; he decides he must hunt it down and kill it to cleanse himself of his fear. Sampson regards the animal as a holy bull that he must kill to wrap its white pelt around the corpse of his deeply mourned infant daughter, who otherwise would not safely pass over into the other world.

Arriving in Cheyenne, Wyoming, Bronson learns that his old flame, Novak, is now running a boarding house and is a recent widow. He heads for her place. Wearing blue glasses that cover his eyes, he is not recognized by Novak immediately. She is seated at a desk as he warms himself at the potbelly stove. Bronson's back is to her as he speaks, and, after a few words, she realizes who the stranger is when he refers to her by name. When Bronson turns around, in full view, Novak says, "You four-flushin' son of a bitch! You cold-decked me." She embraces him and kisses him before going into action by grinding her hips against him.

Still continuing her hard-sell, Novak says, "If you ain't a sight for a widow in weeds . . . always could get you mounted fast, couldn't I?" There is remembrance in both of their eyes of days when times were happier between them. (This is a memorable moment for Novak and Bronson; they and their chemistries work well together.) Seated at the dining room table, they continue to bring each other up to date.

| | |
|---|---|
| Novak: | Guess you heard about me and Lucas Schermerhorn getting noosed? |
| Bronson: | Just about the same time I heard you were a widow again. How many times is that? |
| Novak: | Don't be a bastard! |
| Bronson: | Lucas was a lucky man, Jen. |
| Novak: | Thank you, cat-eyes. |
| Bronson: | Why do you always call me cat-eyes? |
| Novak: | Ain't you ever seen those wild eyes of yours when you're lovin' it up or when you're hitchin' your pistols on for a shindy? |
| Bronson: | I'm a man of comity. I've always dodged a fight. |
| Novak: | Comity? Sure, you're the most politest shootist who ever blew a man's brains out. |

It is plain to see that Novak does not approve of Bronson's way of life. It is also clear that she has a plan of action and wants to bring things back to the way they once were when she says, "Why don't you let me put you to bed in my room?"

In her room, Bronson smiles at her although he is visibly exhausted. She returns his smile, temptingly, and sits at the foot of the bed while unfastening the buttons of her bodice. Bronson stops her (knowing what she has in mind) with, "Aw, Jen, I ain't got the gumption." Novak snaps back with, "That'll be the day. You just lie still and I'll fly the eagle." Bronson explains, "No, Jen. Sometime back, one of your scarlet sisters dosed me proper. I'm not about to ride the high horse." Novak shrugs and says, "Hell, I probably gave

it to you myself. I'll take the chance." Bronson says, "But I won't." Novak flips back, "Alright, cat-eyes, you take yourself a sound snooze. Since you're a gamblin' man, I'll bet you six, two and even when you wake up, I'll talk you into it! I'll leave the door open in case you need anything."

This scene, as originally written, was to have shown Novak standing nude after undressing. As a new bride in real life, she didn't think her husband would approve. Furthermore, she saw no need for the nudity. She therefore played the scene clothed, and it worked beautifully. (The black dress—her only costume in the film—was the same one she had previously worn in *The Great Bank Robbery*.)

Asleep in Novak's bedroom, Bronson is troubled by his recurring dream. From behind a huge black rock, the snow boils and steams and the white buffalo appears with his terrifying bellow. As he charges, the huge head fills the screen. Bronson, awakening, reaches for his gun and fires at the opposite wall where, reflected in a mirror, we can see the head of a white buffalo. After the shots, it falls to the floor as he sits up, doused in water that Novak has poured on him to bring him back to reality. Terrified, she stares at him in disbelief. Bronson promises to buy her another buff head for the wall, but she says, "I don't ever want to see it again."

Bronson comes to the full realization that the dream is taking over, and knows that, if he is to find peace, he must track down the white buffalo and put an end to the dream once and for all. He is fully dressed now and ready to move on as he enters Novak's parlor, where she's busily working on her needlepoint.

She looks up fearfully and eyes him suspiciously, not knowing what frame of mind he is in. As a result of the nightmare, she knows he is sick and that there is no chance for them to continue any kind of relationship. However, she is still concerned for his safety.

Novak: The Frozen Dog [where he is headed] is a hellhole. Keep a wall at your back. You're alone up there.
Bronson: I'm used to that.
Novak: Bill, I lost my bet.
Bronson: No, Jenny, I did.

Novak is still seated in her chair. The camera holds on her sad face in the background, her eyes misting, as Bronson walks out the door.

Eventually, Bronson's nightmare ends when he and Sampson kill the white buffalo. Sampson, too, has solved his problem and carries the animal's pelt to avenge his daughter's death and allow him, once more, to hold his head up among the members of his tribe.

\*　　　\*

Kim's scenes, although brief, were among the high spots of the film. This was an opportunity for her to project mature emotion on a different level, and she was successful. This was an interesting characterization, one that would have benefited greatly if it had been allowed more screen time. Here was a lustier Novak than before, projecting her voice in a lower register than any she had previously used. Her participation brightened the film considerably and left you wanting to see more of her.

The picture was not released until well over a year after its completion. It was screened in test engagements and withheld from reviewers for months. When it was finally presented, *Variety* said, "*The White Buffalo* is a turkey." They criticized "arch scripting . . . and forced direction," and further took it to task with "the trade has to wonder how a project like this gets off the ground, when the dialogue is enough to invite jeers from an audience." They complained of "hokey sound track noise, busy John Barry scoring, murky photography and fast editing. The showmanly vision of De Laurentiis isn't always clear in contemporary subject matter, but it's positively myopic on period Americana." They dismissed it with:

> Wandering in and out of mini-cameo roles are the likes of Kim Novak, Clint Walker, Stuart Whitman, Jack Warden, Cara Williams, John Carradine, Ed Lauter, Douglas V. Fowley, etc. Cast will look good for [television] licensing, though some of the PG-type vulgarity will have to be cleaned up.

Robert Osborne, in the *Hollywood Reporter,* said:

> The cast, headed by macho Bronson, is fine; it's also a pleasure to see small roles played by big actors. Kim Novak, in for four scenes as an unweeping widow named Poker Jenny, is particularly dandy and looks gorgeous. Jack Warden (almost unrecognizable with bushy white hair and beard), Clint Walker, Stuart Whitman, Cara Williams, John Carradine, Slim Pickens and Sampson all do their turns with the professional polish one would expect of them. It's too bad the final product doesn't justify their efforts, or time.

The role had interested Kim. She had seen possibilities in it and given it everything she could. The result showed great change in her work and her style. There was more subtlety and more relaxation. There was also a preview of what could be expected in the future—from a more mature, yet equally appealing, charisma.

\*　　　\*

In July of the same year, Kim and Bob Malloy made a brief trip to New York City where Kim combined business with pleasure. Kim's reason for going was to film some television commercials for Ralston Purina's catfood product "Lovin' Spoonfuls." This was the first time she had attempted to do anything of this nature, and it was a new experience for her in many ways. As in the past, she couldn't promote anything unless she believed in it herself. "Lovin' Spoonfuls" was a product she was familiar with and one for which she could feel a sincere regard. Her animal-lover instincts and, especially, her love for cats since she was a tot, made her even more convincing, and gave everyone satisfaction.

During the time when she wasn't needed for filming, Kim and Bob managed to spend their free hours sight-seeing and doing things they really wanted to do. Photographed in the lobby of their posh Fifth Avenue hotel, the couple radiated the happiness they felt. Kim was delighted that Bob was able to make the trip with her and spoke briefly about her new-found happiness.

> I have had so much good luck in my life but I still feel very lucky that Bob and I found each other. If I'd stayed in Hollywood, I'd never have met my ideal man because that type just doesn't exist there. I'd never have found Bob on the freeways of Los Angeles—but [home at Big Sur] we both share the joys of walking through life the same way. It still amazes me that I found Bob.

Kim also made it clear that her husband is the boss and he comes before her career. A case in point was the recent assignment in *The White Buffalo* when she had been asked to shoot the nude scene and she and Bob had both said, "No." As Kim told producer De Laurentiis, "It's not nice for Bob to have a wife who does that sort of thing." Kim had decided that she must think of her husband's feelings and be fair to him at all times.

\*　　　\*

Kim was happy to return to Big Sur where, now, she and Bob could wander through the woods, hand-in-hand, along untouched trails. The animals, too, were glad to see the lady of the house back where she belonged, and they welcomed Bob too. With one exception.

The one exception was Uno, Kim's pet llama, who seemed to dislike everyone except Kim. Uno was great protection around the property and would keep anyone away who wasn't supposed to be there. The llama could spew a green fluid at people she didn't like, and she was always deadly accurate. At a distance of up to fifteen feet, Uno usually caught her victims straight between the eyes. This prompted Malloy to carry a water squirt gun to protect himself from the sure-shot spitter. In defense of her llama, Kim's words were, "Uno always waits until you're facing her before she lets you have it."

Outside of Uno, the other animals on the place were all friendly and contented. Kim's menagerie included two goats named Moonshine and Sunshine, three dogs, six horses, cats, chickens, and a mynah bird named Choika (meaning seagull in Russian) that spoke with a Japanese accent. As Kim laughingly explained, "My Japanese maid taught him every word he knows."

Since Kim's marriage, only one of the animals in her happy menagerie was missing. This was her pet raccoon. As Kim put it:

Ume was probably closer to me, and needed me more than any other living creature, until I met Bob. He slept on my bed every night for three years—all the time I had him. But it was very important for Ume to realize that human companionship comes first. He sensed this and knew the time had come to find another raccoon and start a family.

And though she missed her masked-bandit friend, Kim hoped that Ume was happy wherever he had journeyed. Eventually, she was able to accept the loss of the raccoon, who had waited until the day of Kim's wedding before vanishing, apparently knowing that Kim would be protected by the new man of the house.

One would never find a glamorous sex goddess around Big Sur. What he would find is a beautiful, out-of-doors individual who is happy and healthy in her environment. In this natural setting, with the gentle atmosphere and the general feeling of peace and contentment that seems to pervade every nook, Kim described her feelings in this way:

The animals really are my family. And, just as Bob brought his two children into our marriage because they are a part of his family, so I brought the llama and my other animals.

Many nights Bob and I just sit on our verandah listening to the sounds of nature. We don't speak for hours. But it's a complete oneness we share—he knows my thoughts and I know his. We don't spoil it with words.

And Malloy echoed Kim's sentiments and added:

We live a simple life, very quiet. We both love the outdoors. I love fishing and Kim comes with me but if she catches any fish, she throws them back. She doesn't like to kill and I appreciate her way of thinking. In the evenings, Kim and I play gin rummy or pinochle. On the weekends, we ride our horses. We don't really need a lot of things to make us happy. Kim is happier helping me with my work as a veterinarian than being down there in Hollywood.

At last, all the pieces in Kim's world had fit together. She had wended her way to her very own haven, surrounded herself with the animals she dearly loved, and married the man she had always hoped to find. Together, they were sharing mutual interests and their special way of life.

Hollywood and the days when the press reported Kim's romantic entanglements with the world's most eligible men seemed a million miles away from this remote, tree-studded area. The fact that she was acclaimed a bona fide movie star by the rest of the world didn't matter, for here she was just Mrs. Robert Malloy. As Bob put it, "I watched *Picnic* once on television but I've never known Kim Novak the film star." The free-spirited nature girl had her own way of saying it. "Who's Kim Novak to my horse?" Now she was her own person—the one thing she had always wanted to be.

# 18

In December 1977, Kim found herself in Berlin to make her first film in Germany, teamed opposite pop favorite David Bowie. The international cast of *Just a Gigolo* included Sydne Rome, David Hemmings, Maria Schell, and Curd (a/ka Curt) Jurgens—with the added coup of the legendary Marlene Dietrich, signed for a cameo role after the film was in production. David Hemmings, who was directing as well as acting, had known Kim since their previous work together on the ill-fated *Eye of the Devil,* which Kim had been unable to complete.

Set in the Twenties, *Just a Gigolo* depicts a young hussar officer who falls to the lowly state of being a ladies' tea-time dancer. Kim was cast as an officer's widow who seduces Bowie and changes the course of his life.

During the filming, in a setting of the flaming-orange cavern known as the Cafe Wien, Kim and Bowie gave their best shots as they tangoed among empty tables, the vast room echoing the strain of the nostalgic music and the clicking heels of their dance shoes.

Kim wore the short bobbed hairstyle that she had used previously in portions of *The Legend of Lylah Clare;* this time it was surmounted by a large white feather attached to a jeweled headband of the period.

Her dress was royal blue, one that had also been designed for her to wear in *Lylah Clare* although it had not been seen on the screen. She had used only the jeweled transparent overblouse to pose for stills, the most famous of which adorns the cover of this book. Together, she and Bowie wheeled and dipped, advancing with outstretched arms, as they performed this dance that was spawned in the brothels of Buenos Aires.

There were many grueling hours of polishing their routine until they had it down to perfection on the third day of filming. Although Kim had danced on the screen in other films, she had never done anything that could match what she did here. The end result looked as if she had been dancing the tango for years, and she was both convincing and sexually interesting as Bowie's partner.

About working with Kim, David Bowie said:

[Kim] is a splended woman and she oozes femininity. I've been a fan of hers forever. For me, she's the peer of Marilyn [Monroe], and equally as exciting. She is more real, and in a way that makes her more relevant. Monroe was the embodiment of our dream lives; Novak is the embodiment of delicious, attainable daydreams.

She has a marvelous sense of herself and what she wants out of life, that she didn't have in the 50s or 60s. She now makes films only when she wants to and she doesn't particularly care about box office or status projects. She says she is happier than she has ever been [and] I find working with such diverse people who can teach and disseminate knowledge an inspiration.

Kim, like all the other stars of the film, was suggested by the scriptwriter, an American expatriate in Europe named Joshua Sinclair. He felt she would be convincing in the role of a society matron who seduces Bowie and starts him on his professional career in the taxi dance. When asked if Kim had been signed for the part because of her associations as a sex goddess, in a movie that he admits is tongue-in-cheek, director David Hemmings answered slyly, "Let's say the possible irony had not escaped my notice."

It was certainly not lost either on the Italian husband of Sydne Rome, a photographer named Emilio Lari, who had taken exclusive shots of Kim when she married Richard Johnson, over a decade before, in Aspen, Colorado. Lari said, "I remember paying the *Daily Express* photographer 1,000 pounds to lure the other photographers away and then we shot her on a platform in the snow. She remembers it, too."

Like many another male associated with *Just a Gigolo*, Lari retained ripe memories of the younger Novak, and found her appeal still very much in evidence. All who came in contact with her were quick to agree with Bowie's sentiments: "a splendid woman who oozes femininity."

On the set, there was an attitude of discreet distance about Kim as she, far from home and in the foreign atmosphere of this production, carefully maintained her aloofness. Those working with her were aware that she was a star and most of them were in awe of her presence. For them, she remained the eternal sex goddess.

Although Kim was away from her animals in Big Sur, she managed to make a new friend while in Germany in the name of charity. This time, the friend turned out to be an elephant. Kim took time from filming chores to be part of a celebrity-studded performance for charity at the Circus Krone in Munich. There, looking as lovely as ever—and a lot braver than most of us might be—Kim went through an elephant-training act with ease, then mounted and rode the elephant. Her appearance was a highlight; she was breathtaking in a black pants suit with a tunic-style top trimmed in rhinestones at the neck, cuffs, and hem. Her shoulder-length blonde hair fell freely, in the casual style she prefers, adding further charm to her first performance under the big top.

There was a story that, for one crucial scene, she was supposed to wear a dress in the style of the period but insisted on one from her own wardrobe instead. During the filming schedule, when she had time off, she returned to America and came back with the dress she preferred: a pink chiffon creation that set off her spendidly proportioned figure to perfection. The scene where she was to instruct Bowie in various social graces and get carried away in voluptuous ecstasies, found her trailing pink gauze skillfully as she slinked across the room. With her hands sliding over her body, the overtures she was making to Bowie were unmistakeably and precisely to the point.

David Bowie had additional comments to make:

Working with these two women [Kim Novak and Marlene Dietrich] has been worth all that's gone before [in my career], and I only want to work with them again. I can't tell you how eager I am to see the finished product even though I don't expect it to be a major commercial success. In fact, I'd be somewhat disppointed if it became a smash. The public at large has such appalling taste that its approval is an artistic kiss of death.

Kim was fortunate in having a director who was, and still is, an actor and who understands some of the pressures a performer experiences during the making of a film. David Hemmings is firm, but he is also pleasant and flexible. About the experience of working on the picture, he said:

We set out to capture the style of the Roaring Twenties and [*Just a Gigolo*] is both a comedy and a tragedy—sometimes a bit happy and sometimes a bit sad. In the end, all the characters opt for the easy way out. They all sell themselves. But it's lightly ironic, tongue-in-cheek, about the period. It's been a gratifying experience for me to work with and direct Kim Novak. She is an actress with extraordinary talent and I thank God for her return to the screen in this film.

The presence of Kim, David Bowie, and Sydne Rome (Marlene Dietrich's scenes were filmed in Paris) in Berlin, during the shooting of the picture, sparked hopes that the island city might recapture some of its past glory as a film production center. This was the first of a number of Berlin-financed projects, a $5 million production made for the Leguan Film Company.

*Just a Gigolo* (and its German title *Schöner Gigolo-Armer Gigolo*) is described as a song, a story, a film. It proved to be the biggest and most expensive German film made since the end of the War, and the producers

*Just a Gigolo*, with David Bowie

*Just a Gigolo*

*Just a Gigolo*

chose to shoot it at the former CCC Studios, now Studios Berlin, which offer all technical facilities. In addition to the principals in the star-studded cast, 1000 extras were employed. There were also various locations used, all of them adding authenticity to the "decadent period" covered in the story. Among them were the old and dilapidated nightclub "Lutzower Lampe," the luxurious palace hotel Gehrhus, Cafe Wien (as if left over from 1920), and the genuine Berlin-Kreuzberg-Chamisso Square with its neo-baroque facades dating back to 1850.

The film's setting is that of a post-World War I Germany suffering from the ideological, financial, and social implications of a massive defeat that had left the once glorious but now decaying Prussian breed in a stupor, hurdling it into a "roaring twenties" of oblivion and nostalgia. For two decades, an entire civilization chose to ignore and undervalue the fatal growth of the germ of National Socialism: a political and ideological movement that, like christianity in the Roman Empire, officially surfaced only when its roots were so deeply embedded in the social and psychological framework of the historical moment that retaliation was impossible.

*Just a Gigolo*

\*     \*

The story of *Just a Gigolo* is that of an antihero, David Bowie, who arrived on the scene of the "Great War" when it was too late to become a hero and returned to his native Berlin when it was too late to remain a Prussian. His is the anguish of being left not only without a country, but without a purpose as well. He is a man groping for identity, his confusion causing an avalanche of emotional changes in both himself and those closest to him.

Bowie's childhood sweetheart, Sydne Rome, has become politically active, a left-wing crusader who pushed her way into fame and fortune in show business and supplemented her political affiliations with a passion for wealth supplied by Curd Jurgens. His mother, Maria Schell, carefully trained by her upbringing to be the faithful wife of a Prussian colonel, now paralyzed, has been forced by sociological situations and a strong desire to survive where others, like her, had given up, to improvise a more actively materialistic life as the manageress of a Turkish Bath. David Hemmings, Bowie's ex-regimental captain, a psychopathic schizophrenic with rampant sexual perversions and the in-

tellectual lucidity of the lunatic, attempts to manipulate Bowie's naiveté in the hope of involving him both sexually and politically in the ranks of a new regiment: the "Forces of Destiny," the embryonic National Socialist Movement.

Bowie is a total anachronism, but he does have one quality upon which he can capitalize. His vulnerability makes him extremely attractive to women. He is swept through the whirlwind of Berlin in the Twenties, desperately searching for a reflection of himself in the hearts and minds of those he encounters. His is the anguish of a man trained to become a hero in a world where illusions have vanished and bravery is laced with insanity.

Bowie meets a Prussian general's widow, Novak, who flirts with him and likes what she sees. They do a seductive tango and are excited by the music and each other. Later, Novak seduces Bowie under her dead husband's flower-decked crypt. Novak contributes to Bowie's education in physical love and equips him with a decent wardrobe. She also introduces him to the kind of sophisticated elegance only an older woman can provide. Eventually, their relationship ends and his despair sends him in another direction.

*Just a Gigolo*

*Just a Gigolo*

The experience with Novak jogs him into the "troops" of Marlene Dietrich, where he becomes a gigolo, renouncing all claims to heroism after having also drowned his romance with Rome because of a lack of communication, and fled from a claustrophobic relationship with Hemmings. Bowie, too, has joined those who are willing to sell themselves for the period.

After hearing Dietrich sing "Just a Gigolo," which describes his inconsequential way of life, Bowie leaves the Eden Bar as communists and Nazis fight in the streets. Lost in his own thoughts, he hardly notices it when he is struck down by a stray bullet. He lies dying on the pavement, dressed to perfection and handsome as he has always been.

Afterwards, each side wishes to claim the body as a martyr for its individual cause, but Hemmings, whose para-military organization is now fully integrated into the party, succeeds, and Bowie is laid out with full military honors at the Nazi headquarters. As fate would have it, Bowie becomes a hero in spite of himself—at a time when it is least expected and in a

manner that is far from valiant: by pure mistake. He is turned into the symbol of a movement he neither joined nor understood, and laid to rest as a hero of the new Germany, Hitler's Germany.

\*　　　\*

Her role in *Just a Gigolo* offered Kim an opportunity to develop a character unlike any she had previously attempted. The aging beauty who attracts a younger man with her seductiveness and position called for unlimited depth and provided Kim with a challenge she was eager to meet.

Kim's work has always appealed to her particular needs on a personal, if not always an artistic, level. Here, she had a chance to combine both. If her work is something she believes in when she is doing it, she measures its success by its ability to move and touch her in the creation of the role. If it doesn't please anyone else, that's fine, because everyone should have the opportunity to film, to paint, and to see what the experience is like. The test is how stimulating the work is. Kim met the role's challenge to the best of her ability and enjoyed making the film.

Critical approval of any given project is important, but *Just a Gigolo* has not been released in this country as this book is being finished. The film was shown shortly after its completion at the Cannes Film Festival. Extensive editing delayed the film's release until February 1979, when it premiered in London, England.

In its appraisal of the film, *Variety* noted:

Those who liked *Cabaret* probably will also admire *Just a Gigolo,* possibly more so, as a kindred harkback to the post-World War I Germany of lost souls and rising Aryan nationalism. No less romanticized, perhaps, but with an added, effective edge of satire.

The fascinating, and obviously exploitable, casting includes Marlene Dietrich as a kind of gigolo den mother and the return of Kim Novak portraying a libidinous widow . . . Novak, another longtime-no-see name, also makes a strong impression, with commanding presence as well as mature beauty. The role suits her and vice-versa, which adds up to clever rather than mere gimmick casting.

The film still delivers a lot of bittersweet entertainment and is never less than engrossing. Period mood is a great strength, with an effective visual mixture of sepia and soft color tints, and a music track of period ballads and jolly ragtime tunes.

\*　　　\*

At the Academy Awards ceremonies, 1979

Presenter at the Academy Awards

On 9 April 1979, Kim took part in the fifty-first annual Academy of Motion Picture Arts and Sciences Awards held at the Dorothy Chandler Pavillion in Los Angeles. In his opening monologue, host Johnny Carson jokingly described the Oscar affair as "Two hours of sparkling entertainment spread out over four hours." It proved to be three hours and twenty-two minutes, with the show being carried nationally over ABC Television to an estimated 70,000,000 viewers. Overseas the show beamed to fifty-four countries and 350,000,000 viewers.

This was Kim's first appearance as a presenter in thirteen years, and she received a warm and hearty welcome from all of her peers in the industry on Hollywood's most exciting night of the year. Breathtakingly beautiful, Kim was stunningly outfitted in a black satin spaghetti-strap gown, designed by Ron Talsky, which accented her still fabulously provocative

figure to perfection. She wore diamond earrings and a diamond and ruby pin which added the right finishing touch. Kim looked every inch the goddess her image has always proclaimed her to be.

Introducing Kim and her copresenter to the audience, Johnny Carson said:

It's been some time since our next two presenters have graced the Oscar festivities. We're pleased to have them back again. Would you welcome, please, James Coburn and Kim Novak.

The theme music from *Picnic* was played by the orchestra as Kim descended the stairs on the arm of Coburn. As she walked to the podium, the sound of thunderous applause greeted her from a most enthusiastic audience.

Coburn:    A lot of people are surprised you came down,

Academy Awards, with Nestor Almendros and James Coburn

Academy Awards, with Nestor Almendros and James Coburn

missed everybody. Kind of nice to see all those cameras and faces and good people again.

Among the "good people" were such old friends as Cary Grant, Sammy Davis, Jr., and Dean Martin. In addition, such contemporaries as Shirley MacLaine, Audrey Hepburn, Natalie Wood, and Lauren Bacall were also on the program along with a host of others.

When questioned about her career, Kim stated her views about future work possibilities in this way:

> I'm kind of itchy to come back. I don't have anything definitely set and I have been turning down all scripts that had sex and violence in them. I have started thinking about doing movies again. I sense a change in Hollywood of getting back to the type of pictures that I really want to do. *An Unmarried Woman* is the kind of film that I mean—something without exploiting sex and violence but with something to say.

At the end of the telecast, Carson invited all of the participants back onstage to greet veteran actor John Wayne. Wayne was making his first public appearance after a recent and much publicized illness. This turned out to be his final public appearance before his death. Kim was on the stage with the other presenters and warmly greeted Duke Wayne with a kiss and hug before mingling with other old friends that she had not seen in a decade.

She thoroughly enjoyed the evening, and Kim proved to be one of the biggest hits of this star-studded night, looking sensational and receiving a warm, rousing welcome on her first visit back to Hollywood in a long time.

\*           \*

For years Hollywood has been trying to solve the puzzle of Kim Novak—or at least to understand her as a person. Not since the days of Greta Garbo has any star generated as much mystery concerning her private life. However, as in the case of her films, Kim's way of life has weathered the test of time.

There are two kinds of successful actors—those who project by craftsmanship and those who project an image by the sheer force of personality. Kim succeeded, at first, by projecting an image of personality. She survived because she was sufficiently intelligent and hard working enough to learn the acting craft and all that went with it in order to become the respected professional most of her coworkers have found her to be.

all the way from Carmel, to be here with us tonight.

Novak:     Well, I do have a very, very fine life there. I think everyone would like living there. It's beautiful.

Coburn:     Well, why don't we find out? We could all go up there after the show tonight.

Novak:     (Laughing) Let's talk about that one later. But, in the meantime, I just want to say I'm really honored and very proud to be here with the industry tonight.

They proceeded with the business at hand and named the artists that were nominated for the outstanding achievement in Cinematography. Kim joyously announced the winner to be "Nestor Almendros for *Days of Heaven*." Almendros happily accepted his award and walked offstage with Kim and Coburn, where they were greeted by photographers and the press.

Backstage, all eyes were on Kim, and the press eagerly questioned her about her future. Kim said:

> I really have no plans other than I just had a feeling to be here this time and to share with the industry. I've kind of

Although her publicity made her out to be just another stereotyped Hollywood glamour girl, it is remarkable how misleading this impression was. She has great sensitivity, great warmth, and is very humble. Grossly misrepresented and caricatured, she is something of an anomaly in movie circles—a free spirit who, long before such things were possible, claimed her right to live her life in the way that suited her best.

No actress, in the course of a career, has had more pot shots taken at her than Kim. Unkind critics have had fine sport at her expense, referring to her as everything from "wooden" to "emotionless." Although she has been the recipient of numerous honors, she has never won a major award for her acting—but then, neither have scores of others who are considered all-time greats. The fact that her performances hold up and continue to entertain is a tribute in itself to her artistry in the motion picture industry. Her stardom has been well-earned.

In all her best work *Picnic, The Man with the Golden Arm, The Eddy Duchin Story,* portions of *Jeanne Eagels, Vertigo, Bell, Book and Candle, Middle of the Night, Of Human Bondage, Kiss Me, Stupid, The Amorous Adventures of Moll Flanders, The Legend of Lylah Clare* and *Third Girl from the Left),* her pathos and vulnerability go straight to your heart. Her excitement is infectious, and a little of the real Novak always surfaces from beneath the strange, haunting quality reflected in her performances. The fact that she has talent has often been obscured by the enormous popularity of her public image. Kim Novak is not the greatest actress in the world, but she has succeeded—and even triumphed—on far more occasions than those with which she has been credited.

In spite of the panning she has taken from some of her critics (usually the same ones), there are a multitude of newsmen who have lauded her with the highest accolades for her gifts as an actress, a fitting answer to those who felt she gave "undisciplined" performances. Kim had all the qualities required for stardom, and, when they were completely assembled, they were more than ample. Millions of adoring viewers, in darkened theaters throughout the world, have appreciated and welcomed her special brand of charisma.

\*          \*

There is a private side to Kim that has never really been expressed. Probably one of the reasons for her silence is the fact that, early in her career, a remark was made to this effect: "Never forget that all you are is a piece of meat, like in a butcher shop." This, and the death of Marilyn Monroe, probably brought home to her the fact that there was more to life than just making films. Highly underrated as an actress during most of her career, Kim has taken it in her stride. About her work, she says succinctly:

> During my entire career, I have never felt that I attained the total of my potential possibilities. Sometimes you have a good script and not the best director, or then you may have a good director and not a very good script. You take your chances and hope for the best.

Home at Big Sur has given her more than her career ever could. In addition to her own animals, there are hundreds of wild creatures—birds, rabbits, raccoons, etc.—that Kim feeds and cares for, and she loves every minute of it. She says:

> My father inspired my love of nature when he took me and my sister on hikes in the woods and collected insects and small birds. The animals are my comrades more than anything. They teach me more than I teach them.

Kim's recollection of her contractual period, when she was exploited by the studio, is very convincing. It also explains her feelings about the need for privacy regarding her artistic talents. As she puts it:

> I know I was exploited during those early days, but acting at any time is exploiting oneself. I don't regret those days because I learned much from them. In a way, it was much the same as being a public park but yearning to be a private garden.
>
> That is one of the reasons that when I paint—I don't sell my paintings because that would be exploiting something. It's enough for me to enjoy my art. I don't need the other thing.
>
> It's the same with my poetry. I don't want it published. Just writing it gives me joy. It's like waking up one morning and seeing a beautiful rainbow. Am I going to rush and get my camera, take a picture of it, and risk missing seeing it for a few seconds, or am I just going to stand there and take it in at its full peak and get the most pleasure out of it?
>
> If I give my paintings or poems away, that's a different thing. That's special. But I would never sell them. One day, I might write poetry for children and illustrate it and put it into a book, but if it's for their joy, that's not exploiting my work.

Kim Novak is an intelligent, sensitive, and creative human being. She is none of the images that publicity created. Although an actress brings a part of herself to every role, the public sees only what it wants to see in these varied characters. It never sees *her*. As she has said:

People always ask me which character I've played in movies is the closest to myself, and I'll tell you something. I haven't played her yet. I loved *Picnic* because it was such a simple story and I think Hollywood is getting back to that. I personally enjoyed doing *Vertigo* best of all, and I liked *Lylah Clare*. I think it says something about Hollywood and it was ahead of its time.

She has left a lasting impression on the movie-going public and will most likely continue to return in roles of her own choosing to please those millions who will always welcome her as an old friend whenever she appears on the screen. About future work, Kim says:

I expect to do films if I am offered roles that I find interesting. I'll do a picture providing, of course, I like the script and feel I have something to contribute to it.

Escaping all the horrors of ex-sex-goddesses, Kim has not found a need to turn to alcoholism, drugs, or suicide. Surmounting all of the pitfalls of creating an image, she has survived simply by knowing when to turn it off. As she explained:

I believe survival lies in simple answers, the same kind that animals live by. You can't fool the animals because they react on basic instincts and it wouldn't hurt human beings to do the same.

And now Kim can look back and reflect on it all as a victor, not a victim. She has summed up her feelings in this way:

It was my childhood dream to own horses but, for a long time, I was too poor to lead the life I dreamt of. Now I'm able to do it. The patterned, routine life is impossible for me. No two days are alike in Big Sur. The only routine I have is feeding the animals, and they are my comrades.

When I was a girl, I always wanted to be a veterinarian. That was my dream. Acting was a detour for me—an enjoyable one—but not a career I really planned. I was never into becoming a star because it had taken me away from my privacy. Fame destroyed my anonymity. But now I'm free. I've paid my dues and I've won something beautiful. My world is rich and full and I am living in my own personal heaven in a setting that no movie could have.

Life for me is more than motion pictures. I have other avenues of self-expression. If I'm selfish, at least I'm not dishonest about it. Kim Novak is the glamour girl but I've always had to revert to what I am. I'm really Marilyn Novak, a girl from Chicago.

In trying to define the essence of Kim Novak, one would have to say that she is a woman who has reached out in her life, as well as in the work she does in films—sometimes for the impossible—and succeeded. She has never been one to walk dry-shod along a safe shore while the waves were challenging. Kim Novak is a woman who has taken chances, defied convention and conventional approaches, and gambled in order to be not just an actress—but a person who remains true to herself.

# Filmography

(All films are listed according to release dates. The order of production is provided in the text.)

**The French Line**   (RKO, 1954)   Technicolor/3-D
102 Minutes

A Howard Hughes Presentation; producer, Edmund Grainger; director, Lloyd Bacon; story, Matty Kemp, Isabel Dawn; screenplay, Mary Loos, Richard Sale; art directors, Albert S. D'Agostino, Carroll Clark; songs, Josef Myrow, Ralph Blane, Robert Wells; music; Walter Scharf; choreography, Billy Daniel; camera, Harry J. Wild; editor, Robert Ford.

Jane Russell, Gilbert Roland, Arthur Hunnicutt, Mary McCarty, Joyce MacKenzie, Paula Corday, Scott Elliott, Craig Stevens, Laura Elliot, Steven Geray, John Wengraf, Michael St. Angel, Barbara Darrow, Barbara Dobbins, Jean Moorhead, Mary Rodman, Charmienne Harker, Dolores Michaels, Suzanne Alexander, Eileen Coghlan, Rosemary Colligan, Millie Doff, Jane Easton, Helene Hayden, Ellye Marshall, Jarma Lewis, *Marilyn Novak (Model)*, Pat Sheehan, Maureen Stephenson, Shirley Tegge, Beverly Thompson, Doreen Woodbury, Devvy Davenport, Barbara Lohrman, Dolly Summers, Phyllis St. Pierre, Shirley Buchanan, Ray Bennett, Lane Bradford.

**Pushover**   (Columbia, 1954)   Black and White
88 Minutes

Producer, Jules Schermer; associate producer, Philip A. Waxman; director, Richard Quine; screenplay, Roy Huggins; based upon the serialized story "The Killer Wore a Badge," the novel *The Night Watch* by Thomas Walsh, and the novel *Rafferty* by William S. Ballinger; makeup, Clay Campbell; hair styles, Helen Hunt; gowns, Jean Louis; art director, Walter Holscher; assistant director, Jack Corrick; music, Arthur Morton; camera, Lester H. White; editor, Jerome Thoms.

Fred MacMurray, *Kim Novak (Lona McLane)*, Phil Carey, Dorothy Malone, E. G. Marshall, Allen Nourse, Phil Chambers, Alan Dexter, Robert Forrest, Don Harvey, Paul Richards, Ann Morriss, Dick Crockett, Marion Ross, Kenneth L. Smith, Joe Bailey, Hal Taggart, John De Simone,
Ann Loos, Mel Welles, Jack Wilson, Walter Beaver, John Tarangelo, Richard Bryan, Paul Picerni.

**Phffft**   (Columbia, 1954)   Black and White
91 Minutes

Producer, Fred Kohlmar; director, Mark Robson; story-screenplay, George Axelrod; assistant director, Carter De Haven, Jr.; music, Frederick Hollander; makeup, Clay Campbell; hair styles, Helen Hunt; gowns, Jean Louis; art director, William Flannery; camera, Charles Lang; editor, William Kiernan.

Judy Holliday, Jack Lemmon, Jack Carson, *Kim Novak (Janis)*, Luella Gear, Donald Randolph, Donald Curtis, Arny Freeman, Merry Anders, Eddie Searles, Wendy Howard, William Lechner, Sue Carlton, Olan Soule, Geraldine Hall, Harry Cheshire, William Newell, Eugene Borden, Alphonse Martell, Jerry Hausner, Charlotte Lawrence, Patrick Miller, George Hill, Tom Kingston, Fay Baker, Sally Mansfield, Vivian Mason, Maxine Marlowe, Shirlee Allard, Joyce Jameson.

**Son of Sinbad**   (RKO, 1955)   Technicolor/Superscope
88 Minutes

A Howard Hughes Presentation; producer, Robert Sparks; director, Ted Tetzlaff; screenplay, Aubrey Wisberg, Jack Pollexfen; art decorators, Albert S. D'Agostino, Walter E. Keller; set decorator, Darrell Silvera; music director, C. Bakaleinikoff; camera, William Snyder; editors, Roland Gross, Frederick Knudtson.

Dale Robertson, Sally Forrest, Lili St. Cyr, Vincent Price, Mari Blanchard, Leon Askin, Jay Novello, Raymond Greenleaf, Nejla Ates, Kalantan, Ian MacDonald, Donald Randolph, Larry Blake, Edwina Hazard, Fred Aldrich, John Merton, George Sherwood, M. U. Smith, Woody Strode, George Barrows, Marilyn Bonney, Janet Comerford, Alyce Cronin, Mary Ann Edwards, Dawn Oney, Maryleen Prentice, Joan Pastin, Judy Ulian, Suzanne Alexander, Randy Allen, Jane Easton, Jeanne Evans, Helene Hayden, Joanne Jordan, Wayne Berk, James Griffith, Bette Arlen, Joann Arnold, Gwen Caldwell, Anne Carroll, Carolea Cole, Claire De Witt Nancy Dunn, Marjorie Holliday, Judy Jorell, Joi

Lansing, Diane Mumbry, Jonni Paris, Jeanne Shores, Maureen Stephenson, Libby Vernon, Doreen Woodbury, Betty Onge, Dee Gee Sparks, DeDe Moore, Sue Casey, Carol Brewster, Chris Fortune, Helen Chapman, Barbara Drake, Bobette Bentley, Joan Whitney, Dolores Michaels, Barbara Lohrman, Zanne Shaw, Gloria Watson, Ann Ford, Donna Hall, Pat D'Arcy, Charlotte Alpert, Roxanne Arlen, Eleanor Bender, Evelyn Bernard, Shirley Buchanan, Roxanne Delman, Mary Ellen Gleason, Diane James, Keith Kerrigan, Mary Langan, Gloria Laughlin, Vonne Lester, Nancy Neal, Gloria Pall, Lynne Forrester, Audrey Allen, Nancy Moore, Phyllis St. Pierre, Evelyn Lovequist, Gerri Patterson, *Marilyn Novak (Raider)*, Rosemary Webster, Laura Carroll, Penny Sweeny, Trudy Wroe, Joyce Johnson, Bob Wilke, Tom Monroe, Peter Ortiz, Virginia Bates, Katherine Cassidy, Honey King, Sally Musik, Leonteen Danies, Elaine Dupont, Gilda Fontana, Joy Lee, La Rue Malouf, Anna Navarro, Paula Vernay, Michael Ross, Michael Mark.

### 5 Against the House (Columbia, 1955)
Black and White
84 Minutes

Producers, Stirling Silliphant, John Barnwell; associate producer, Helen Ainsworth; director, Phil Karlson; story, Jack Finney; screenplay, Stirling Silliphant, William Bowers, John Barnwell; art director, Robert Peterson; music director, Morris Stoloff; assistant director, Milton Feldman; gowns, Jean Louis; music, George Duning; camera, Lester White; editor, Jerome Thoms.

Guy Madison, *Kim Novak (Kay Greylek)*, Brian Keith, Alvy Moore, William Conrad, Kerwin Mathews, Jack Dimond, Jean Willes, Kathryn Grant.

### Picnic (Columbia, 1955)  Technicolor/Cinemascope
115 Minutes

Producer, Fred Kohlmar; director, Joshua Logan; based on the play by William Inge; screenplay, Daniel Taradash; art director, William Flannery; music director, Morris Stoloff; music, George Duning; orchestrator, Arthur Morton; makeup, Clay Campbell; hair styles, Helen Hunt; gowns, Jean Louis; assistant director, Carter De Haven, Jr.; camera, James Wong Howe; editors, Charles Nelson, William A. Lyon.

William Holden, Rosalind Russell, *Kim Novak (Madge Owens)*, Betty Field, Susan Strasberg, Cliff Robertson, Arthur O'Connell, Verna Felton, Reta Shaw, Nick Adams, Raymond Bailey, Elizabeth W. Wilson, Phyllis Newman, Don C. Harvey, Steven Benton, Henry P. Watson.

### The Man with the Golden Arm (United Artists, 1955)  Black and White
119 Minutes

Producer-director, Otto Preminger; based on the novel by Nelson Algren; screenplay, Walter Newman, Lewis Meltzer; music and music conductor, Elmer Bernstein; or-

chestrator, Frederick Steiner; titles, Saul Bass; art director, Joseph Wright; set decorator, Darrell Silvera; hair styling, Helene Parrish, Hazel Keats; costume supervisor, Mary Ann Nyberg; men's wardrobe, Joe King; women's wardrobe, Adele Parmenter; makeup, Jack Stone, Bernard Ponedel, Ben Lane; assistant directors, Horace Hough, James Engle; sound, Jack Solomon; camera, Sam Leavitt; editor, Louis R. Loeffler.

Frank Sinatra, Eleanor Parker, *Kim Novak (Molly)*, Arnold Stang, Darren McGavin, Robert Strauss, John Conte, Doro Merande, George E. Stone, George Mathews, Leonid Kinskey, Emile Meyer, Shorty Rogers, Shelly Manne, Frank Richards, Will Wright, Tommy Hart, Frank Marlowe, Joe McTurk, Ralph Neff, Ernest Raboff, Martha Wentworth, Jerry Barclay, Lennie Bremen, Paul E. Burns, Charles Seel.

### The Eddy Duchin Story (Columbia, 1956)
Technicolor/Cinemascope
123 Minutes

Producer, Jerry Wald; associate producer, Jonie Taps; director, George Sidney; story, Leo Katcher; screenplay, Samuel Taylor; art director, Walter Holscher; music supervisor and music conductor, Morris Stoloff; piano recordings, Carmen Cavallaro; incidental music, George Duning; makeup, Ben Lane; hair styles, Helen Hunt; gowns, Jean Louis; assistant director, Seymour Friedman; camera, Harry Stradling; editors, Viola Lawrence, Jack W. Ogilvie.

Tyrone Power, *Kim Novak (Marjorie Oelrichs)*, Victoria Shaw, James Whitmore, Rex Thompson, Mickey Maga, Shepperd Strudwick, Frieda Inescort, Gloria Holden, Larry Keating, John Mylong, Gregory Gay, Warren Hsieh, Jack Albertson, Carlyle Mitchell, Richard Sternberg, Andy Smith, Lois Kimbrell, Oliver Cliff, Ralph Gamble, Richard Walsh, Howard Price, Richard Cutting, Richard Crane, Brad Trumbull, Gloria Ann Simpson, Arline Anderson, Michael Legend, Rick Person, Butler Hixson, Peter Norman, Betsy Jones Moreland, Joan Raynolds, Jacqueline Blanchard, Kirk Alyn.

### Jeanne Eagels (Columbia, 1957)  Black and White
109 Minutes

Producer-director, George Sidney; story, Daniel Fuchs; screenplay, Daniel Fuchs, Sonya Levien, John Fante; art director, Ross Bellah; music director, Morris Stoloff; music, George Duning; orchestrator, Arthur Morton; assistant director, Charles S. Gould; makeup, Ben Lane; hair styles, Helen Hunt; gowns, Jean Louis; camera, Robert Planck; editors, Viola Lawrence, Jerome Thoms.

*Kim Novak (Jeanne Eagels)*, Jeff Chandler, Agnes Moorehead, Charles Drake, Larry Gates, Virginia Grey, Gene Lockhart, Joe DeSantis, Murray Hamilton, Will Wright, Sheridan Comerate, Lowell Gilmore, Juney Ellis, Beulah Archuletta, Jules Davis, Florence MacAfee, Snub Pollard, Joseph Novak (Kim's father as a Patron), Johnny Tarangelo, Bert Spencer, Richard Harrison, Ward Wood, Myrtle Anderson, Michael Dante, Joseph Turkel, George Neise.

**Pal Joey**  (Columbia, 1957)  Technicolor
111 Minutes

An Essex-George Sidney Production; producer, Fred Kohlmar; director, George Sidney; based on the play by John O'Hara, Richard Rodgers, Lorenz Hart; screenplay, Dorothy Kingsley; songs, Rodgers and Hart; music supervisor and conductor, Morris Stoloff; music arranger, Nelson Riddle; music adaptors, George Duning, Nelson Riddle; orchestrator, Arthur Morton; art director Walter Holscher; set decorators, William Kiernan, Louis Diage; makeup, Ben Lane; hair styles, Helen Hunt; gowns, Jean Louis; assistant director, Art Black; sound, Franklin Hansen; camera, Harold Lipstein; editors, Viola Lawrence, Jerome Thoms.

Rita Hayworth, Frank Sinatra, *Kim Novak (Linda English)*, Barbara Nichols, Bobby Sherwood, Hank Henry, Elizabeth Patterson, Robin Morse, Frank Wilcox, Pierre Watkin, Barry Bernard, Ellie Kent, Mara McAfee, Betty Utey, Bek Nelson, Henry McCann, John Hubbard, James Seay, Hermes Pan, Ernesto Milnari, Jean Corbett, Robert Rietz, Jules Davis, Judy Dan, Gail Bonney, Cheryl Kubert, Tol Avery, Robert Anderson.

**Vertigo**  (Paramount, 1958)  Technicolor/Vista Vision
123 Minutes

Producer-director, Alfred Hitchcock; associate producer, Herbert Coleman; based on the novel *D'Entre les Morts* by Pierre Boileau, Thomas Narcejac; screenplay, Alex Coppel, Samuel Taylor; art directors, Hal Pereira, Henry Bumstead; set decorators, Sam Comer, Frank McKelvy; assistant director, Daniel McCauley; titles, Saul Bass; costumes, Edith Head; special sequences designer, John Ferren; music, Bernard Herrmann; makeup, Wally Westmore; sound, Harold Lewis, Winston Leverett; special camera effects, John P. Fulton; process camera, Farciot Edouart, Wallace Kelley; camera, Robert Burks; editor, George Tomasini.

James Stewart, *Kim Novak (Madeleine Elster/Judy Barton)*, Barbara Bel Geddes, Tom Helmore, Henry Jones, Raymond Bailey, Ellen Corby, Konstantin Shayne, Lee Patrick, Paul Bryar, Margaret Brayton, William Remick, Sara Taft.

**Bell, Book and Candle**  (Columbia, 1958)  Technicolor
103 Minutes

Producer, Julian Blaustein; director, Richard Quine; based on the play by John Van Druten; screenplay, Daniel Taradash; assistant director, Irving Moore; gowns, Jean Louis; music, George Duning; art director, Cary Odell; set decorator, Louis Diage; native primitive art, Carlebach Gallery; makeup, Ben Lane; sound, Franklin Hansen, Jr., camera, James Wong Howe; editor, Charles Nelson.
James Stewart, *Kim Novak (Gillian Holroyd)*, Jack Lemmon, Ernie Kovacs, Hermione Gingold, Elsa Lanchester, Janice Rule, Philippe Clay, Bek Nelson, Howard McNear, The Brothers Candoli, Wolfe Barzell, Joe Barry, Gail Bonney, Monty Ash.

**Middle of the Night**  (Columbia, 1959)
Black and White
118 Minutes

A Sudan Production; producer, George Justin; director, Delbert Mann; based on the play by Paddy Chayefsky; screenplay, Paddy Chayefsky; music and music conductor, George Bassman; assistant director, Charles H. Maguire; art director, Edward S. Haworth; set decorator, Jack Wright, Jr.; costumes, Frank L. Thomson; clothes for Miss Novak, Jean Louis; technical advisor, Lionel Kaplan; makeup, George Newman; sound, Richard Gramaglia, Richard Vorisek; camera, Joseph Brun; editor, Carl Lerner.

*Kim Novak (Betty Preisser)*, Fredric March, Lee Philips, Glenda Farrell, Albert Dekker, Martin Balsam, Lee Grant, Edith Meiser, Joan Copeland, Betty Walker, Rudy Bond, Effie Afton, Jan Norris, Anna Berger, David Ford, Audrey Peters, Lou Gilbert, Dora Weissman, Alfred Leberfield, Lee Richardson, Nelson Olmsted.

**Strangers When We Meet**  (Columbia, 1960)
Eastman Color by Pathé/Cinemascope
117 Minutes

A Bryna-Quine Production; producer-dorector, Richard Quine; based on the novel by Evan Hunter; screenplay, Evan Hunter; art director, Ross Bellah; set decorator, Louis Diage; music, George Duning; music supervisor, Morris Stoloff; orchestrator, Arthur Morton; assistant director, Carter De Haven, Jr.; Miss Novak's clothes, Jean Louis; hair styles, Helen Hunt; makeup, Ben Lane; sound, Charles J. Rice, Lambert Day; camera, Charles Lang, Jr.; editor, Charles Nelson.

Kirk Douglas, *Kim Novak (Maggie Gault)*, Ernie Kovacs, Barbara Rush, Walter Matthau, Virginia Bruce, Kent Smith, Helen Gallagher; John Bryant, Roberta Shore, Nancy Kovak, Carol Douglas, Paul Picerni, Ernest Sarracino, Harry Jackson, Bart Patton, Robert Sampson, Ray Ferrell, Douglas Holmes, Timmy Molina, Betsy Jones Moreland, Audrey Swanson, Cynthia Leighton, Judy Lang, Sharyn Gibbs, Charles Victor, Joe Palma, Tom Anthony, Sheryl Ellison, Mark Beckstrom, Sue Ane Langdon, Ruth Batchelor, Dick Crockett, Lorraine Crawford.

**Pepe**  (Columbia, 1960)
Eastman Color by Pathé/Cinemascope
195 Minutes

Producer-director, George Sidney; associate producer, Jacques Gelman; based on the play *Broadway Zauber* by Ladislaus Bus-Fekete; screen story, Leonard Spigelgass, Sonya Levien; screenplay, Dorothy Kingsley, Claude Binyon; assistant director, David Silver; art director, Ted Haworth; set decorator, William Kiernan; music supervisor and background score, Johnny Green; special material, Sammy Cahn, Roger Eden; songs, Andre Previn, Dory Langdon—Hans Wittstatt, Dory Langdon, Andre Previn—Augustin Lara, Dory Langdon; choreography, Eugene Loring, Alex Romero; makeup, Ben Lane; gowns, Edith Head; camera, Joe MacDonald; editors, Viola Lawrence, Al Clark.

Cantinflas, Dan Dailey, Shirley Jones, Carlos Montalban, Vicki Trickett, Matt Mattox, Hank Henry, Suzanne Lloyd, Carlos Rivas, Stephen Bekassy, Carol Douglas, Francisco Reguerra, Joe Hyams, Joey Bishop, Michael Callan, Maurice Chevalier, Charles Coburn, Richard Conte, Bing Crosby, Tony Curtis, Bobby Darin, Sammy Davis, Jr., Jimmy Durante, Zsa Zsa Gabor, the voice of Judy Garland, Greer Garson, Hedda Hopper, Ernie Kovacs, Peter Lawford, Janet Leigh, Jack Lemmon, Dean Martin, Jay North, *Kim Novak (Herself)*, Andre Previn, Donna Reed, Debbie Reynolds, Edward G. Robinson, Cesar Romero, Frank Sinatra, Billie Burke, Ann B. Davis, William Demarest, Jack Entratter, Colonel E. E. Fogelson, Jane Robinson, Bunny Waters, Shirley DeBurgh, Steve Baylor, John Burnside, James Bacon, Jimmy Cavanaugh.

### Boys' Night Out (MGM, 1962)
Metrocolor/Cinemascope
115 Minutes

A Joseph E. Levine Presentation of a Kimco-Filmways Picture; producer, Martin Ransohoff; associate producer, James Pratt; director, Michael Gordon; based on the story by Marvin Worth, Arne Sultan; adaptation, Marion Hargrove; screenplay, Ira Wallach; music, Frank De Vol; songs, James Van Heusen, Sammy Cahn; art directors, George W. Davis, Hans Peters; set decorators, Henry Grace, Jerry Wunderlich; Miss Novak's costumes, Bill Thomas; assistant director, Ivan Volkman; sound, Franklin Milton, camera, Arthur E. Arling; editor, Tom McAdoo.

*Kim Novak (Cathy)*, James Garner, Tony Randall, Howard Duff, Janet Blair, Patti Page, Jessie Royce Landis, Oscar Homolka, Howard Morris, Anne Jeffreys, Zsa Zsa Gabor, Fred Clark, William Bendix, Jim Backus, Larry Keating, Ruth McDevitt.

### The Notorious Landlady
(Columbia, 1962)   Black and White
123 Minutes

A Fred Kohlmar-Richard Quine Production; producer, Fred Kohlmar; director, Richard Quine; based on the story by Margery Sharp; screenplay, Larry Gelbart, Blake Edwards; music, George Duning; orchestrator, Arthur Morton; art director, Cary Odell; set decorator, Louis Diage; Miss Novak's gowns designed by herself and executed by Elizabeth Courtney; assistant director, Carter De Haven, Jr.; makeup, Ben Lane; sound, Charles J. Rice, Josh Westmoreland; camera, Arthur Arling; editor, Charles Nelson.

*Kim Novak (Carlye Hardwicke)*, Jack Lemmon, Fred Astaire, Lionel Jeffries, Estelle Winwood, Maxwell Reed, Philippa Bevans, Henry Daniell, Ronald Long, Doris Lloyd, Richard Scott Davey, Jack Livesey, Tom Dillon, Benno Schneider, Clive Halliday, Antony Eustrel, Carter De Haven, Sr., David Hillary Hughes, Nelson Welch, Cecil Weston,

Mavis Neal, Cicely Walper, Queenie Leonard, Blanche Novak (Kim's mother as spa patron under umbrella), John V. Lemmon, Betty Fairfax, Clive Morgan, Julie Scott, Eric Micklewood, Mary Burke, Ottola Nesmith, Milton Parsons.

### Of Human Bondage (MGM, 1964)   Black and White
99 Minutes

A Seven Arts Production; producer, James Woolf; associate producer, Ernest Holding; director, Ken Hughes; additional scenes directed by Henry Hathaway; based on the novel by W. Somerset Maugham; screenplay, Bryan Forbes; production designer, John Box; music and music conductor, Ron Goodwin; makeup, George Prest; hairdresser, Olga Angelinetta; costume designers, Bob Jones, Beatrice Dawson; camera, Oswald Morris; additional camera, Denys Coop; editor, Russell Lloyd.

*Kim Novak (Mildred Rogers)*, Laurence Harvey, Robert Morley, Siobhan McKenna, Roger Livesy, Jack Hedley, Nanette Newman, Ronald Lacey, Anthony Booth, Anna Manahan, Derry O'Donovan, Jacqueline Taylor, Helen Robinson, Michael Doolan.

### Kiss Me, Stupid (Lopert Pictures Corporation, 1964
Black and White/Panavision
126 Minutes

A Mirisch Corporation Presentation; producer-director, Billy Wilder; associate producers, I.A.L. Diamond, Doane Harrison; based on the play *L'Ora Della Fantasia* by Anna Bonacci; screenplay, Billy Wilder, I.A.L. Diamond; songs, George and Ira Gershwin; music, Andre Previn; choreography, Wally Green; costume designer, Bill Thomas; wardrobe, Wes Jeffries, Irene Caine; makeup, Emile LaVigne, Loren Cosand; hairdressers, Alice Monte, Maudlee McDougall; art director, Robert Luthardt; set decorator, Edward G. Boyle; assistant director, C. C. Coleman, Jr.; sound, Robert Martin, Wayne Fury; special effects, Milton Rice; camera, Joseph LaShelle; editor, Daniel Mandell.

Dean Martin, *Kim Novak (Polly the Pistol)*, Ray Walston, Felicia Farr, Cliff Osmond, Barbara Pepper, James Ward, Doro Merande, Howard McNear, Bobo Lewis, Tommy Nolan, Alice Pearce, John Fiedler, Arlen Stuart, Cliff Norton, Mel Blanc, Eileen O'Neill, Susan Wedell, Bern Hoffman, Henry Gibson, Alan Dexter, Henry Beckman.

### The Amorous Adventures of Moll Flanders
(Paramount, 1965)   Technicolor/Panavision
126 Minutes

A Winchester Film Production; director, Terence Young; based on the novel by Daniel Defoe; screenplay, Denis Cannon, Roland Kibbee; production designer, Syd Cain; assistant director, David Adderson; music, John Addison; camera, Ted Moore; editor, Frederick Wilson.

*Kim Novak (Moll Flanders)*, Richard Johnson, Angela Lansbury, George Sanders, Leo McKern, Vittorio DeSica, Lilli Palmer, Dandy Nichols, Daniel Massey, Derren Nesbitt,

Noel Howlett, Roger Livesey, Cecil Parker, Barbara Couper, Richard Wattis, Hugh Griffith, Michael Trubshawe, David Lodge, Richard Gooden, Basil Dignam.

## The Legend of Lylah Clare
(MGM, 1968)   Metrocolor
130 Minutes

An Associates and Aldrich Company Production; producer-director, Robert Aldrich; associate producer, Walter Blanke; based on the teleplay by Robert Thom, Edward De Blasio; screenplay, Hugo Butler, Jean Rouverol; music, Frank De Vol; song, Frank De Vol, Sibylle Siegfried; art directors, George W. Davis, William Glasgow; set decorators, Henry Grace, Keogh Gleason; makeup, William Tuttle, Robert Schiffer; assistant director, Cliff C. Coleman; hair styles, Sydney Guilaroff; costumes, Renie; recording supervisor, Franklin Milton; camera, Joseph Biroc; editor, Michael Lucinao.

*Kim Novak (Lylah Clare/Elsa Brinkmann Campbell),* Peter Finch, Ernest Borgnine, Milton Selzer, Rossella Falk, Gabriele Tinti, Coral Browne, Valentina Cortesa, Jean Carroll, Michael Murphy, George Kennedy, Lee Meriwether, James Lanphier, Hal Maguire, Robert Ellenstein, Nick Dennis, Dave Willock, Peter Bravos, Ellen Corby, Michael Fox, Vernon Scott, Queenie Smith, Sidney Skolsky, Barbara Ann Warkmeister, Mel Warkmeister, Tom Patty.

## The Great Bank Robbery  (Warner Brothers-Seven Arts, 1969)   Technicolor/Panavision
98 Minutes

Producer, Malcolm Stuart; associate producer, Richard Freed; director, Hy Averback; based on the novel by Frank O'Rourke; music, Nelson Riddle; music supervisor, Sonny Burke; songs, Sammy Cahn, James Van Heusen; vocal arranger, Ken Darby; orchestrator, Gil Grau; production designer, Jack Poplin; set decorator, William L. Kuehl; titles, Don Record; choreography, Miriam Nelson; costumes, Moss Mabry; hair stylist, Jean Burt Reilly; makeup, Al Greenway; assistant director, Jack Cunningham; sound, Everett A. Hughes; special effects, Ralph Webb; aerial camera, Jack Willoughby; camera, Fred J. Koenekamp; editor, Gene Milford.

Zero Mostel, *Kim Novak (Lyda Kabanov),* Clint Walker, Claude Akins, Akim Tamiroff, Larry Storch, John Anderson, Sam Jaffe, Mako, Elisha Cook, Jr., Ruth Warrick, John Fiedler, John Larch, Peter Whitney, Norman Alden, Grady Sutton, Homer Garrett, Byron Keith, Bob Steele, Ben Aliza, Mickey Simpson, Guy Wilkerson, Burt Mustin, Royden Clark, Janet Clark, Jerry Brown, Chuck O'Brien, Philo McCullough, Fred Krone, Dick Hudkins, Emile Avery, Everett Creach, William Zuckert, Jerry Summers, Bob Mitchell Boys Choir.

## The Third Girl from the Left
(ABC-TV, 1973)   Color
74 Minutes

A Playboy Production; executive producer, Hugh M. Hefner; producer, Ron Roth; director, Peter Medak; screenplay, Dory Previn; songs, Dory Previn; music supervisor, Nikolas Venet; music arranger, James E. Bond, Jr.; choreography, Miriam Nelson; art director, Frank Arrigo; Miss Novak's wardrobe, Bill Thomas; camera, Gayne Rescher; editor, Jim Benson.

*Kim Novak (Gloria Joyce),* Tony Curtis, Michael Brandon, George Furth, Michael Conrad. Bern Hoffman, Jenifer Shaw, Louis Guss, Barbi Benton, Anne Ramsey, Larry Bishop.

## Tales That Witness Madness
(Paramount, 1973)   In Color
90 Minutes

A World Film Services Limited Production; producer, Norman Priggens; director, Freddie Francis; screenplay, Jay Fairbank; art director, Roy Walker; music and music conductor, Bernard Ebbinghouse; assistant director, Peter Saunders; makeup, Eric Allwright; hairdresser, Barbara Ritchie; wardrobe supervisor, Bridget Sellers; sound, Ken Ritchie, Nolan Roberts; camera, Norman Warwick; editor, Bernard Gribble.

*Clinic Link Episodes:* Jack Hawkins, Donald Pleasence. *Mr. Tiger:* Georgia Brown, Donald Houston, Russell Lewis, David Wood.

*Penny Farthing:* Suzy Kendall, Peter McEnery, Neil Kennedy, Richard Connaught, Beth Morris, Frank Forsyth. *Mel:* Joan Collins, Michael Jayston.
*Luau: Kim Novak (Auriol Pageant),* Michael Petrovitch, Mary Tamm, Lesley Nunnerley, Leon Lissek, Zohra Segal.

## Satan's Triangle  (ABC-TV, 1975)   Color
74 Minutes

A Danny Thomas Production; executive producers, Paul Junger Witt, Tony Thomas; producer, James Rokos; director, Sutton Roley; teleplay, William Read Woodfield; music, Johnny Pate; director of photography, Leonard J. South; special effects, Gene Griff, editors, Bud Molin, Dennis Virkler.

*Kim Novak (Eva),* Doug McClure, Alejandro Rey, Ed Lauter, Jim Davis, Michael Conrad, Titos Vandis, Zitto Kazann, Peter Bourne, Hank Stohl, Tom Dever, Trent Dolan.

## The White Buffalo  (United Artists, 1977)
DeLuxe Color
97 Minutes

A Dino De Laurentiis Presentation; producer, Pancho Kohner; director, J. Lee Thompson; screenplay, Richard Sale; based upon novel by Richard Sale; music composed and conducted by John Barry; production designer, Tambi Larsen; set decorator, James Berkey; costumes, Eric Seelig; makeup, Phil Rhodes, Michael Hancock; hairstylist, Shirley Padgett; assistant director, Jack Aldworth; sound, Harlan

319

Riggs; special effects, Richard M. Parker; buffalo sequences, Carlo Rambaldi; camera, Paul Lohmann; editor, Michael F. Anderson.

Charles Bronson, Jack Warden, Will Sampson, *Kim Novak (Poker Jenny Schermerhorn),* Clint Walker, Stuart Whitman, Slim Pickens, John Carradine, Cara Willaims, Shay Duffin, Douglas V. Fowley, Cliff Pellow, Ed Lauter, Martin Kove, Scott Walker, Ed Bakey, Richard Gilliland, David Roy Chandler, Philip Montgomery, Linda Moon Redfearn, Chief Tug Smith, Douglas Hume, Cliff Carnell, Ron Thompson, Eve Brent, Joe Roman, Bert Williams, Dan Vadis, Christopher Cary, Larry Martindale, Scott Bryson, Will Walker, Gregg White.

**Just a Gigolo** *(Schöner Gigolo-Armer Gigolo)* (Tedderwick Ltd. release (in U.K.) of a Leguan Film presentation. Warner-Columbia distribution elsewhere, 1979)

German-Color
105 Minutes

Producer, Rolf Thiele; director, David Hemmings; screenplay, Joshua Sinclair, Ennio De Concini; production designer, Peter Rothe; choreography, Herbert F. Schubert; costumes, Ingrid Zore; makeup, Anthony Clavet, Ingrid Thier, Alfred Rasche, Karin Bauer; sound, Gunter Kortwich; music, Gunther Fischer; special effects, Erwin Lange; camera, Charly Steinberger; assistant director, Eva-Maria Schonecker; editors, Siegrun Jager (Susan Jaeger), Fred Srp, Maxine Julius, David Hemmings.

David Bowie, Sydne Rome, *Kim Novak (Helga),* David Hemmings, Maria Schell, Curd (a/ka Curt) Jurgens, Marlene Dietrich, Erika Pluhar, Rudolf Schundler, Hilde Weissner, Werner Pochath, Bela Erny, Friedhelm Lehmann, Rainer Hunold, Evelyn Kunneke, Karin Hardt, Gudrun Genest, Ursula Heyer, Christiane Maybach, Martin Hithe, Rene Kolldehoff, Gunter Meisner, Peter Schlesinger.

*Kim Novak completed filming on this production as this book was being printed. Film editing had not been completed and, therefore, discussion of the film is not included in the text:*

**The Mirror Crack'd** (EMI, 1981) Color

Producers, John Brabourne, Richard Goodwin; director, Guy Hamilton; screenplay, Jonathan Hales, Barry Sandler; from the novel, *The Mirror Crack'd,* by Agatha Christie; production manager, Jim Brennan; assistant director, Derek Cracknell; photography, Chris Challis; sound, John Mitchell; production design, Michael Stringer; art director, John Roberts; costume design, Phyllis Dalton; editor, Richard Marden.

Angela Lansbury as Miss Marple, and starring in alphabetical order, Geraldine Chaplin, Tony Curtis, Edward Fox, Rock Hudson, *Kim Novak (Lola Brewster),* Elizabeth Taylor, with Marella Oppenheim, Charles Gray, Richard Pearson, Anthony Steel, Dinah Sheridan, Hildegard Neil, Nigel Stock, Allan Cuthbertson.